Keats's Boyish Imagination

John Keats, famously, is the poet who aspired to, and managed to achieve, a supreme maturity; who progressed from the 'namby-pamby' early lyrics to the 'calm power' of the great Odes and the *Hyperion* poems. His 'maturity' has become a cornerstone of recent political appraisals of his work. This book explores its subject over a range of poetical and psychological terrain to contend that *immaturity* – the 'Boyish imagination' – is not only a more appropriate place from which to scrutinize Keats's political consciousness, but is itself the emphatic site of that consciousness.

If Keats could deploy puerility purposefully as a system of political interruption, his ambivalent stance towards the forms and functions of adulthood also exacerbated personal anxieties concerning 'manly' behaviour, finding what he called a 'right feeling towards Women', and locating a poetic idiom that would be accepted by 'grown-up' reading audiences. In a series of profoundly surprising readings, focusing on themes such as feet and foot-related imagery, the breaking voice and female anatomy, this study of a major canonical figure alerts us to – and opens a new perspective on – the rich complexity of Keats the poet, and Keats the man.

This book will be of essential interest to academics and students of Romanticism.

Richard Marggraf Turley is Lecturer in Nineteenth-Century Literature at the University of Wales, Aberystwyth. He is the author of *The Politics of Language in Romantic Literature* (2002) and *Writing Essays: A Guide for Students in English and the Humanities* (2000). He is currently working on a co-edited collection of essays tracing Romantic influence in twentieth-century literature.

Routledge Studies in Romanticism

1 **Keats's Boyish Imagination**
Richard Marggraf Turley

2 **Leigh Hunt**
Life, poetics, politics
Edited by Nicholas Roe

3 **Leigh Hunt and the London Literary Scene**
A reception history of his major works, 1805–1828
Michael Eberle-Sinatra

Preface

My first book, *The Politics of Language in Romantic Literature* (2002), was a traditional, if occasionally quirky, work of scholarship. In addition to exploring Romanticism's complex negotiation of radically new French and German theories of language as these percolated into the British intellectual and poetic consciousness between the 1790s and 1830s, it also sought to delineate the *political* contours of Romanticism's engagement with Continental philology. At first glance, the present volume is rather differently detained. Focusing on the work of a single author, *Keats's Boyish Imagination* is not concerned (first and foremost) with tracing the history of ideas, nor with identifying wider unifying tendencies within Romanticism. None the less, it has some important features in common with my earlier project. Chief among these is its commitment to drawing out the oppositional politics of key Romantic figures, in this case John Keats. In our difficult times, it is especially instructive and edifying to learn how great men and women of the past responded to, and found ways to protest against, the tyrannies and brutalities of their own days.

There are signal differences, too, in tone, frame, and approach, between the respective books. *The Politics of Language in Romantic Literature* pressed its claim by carefully marshalling newly uncovered details: revealing, for example, that Keats found key phrases from 'Ode on a Grecian Urn' and 'Ode on Melancholy' (including 'Beauty is truth, truth beauty', and 'when the melancholy fit shall fall / Sudden from heaven') in Etienne Bonnot de Condillac's now neglected volume of linguistic philosophy, *An Essay on the Origin of Human Knowledge* (translated into English by Thomas Nugent in 1756). By contrast, *Keats's Boyish Imagination*, which shows how objects/conditions such as feet and puberphonia lead us towards a fuller and richer understanding of Keats's hybrid oppositional persona, is more vibrantly conceptual and eclectically resourceful, and seeks to put the cat among the pigeons. I hope my often 'left-field' approach to a major poet, while quite possibly not in chime with current criticism, will prove stimulating and prompt further discussion. If Keats was right about one thing – and he was right about many things – it was undoubtedly that 'there must be conversation of some sort' (unpublished Preface to *Endymion*).

I am indebted to friends and colleagues who discussed ideas or commented on early versions of chapters, particularly to Damian Walford Davies, Peter Barry, Andrew Wawn, Martin Padget, Tiffany Atkinson, Claire Jowitt, Diane Watt, David Shuttleton; and to Anne Marggraf-Turley. Any errors of judgement that remain are my own. Other friends have helped along the way, especially Anett Ramme, Birte Marggraf, Mattis Steier, Teresa Gehrs, and Karim McCleod. Thanks are due to staff of the Hugh Owen Library, Aberystwyth, and the National Library of Wales; also to staff of the Bodleian Library, the British Library (especially Reproductions), and to Jane Henderson at the Wellcome Library for the History and Understanding of Medicine. I am grateful, too, for the cheerfulness and energy with which my editor at Routledge, Amritpal Bangard, saw this project through to completion. Finally, I would like to thank Routledge's anonymous readers for their suggestions, encouragement, and intellectual generosity.

Ötztal, April 2003

Acknowledgements

A version of Chapter 1 has previously appeared in *Studies in Romanticism*, 41 (2002), 89–106. I am grateful to the editor of this journal, and to the Trustees of Boston University, for permission to recast my work here. A shorter version of Chapter 2 appeared in *Romanticism on the Net*, 28 (November, 2002) http://www.ron.umontreal.ca, and is reprinted here by permission of the editor. Poems in the Appendix are reprinted by permission of the publisher from *John Keats: Complete Poems*, ed. Jack Stillinger, pp. 20–4, 360–1, Cambridge, MA: The Belknap Press of Harvard University Press, Copyright © 1978, 1982 by the President and Fellows of Harvard College.

Contents

	Preface	ix
	Acknowledgements	xi
	Note on texts	xiii
	Introduction	1
1	'Strange longings': Keats and feet	11
2	'Full-grown lambs': immaturity and 'To Autumn'	27
3	'Give me that voice again': Keats and puberphonia	46
4	Japing the sublime: naughty boys and immature aesthetics	73
5	'Stifling up the vale': Keats and 'c——ts'	104
	Afterword	126
	Appendix	129
	Notes	134
	Bibliography	148
	Index	154

'I am certain I have not a right feeling towards Women . . . Is it because they fall so far beneath my Boyish imagination?'
(John Keats to Benjamin Bailey, 18 July 1818)

'Are we to expect that poets are to be given to the world, as our first parents were, in a state of maturity? Are they to have no season of Childhood?'
(Richard Woodhouse to Mary Frogley, 23 October 1818)

Keats's Boyish Imagination

Richard Marggraf Turley

Routledge
Taylor & Francis Group
LONDON AND NEW YORK

First published 2004
by Routledge
11 New Fetter Lane, London EC4P 4EE

Simultaneously published in the USA and Canada
by Routledge
29 West 35th Street, New York, NY 10001

Routledge is an imprint of the Taylor & Francis Group

© 2004 Richard Marggraf Turley

Typeset in Garamond by
BOOK NOW Ltd
Printed and bound in Great Britain by
TJ International Ltd, Padstow, Cornwall

All rights reserved. No part of this book may be reprinted or reproduced or utilised in any form or by any electronic, mechanical, or other means, now known or hereafter invented, including photocopying and recording, or in any information storage or retrieval system, without permission in writing from the publishers.

British Library Cataloguing in Publication Data
A catalogue record for this book is available from the British Library

Library of Congress Cataloging in Publication Data
A catalog record for this book has been requested

ISBN 0–415–28882–7

Note on texts

Unless otherwise indicated, all references to Keats's poetry are to Jack Stillinger's edition, *The Poems of John Keats* (Cambridge, MA: Belknap Press, 1978), hereafter *Poems*.

All quotations from Keats's letters are from Hyder Edward Rollins, *The Letters of John Keats, 1814–1821*, 2 vols (Cambridge, MA: Harvard University Press, 1958), hereafter *Letters*. Keats's original punctuation, spellings, and misspellings, have been retained.

Unless otherwise indicated, all reviews of Keats's poetry referred to in the following chapters can be found in Donald H. Reiman (ed.), *The Romantics Reviewed: Contemporary Reviews of British Romantic Writers*, 9 vols (New York: Garland, 1972).

Introduction

Leigh Hunt's verse epistle 'To William Hazlitt', published in *Foliage* (1818), contains a passage that in all probability spoke very directly to Keats:

> Dear Hazlitt, whose tact intellectual is such
> That it seems to feel truth, as one's fingers do touch, –
> Who in politics, arts, metaphysics, poetics,
> To critics in these times, are health to cosmetics,
> And nevertheless, – or I rather should say,
> For that very reason, – can relish boy's play,
> And turning on all sides, through pleasures and cares,
> Find nothing more precious than laughs and fresh airs.
> 			(*Foliage*, pp. xc–xci)

Jeffrey C. Robinson hits things squarely when he says of these lines, and of *Foliage* more generally:

> Upon arriving at the Epistle 'To William Hazlitt', one realises that any association of fanciful poetry with the childish ('boy's play') has been modified to register more positively energy, ingenuousness, social consciousness and idealism, and a desire to disrupt convention.[1]

'To William Hazlitt', Robinson adds, maintains a 'witty intimacy and irreverence towards conventional middle-class life and "bigotry"', linking Hunt's 'fanciful style of playfulness and quickwittedness with serious cultural politics' (p. 172). This seems to me a good place to begin a book on Keats and immaturity.

Keats, Hunt's protégé, was adept at mixing playfulness and serious politics. While traditional criticism has perceived Hunt's influence on Keats as a 'stage' to be passed through, at least one aspect of Hunt's influence – his relish for 'boy's play', for disruptive performances of childishness and puerility – remained a lodestone in Keats's creative and political life. One of my aims in *Keats's Boyish Imagination* is to investigate the ways in which Keats deployed juvenility as a system of interruptions, challenging the mature force of established power over a range of aesthetic and political terrain.

Keats revelled in the deliberate use of immaturity, but at a psychic level he was to experience his boyish imagination as profoundly disorientating, especially when it came to sorting out a 'right feeling towards Women' (*Letters*, I, 341), finding a suitable bearing towards adult responsibilities, and fulfilling readers' expectations of a mature poet. The tensions that existed between what we might call ingenuous and strategic enactments of immaturity in Keats's writing are also explored in the present volume.

Perfect fruit

Where contemporary reviewers had despaired at Keats's apparent inability to grow up, decrying 'boyish petulance' in *Lamia, Isabella, The Eve of St Agnes, and Other Poems* (1820), just as they had deplored 'namby-pamby' phrases in *Poems* (1817), Richard Monckton Milnes's *Life, Letters, and Literary Remains of John Keats* (1848), the first substantial account of the poet's career to appear in print, inaugurated (in surprisingly modern tones) the now familiar narrative of Keats's rapid 'poetical education':[2]

> Day by day, his imagination is extended, his fancy enriched, his taste purified; every fresh acquaintance with the motive minds of past generations leads him a step onwards in knowledge and power . . . And now we approach the consummation of this laborious work, the formation of a mind of the highest order; we hope to see the perfect fruit . . . we desire to sympathize with this realised idea of a great poet, from which he has ever felt himself so far, but which he yet knows is ever approaching.[3]

In *Keats's Craftsmanship* (1933), another key document in the construction of a mature Keats, M. R. Ridley lent to Milnes's 'story' the legitimizing sheen of metrical analysis and a close study of verbal patterning. Ridley set about tracking Keats's growth from the neophyte poetry of 1817 to the genius of the odes and the 'serene perfection' of 'To Autumn', pointing out:

> the 'mere' craftsmanship [of the early poems]; the development in metric skill from the fumblings of *Isabella*, through the brilliant imitativeness of *Hyperion*, to the original creation of the stanza of the Odes . . . the increasing security in the rejection and choice of verbal expression from the errors of *Isabella* through the felicities of *The Eve of St. Agnes* to the magic of the *Nightingale* and the serene perfection of *To Autumn*.[4]

What impressed Ridley above all was the 'rapidity so astonishing' with which Keats 'grew from poetic adolescence to poetic maturity' (p. 17). The same astonishment is palpable in more recent assessments of Keats's achievement. Stephen Coote – whose bearing on Keats and maturity is signalled by chapter titles such as 'Apollo's Apprentice' and 'Getting Wisdom' – marvels at the 'sudden and miraculous flowering' in the odes of a 'major poet working with a deeply felt . . . authority on the great themes of his life and art'.[5] Andrew Motion, sensing the limits of historical determinism where creative genius is concerned, reminds us that Keats:

> was extraordinarily young when he produced his greatest poetry. Although never prodigious in the sense that Mozart was prodigious, and although his friends recognised this by stressing what Hunt called his 'great promise' rather than his maturity, the fact remains that he was only twenty-three years old when he wrote 'The Eve of St Agnes', the six odes, 'Lamia' and the two 'Hyperion's. Accounts of his reading, his friendships, his psychological imperatives, his poetic 'axioms', his politics, and his context can never completely explain this marvellous achievement. The story of his life must also allow for other things . . . inspiration, accident, genius.[6]

Yet the bias of recent biographies and critiques, Motion's included, has been to stress Keats's maturity, rather than what Hunt called his 'great promise'. In 2001, Jack Stillinger, writing 'The "story" of Keats' – which he acknowledges is really 'several stories' – strenuously asserts that while Keats died young, he 'nevertheless left a body of mature work in narrative and lyric forms sufficient to make him a "major" writer by anybody's standards'. Stillinger concludes that 'the imagined poet of promise was in fact a poet of enormous accomplishments'.[7]

Standing between these early and recent advocates of a mature Keats, in the 1960s and early 1970s a triumvirate of 'playful' critics, Lionel Trilling, John Bayley, and Christopher Ricks, drew (back) into focus an essential youthfulness in Keats's idiom that was once seen, damningly so, as characteristic of the poet's 'true' voice. Ricks emphasized that a 'particular strength' of Keats was the implication that the 'youthful, the luxuriant, the immature, can be, not just excusable errors, but vantage-points'.[8] In a ground-breaking short article of 1961, Roger Sharrock suggested that it would be an error to 'excuse Keats from immaturity' and 'accept him as the supreme artist of growth and development', since this would be to assume that 'as a result of any sound development of his art and outlook Keats put away not merely childish things but all the impulses of his youth'.[9] Adopting this position, Sharrock argued, would be tantamount to 'equat[ing] adolescence with delinquency and stoop[ing] to the present-day vulgarity which makes "adult" generally admitted as a term of critical praise'. I wish to explore and extend Sharrock's deeply intelligent insight that Keats 'remains in his most characteristic works not just the supreme poet for adolescents, but supremely the adolescent poet'.

A central purpose of *Keats's Boyish Imagination*, then, is to recover and renovate a truth about Keats that has once more become obscured from view. Since the 1980s, Keats has been painstakingly and determinedly repositioned as a mature poet of turbulent times, who anticipates – and thus verifies – certain political demeanours in our own day. It is my contention that immaturity not only represents an excellent place from which to scrutinize Keats's political consciousness, but is itself the emphatic site of that consciousness. Much of this book's accent is on investigating the strategic infantilism of the poet.

It would be wrong to imply that boyishness in Keats's poetics has been completely ignored since the glittering interventions of Ricks and his companions. Marjorie Levinson's virtuosic, idiosyncratic performance, *Keats's Life of Allegory* (1988), scrutinized the role of class politics in Keats's 'bad' early poetry, identifying childishness as a powerful 'self-fashioning gesture'. Nicholas Roe, too, with characteristic verve, has sharpened our sense of how Keats's 'lisping' poetry was not just *perceived* as seditious by contemporary reviewers, but really was subversively freighted. But students of Keats in the last couple of decades have, by and large, adhered to proto-schemas delineated by Milnes and Ridley when addressing their subject's 'growth' as poet and man. Helen Vendler's monumental *The Odes of John Keats* (1983) speaks unselfconsciously about the later 'perfect' poems; and the entire thrust of Vendler's most recent book, *Coming of Age as a Poet: Milton, Keats, Eliot, Plath* (2003), is directed towards examining the processes poets have to work through in order to produce their 'first "perfect" poem' (defined by Vendler as 'the poem which first wholly succeeds in embodying a coherent personal style').[10] What is more, a brace of new historicist critiques of Keats depend absolutely on narratives of growth from political adolescence to political maturity in order for identifications of, say, grown-up 'conspiracy' in 'To Autumn' with post-Peterloo dissent to make any plausible sense.

Keats was himself fond of suggesting models for poetic and personal maturation, particularly in his correspondence (the concept of progressing through 'Chambers' of developing intellect is perhaps the best known). One part of Keats was undoubtedly eager to be accepted by reviewers and the reading public as a mature writer, worthy of serious attention. Yet such portrayals of regular steppings in knowledge and power in the letters do not always correspond to the way in which Keats envisaged poetic evolution in his poems. To pursue the point, let us turn to a passage from the verse epistle, 'To George Felton Mathew' (1815):

> Felton! without incitements such as these,
> How vain for me the niggard muse to tease:
> For thee, she will thy every dwelling grace,
> And make 'a sun-shine in a shady place':
> For thou wast once a flowret blooming wild,
> Close to the source, bright, pure, and undefil'd,
> Whence gush the streams of song: in happy hour
> Came chaste Diana from her shady bower,
> Just as the sun was from the east uprising;   80
> And, as for him some gift she was devising,
> Beheld thee, pluck'd thee, cast thee in the stream

> To meet her glorious brother's greeting beam.
> I marvel much that thou hast never told
> How, from a flower, into a fish of gold
> Apollo chang'd thee; how thou next didst seem
> A black-eyed swan upon the widening stream;
> And when thou first didst in that mirror trace
> The placid features of a human face:
> That thou hast never told thy travels strange,   90
> And all the wonders of the mazy range
> O'er pebbly crystal, and o'er golden sands;
> Kissing thy daily food from Naiad's pearly hands.
> ('To George Felton Mathew', ll. 72–93)

Keats doesn't depict the youthful travels of Felton – who *he* felt had progressed faster than he had in the poetic realms of gold – as a linear movement. Neither, for that matter, are his friend's literary successes imagined as being in any way dependent on heroic exertion (on 'laborious work', to call back Milnes). Similarly, there is no hint that studious craftsmanship has opened out a path towards future perfection. On the contrary, Felton's poetic advances, his rushes and dashes, have been facilitated by arbitrary gifts from Diana and Apollo – by the 'niggard muse', whose blessings Keats complains have been denied him – and by transformative flashes of inspiration that can change a 'flowret . . . wild' into a 'fish of gold', and then into a 'black-eyed swan'. Felton has not toiled from apprenticeship through to poetic power. There has been no coming of age, no sudden finding of voice, in Vendler's terms. Nor are his travels portrayed by Keats as a voyage of self-discovery. In fact, Keats's conception of artistic development in 'To George Felton Mathew' may be helpfully compared with sentiments embedded in another early verse epistle, 'To Charles Cowden Clarke' (1816), where Keats declared that when he himself ventured on the 'stream of rhyme', he sailed slowly, 'scarce knowing [his] intent' (ll. 16, 18). While the letters frequently lead one to conclude that Keats visualized poetic advance primarily in linear terms, his poetry often depicts a view of creative development that is more contingent, fanciful, fortuitous.

'T wang-dillo-dee'

> T wang dillo dee. This you must know is the Amen to nonsense. I know many places where Amen should be scratched out, rubb'd over with pou[n]ce made of Momus's little finger bones, and in its place 'T wang-dillo-dee,' written. This is the word I shall henceforth be tempted to write at the end of most modern Poems – Every American Book ought to have it. It would be a good distinction in Society. My Lords Wellington, Castlereagh and Canning and many more would do well to wear T wang-dillo-dee written on their Backs instead of wearing ribbands in their

6   *Introduction*

> Button holes . . . Some philosophers in the Moon who spy at our Globe as we do at theirs say that T wang dillo dee is written in large Letters on our Globe of Earth – They say the beginning of the T is just on the spot where London stands. London being built within the Flourish – *wan* reach downward and slant as far a[s] Tumbutoo in africa, the tail of the G. goes slap across the Atlantic into the Rio della Plata – the remainder of the Letters wrap round new holland and the last e terminates on land we have not yet discoverd. However I must be silent, these are dangerous times to libel a man in, much more a world.
>
> (*Letters*, II, 246–7)

This relentlessly inventive, ebullient passage is joyously alive, though written in 1820 when Keats's death was assured. It pokes fun at modern poems, the church, American authors, political rulers – whose punishment recalls the schoolboy trick of surreptitiously pinning a rude notice to somebody's back – and eventually the entire globe. It is a perfect example of how Keats's political being and boyish identity were sinuously and insinuatingly intertwined. In a flourish of his own, Keats depicts the world as one huge, transcendental signifier of nonsense; and yet the whole joke is circumscribed by a sharp awareness of the precarious nature of English freedoms, by the memory of Hunt's incarceration in Horsemonger Lane Gaol for libelling the Prince Regent (Hunt's release on 2 February 1815 was the occasion for an early Keats sonnet). Just as Jeffrey C. Robinson identifies immaturity, 'boy's play', as a 'carefully worked structure' in Hunt's life and work (p. 169), 'boyishness' is a coherent – or at least coherently incoherent – position of contestation, power, and personal liberation for Keats.

A major obstacle to integrating 'boyishness' within political accounts of the poet is our persistence in seeing immaturity as a stage through which Keats had to pass in order to achieve the teleology of a mature outlook, rather than as a 'completed' position in itself. Motion's political biography moves distinctively – but in this sense conventionally – from the childish 'doodles and dabblings' of *Calidore*, to the awakening of political and historical consciousness in *Sleep and Poetry* (where, after having 'given no impression of wanting to construct an argument', Keats is 'overtaken' by maturer thoughts on the 'agonies, the strife' of human life);[11] and then assuredly onwards to the *Hyperion* fragments, with their adult preoccupations with social order, and the dignified great odes, which 'transcend time', yet 'are fully aware of being written within time'.[12]

Identifying this schema is not to denigrate Motion's remarkable achievement as a chronicler of Keats's life and works. My point is simply this – in its own way, Motion's *Keats* reifies earlier attempts by Aileen Ward, Walter Jackson Bate, and Robert Gittings to model the poet's career as a predominantly uni-directional exertion towards self-determination of one kind or another – creative, personal, prophetic, historical. Gittings, for example, speaks of early Keats as 'not far enough advanced in his own taste'. We sense him waiting impatiently for the fully realized poet and man to emerge. Such 'maturational' accounts are prevalent; but they are surprisingly ill equipped to deal with the mercurial, protean, driven but *riven* Keats – the Keats of false starts, fits and starts, but also leaps and bounds; the Keats of *Feu de joie*, *embonpoint*, and 'T wang-dillo-dee', but also of the dark passages of human intellect; the Keats who read Spenser and Hunt, but also Locke and Condillac. What is a maturational critique to make of works by Keats that appear to cut awkwardly across narratives of personal and artistic maturation? Take, for example, the 'nonsense' poem, *The Cap and Bells; or, The Jealousies* – the last major writing project embarked on by Keats – routinely dismissed as 'naïve' and 'minor' (the second label conflating senses of 'insignificant' and 'under-aged'). In Motion's view, *The Cap and Bells* is 'of all the poems written in his maturity . . . the most disappointing';[13] while in Bate's it is 'the poorest of all Keats's poems, leaving aside the juvenile verses'.[14] What disturbs critics most about *The Cap and Bells* is its deep, unapologetic involvement in the forms and language of childhood. Yet we cannot get away from the prickly fact that Keats chose to cast his last long poem – a political satire attacking the Prince Regent – as a fairy tale (a childish genre).[15] Personally, I do not see the rupture deplored by Motion, Bate, and others, which *The Cap and Bells* is supposed to represent in terms of the authorized 'plot' of Keats's development towards poetic apotheosis. The oppositional mode which Keats employs to challenge the unyielding mechanisms of mature authority at the end is congruent with that found throughout his writing.

Indeed, in the letters and poems the politics of landed privilege, and the literary tastes and aesthetic values of a classically educated élite, are unfixed not so much by 'grown-up' disputations (by appropriating the discourse of established power and turning it to one's 'own' uses), as by moments of directed puerility and jejune tastelessness – 'boy's play', to recall Leigh Hunt in the epistle 'To William Hazlitt'. Put another way, Keats's most potent weapon against conservative ideology was precisely that for which he was most severely, and in a sense unsurprisingly, castigated by the mouthpieces of inherited power: 'Z' in *Blackwood's Edinburgh Magazine*, and J. W. Croker in the *Quarterly Review*. This is not to deny that Keats possessed a mature political consciousness; but the true radicalism of this consciousness, I believe, is located in performances of infantilism and absurdism, in what were perceived as his wheyey words and callow versification. It is the present volume's contention that only by resisting maturational narratives can we bring the true extent of Keats's challenge to middle-class values, bourgeois ideology, abusive power, exploitative labour exchange, the strictures of rigidly defined gender roles, dominant representations of masculinity, and the pernicious influence of polite aesthetics/aesthetic pleasure – opposition enacted through attention to puerility, gauche displays of petulance, callowness – finally into clear light. To this end, the discussions that follow investigate the psychological, poetical, and political contours of Keats's boyish imagination.

8   *Introduction*

Material is organized thematically rather than chronologically, individual chapters scrutinizing a single preoccupation in Keats's life and work, such as feet, the breaking voice, or female anatomy. Each, I demonstrate, provides a valuable new insight into the shaping and contesting energies of the poet's creative mind.

Chapter 1, '"Strange longings": Keats and feet', begins by casting in bold political relief the predominantly *un*conscious operations of Keats's childish conception. I read key poems, including *Endymion*, *The Fall of Hyperion*, *The Cap and Bells*, and *The Eve of St Agnes*, through Freud's 1927 paper 'On Fetishism', suggesting that Keats's attention to feet discloses a fascinating libidinal economy, founded on a boyish system of exchange. This structure, I argue, unsettles (with varying degrees of self-reflexivity) prevailing early nineteenth-century notions of virility, manliness, manly prowess, female sexuality, and desire itself; yet at the same time reveals an essential immaturity about Keats, a boyishness that persisted at what might be termed an impulsive level. While Joanna Richardson talks about Keats's 'forced indifference to women', as if this manifestation of crisis were an imposture or arty pose, I show that the poet's discordant relations with members of the opposite sex were, psychologically speaking, far more deeply seated than that.[16]

Where the opening chapter grants primacy to Keats's unconscious challenges to the sexual orthodoxies of mature power, Chapter 2, '"Full-grown lambs": immaturity and "To Autumn"', explores how his work – which a contemporary reviewer recognized was 'involved in ambiguity' – often teeters deliberately and self-consciously on the edge of puerility. Again my focus is on the complexity of Keats's standing to childishness. At times, we discover, Keats is 'sincerely' childish; elsewhere puerility is deployed in a calculating manner, as part of an ideology of resistance. Such teeterings are evident even – or perhaps we should say *especially* – in such celebrated works of 'calm power' as 'To Autumn'. I suggest that the famous ode becomes for Keats a conflicted testing ground of maturity, and that in it Keats is engaged in no less radical a procedure than undermining his own (always disputed) authority as a mature poet.

'Persistent puberphonia' is the medical term used to describe the failure of some adolescents to undergo vocal maturation. Chapter 3, '"Give me that voice again": Keats and puberphonia', explores the proposition that while Keats the maturing son longed to 'find his voice' – the 'mighty voice of Apollo', as he puts it in *I Stood Tip-toe* – he also wished to retain the youthful intonations of 'whining boyhood' (*Sleep and Poetry*). Vocal fluctuation between a deep-toned, manly register and a boyish, high-pitched whine can be detected across Keats's writing, and often within single poems, which are frequently double-voiced. This equivocation was in part an instinctively boyish reaction to what Keats perceived as the disturbing prospect of growing up. Clinical studies of adolescent vocal disorders clarify that a major psychological factor in the aetiology of puberphonia is the fear of assuming adult responsibilities, and my discussion highlights instances where Keats and his poetic surrogates display such a fear paradigmatically. But the poet's reluctance to develop an unambiguously manly voice was also – at certain times simultaneously – a political standpoint of non-conformity, from which Keats refused the demands of reviewers that he modulate his poetic voice in accordance with established models of literary maturation.

The fourth chapter, 'Japing the sublime: naughty boys and immature aesthetics', continues Chapter 2's investigation of more purposeful, directed performances of immaturity. In the summer of 1818, Keats left Hampstead for a walking tour of the Lakes, Highlands, and Ireland. His first sight of Lake Windermere made a deep impression:

> The two views we have had of it are of the most noble tenderness – they can never fade away – they make one forget the divisions of life; age, youth, poverty and riches; and refine one's sensual vision into a sort of north star which can never cease to be open lidded and stedfast over the wonders of the great Power.
>
> (*Letters*, I, 299)

Yet the 'divisions of life' could not be forgotten for very long. Moreover, it was precisely the divisions mentioned in this open-lidded passage – 'age, youth, poverty and riches' – that turned out to be at the very crux of Keats's northern experience. The tour was intended to give Keats a constructive dose of life outside the metropolis, as well as providing an opportunity to 'gorge wonders' (words which resounded in ways Keats could hardly have anticipated as he set out from London). The walks were also envisaged as an occasion to gather poetic raw material. This, Keats hoped, could be used to cultivate a grand style that would persuade established figures within the literary scene that the culturally marginalized poet was worthy of serious attention. However, Keats quickly developed an antipathy towards sublime scenery, and distrusted the standard techniques employed to represent it; he began to sense, indeed, that aesthetic theory was closely bound up with an élite model of political governance. Keats used boyish antics in sublime spots to undermine the coherency of both. Where criticism has traditionally sought to absorb the northern walks within a familiar paradigm of trial and endeavour, hardship and eventual triumph, I argue that, in the summer of 1818, Keats turns the concept of personal and poetic growth gained through experience on its head.

The final chapter, '"Stifling up the Vale": Keats and "c—-ts"', extends Chapter 1's investigation into psychosexual complexity. I examine Keats's possession of two ostensibly discrete traditions of knowledge regarding women's physiological 'reality'. The first was circulated through homosocial communities, passed around at 'Saturday clubs' and rowdy suppers. Keats's second mode of access to the biological function of the female body was gleaned through five years of obstetric and anatomical training with apothecary-surgeon Thomas Hammond, and a year's study with Sir Astley

Cooper at Guy's Hospital. Keats's longing to develop a 'right feeling towards Women' suggests that he wished to reconcile and integrate these two epistemologies: however, as I discuss, *both* were experienced as profoundly debilitating (to the point where they threatened to undermine and destabilize boyishness elsewhere as a viable mode of political resistance). Chapter 5 examines Keats's account of after-dinner etymological enquiries into four-letter words; scrutinizes his excruciating poetic attempts at bawdy – which are contrasted with those more robust, unabashed performances by his literary hero, Robert Burns, in *The Merry Muses of Caledonia* (banned in Britain until 1965); and compares anatomically suggestive passages from *Lamia* and *Isabella* with sections from Keats's student manuals at Guy's, particularly those focusing on the male and female organs of generation.

Collectively, these chapters explore a crucial but now neglected disposition in Keats's life and work that constituted – at different times, but also at the same time – a point of political resistance, a source of acute psychic disquiet, a form of imaginative liberation, and a primary creative resource.

1 'Strange longings'
Keats and feet

There are more feet in Keats's poetry than might be supposed – and by feet, I am referring to those found on the end of legs, not the metrical variety. Feet figure in various ways: for example, Keats visualized his poetic career in terms of the 'daring steps' he hoped to tread along the 'bright path[s] of light' left by Britain's great poets ('Specimen of an Induction to a Poem', ll. 57, 60). Many other references, on first sight at least, are formulaic. A lady's feet are always 'white' (*Endymion*, II, 325),[1] 'light' ('La Belle Dame Sans Merci', l. 15),[2] or 'nimble' (*Lamia*, I, 96). Reading from a psychoanalytic perspective, however, and drawing specifically on Freud's 1927 paper 'On Fetishism', I suggest that Keats's attention to feet – 'things on which the dazzled senses rest / Till the fond, fixèd eyes, forget they stare'[3] – cannot simply be explained, or contained, within the terms of conventional imagery. Closer examination opens a narrative into an intriguing libidinal economy, founded on what Keats himself called his 'Boyish imagination'. As I demonstrate, within this exchange 'normative' early nineteenth-century notions of manliness, female sexuality, and desire itself, are radically unfixed by physiological apprehension.

The boyish imagination

Keats's ambivalent relationship with 'manliness' has often been remarked on. As Anne K. Mellor reminds us, Keats believed his appearance was girlish.[4] Reviewers confirmed this image by portraying him as a 'Cockney' poet, a label that readers would have recognized as containing a sense of effeminacy.[5] Or else, employing what Susan Wolfson calls 'a puerilising rhetoric', Keats was presented to the reading public as an immature boy.[6] In both cases, detractors aimed to discredit Keats's literary productions by questioning his manliness, and thus his right to be taken seriously by a 'grown-up' audience. *Blackwood's* 'Z' (John Gibson Lockhart) called Keats 'a boy of pretty abilities';[7] in 1826, the journal referred to his 'emasculated pruriency'.[8] In private Byron showed less restraint, vehemently dismissing 'Johnny Keats's *p—ss a bed* poetry'.[9]

Keats was conscious that he harboured a vulnerability to attacks of this kind. In 1819 he complained to his brother and sister-in-law: 'My name with the literary fashionables is vulgar – I am a weaver boy to them' (*Letters*, II, 186). Nevertheless, he did not deny the centrality of immaturity to his life and art. On the contrary, in a letter to his friend Benjamin Bailey in July 1818, he refers uneasily to his 'Boyish imagination', which he supposes has prevented him from developing a 'right feeling towards Women':

> I am certain I have not a right feeling towards Women . . . Is it because they fall so far beneath my Boyish imagination? When I was a Schoolboy I though[t] a fair Woman a pure Goddess, my mind was a soft nest in which some one of them slept though she knew it not – I have no right to expect more than their reality . . . When I am among Women I have evil thoughts, malice spleen – I cannot speak or be silent – I am full of Suspicions . . . I am in a hurry to be gone – You must be charitable and put all this perversity to my being disappointed since Boyhood.
> (*Letters*, I, 341)

He adds despairingly: 'I must absolutely get over this – but how?' (*Letters*, I, 342). Later I will suggest ways in which Keats attempted to overcome his wrong feelings. Displaying a precocious talent for self-analysis, Keats identifies a conflict between his boyish conception of women as 'pure goddesses' and his more mature, if troubled, notion of what he calls 'their reality'. I am not merely suggesting that these rival concepts help generate such dualistic figures as La Belle Dame, Moneta, or Lamia, whose head, as every student knows, 'was serpent, but ah, bitter-sweet! / She had a woman's mouth with all its pearls complete' (*Lamia*, I, 59–60). Rather, my discussion discloses a compelling psychological drama in Keats's letters and poetry, in which a reluctance to respond to or represent women in any way other than 'boyishly' is repeatedly demonstrated. While it may not be surprising to suggest that his poetry is frequently immature, given that Keats died at the age of twenty-five, I will show in precise terms how this immaturity manifests itself through the representations of the fetishistic imagination.

In an engaging article on Keats's *Isabella; or, The Pot of Basil*, Diane Long Hoeveler insists that 'just as we know from dream analysis that everything in the dream is a manifestation of the dreamer, so everything in the poem is a projection of some aspect of the poet'.[10] This liberating methodology allows us to perceive in Keats's writing psychological dilemmas that not only inflected the ways in which Keats constructed female sexuality, but ones that were also central to the formation of his own sexuality. The master clue in this respect, and the one that opens a new perspective on Keats's 'boyishness', is the poet's enduring interest in feet. If this sounds frivolous, preposterous even (and I am prepared to concede that at this stage it does), possibly it is because no one, to my knowledge, has commented on the extraordinary frequency – the altogether *extraordinariness* – of feet and foot-related imagery in Keats's work. The following sections explore episodes in which Keats's attention to feet registers deeper anxieties about sex and/with women. Despite Jean Hagstrum's contention that 'Keats delights in consummation', I contend that foot episodes document the conversion in Keats's poetics of 'normative' early nineteenth-century modes of mature desire and sexual fulfilment into a 'boyish' erotics that is voyeuristic, fetishistic, and deferred.[11]

Completed completeness

I begin with a bizarre fiction (but in terms of male psychology, possibly a 'true Story' as Keats claims), recounted by the poet to James Rice in 1819:[12]

> Would you like a true Story "There was a Man and his Wife who being to go a long journey on foot, in the course of their travels came to a River which rolled knee deep over the pebbles – In these cases the Man generally pulls off his shoes and stockings and carries the woman over on his Back. This man did so; and his Wife being pregnant and troubled, as in such cases is very common, with strange longings, took the strangest that was ever heard of – Seeing her Husband's foot, a handsome on[e] enough, look very clean and tempting in the clear water, on their arrival at the other bank she earnestly demand{ed} a bit of it; he being an affectionate fellow and fearing for the comeliness of his child gave her a bit which he cut off with his Clasp knife – Not satisfied she asked another morsel – supposing there might be twins he gave her a slice more. Not yet contented she craved another Piece. "You Wretch cries the Man, would you wish me to kill myself? take that!" Upon which he stabb'd her with the knife, cut her open and found three Children in her Belly two of them very comfortable with their mouth's shut, the third with its eyes and mouth stark staring open. "Who would have thought it" cried the Wid{ow}er<">, and pursued his journey –, Brown has a little rumbling in his Stomach this morning –
>
> (*Letters*, II, 236)

Christopher Ricks links this passage to the 'primacy of eating in Keats' and a 'richly robust fantasy',[13] whereas for Anne Mellor it emphasizes the 'extraordinary degree to which Keats identified the process of poetic creation with the process of female pregnancy and giving birth'.[14] These readings seem to me to skirt the issue. Keats is not concerned, initially at least, with eating, fantasizing, or even, most spuriously of all, giving birth. The focus of his odd tale, like the wife's 'strange longings', is directed at the husband's foot, which appears 'clean and tempting in the clear water'.[15] Additionally, Keats's interest in the wife's fixation tells us at least as much about Keats and his configuration of female sexuality as it does about the wife's strange longings. We do not have to work very hard to find phallic significance in the foot, or to surmise that its mutilation by the wife records a fear of castration. As we shall see, visions of castration define Keats's response to assertive women, and in this respect we might say that the wife is a psychological sibling to other figures whom Keats *perceives* as emasculating, such as Lamia, La Belle Dame, and Moneta. I italicize 'perceives' because, although these poetic personages are in one sense Keats's creations, that is not to say that he exercises full control over their significations. Indeed, the limits of authored determination can be observed in Moneta in *The Fall of Hyperion*, who, on the face of things, is a powerfully immobilizing figure, but who also, as I shall argue, functions at some level to assist the dreamer in developing a 'right feeling towards Women'. But if the castration anxieties in Keats's foot tale are clearly recognizable, the psychological processes underlying the wife's 'strange longings' (and equally importantly, Keats's evident interest in them) need to be unravelled.

In his famous paper on fetishism, delivered in 1927, Freud contends that when young boys first catch sight of the female genitals, their infantile belief that girls possess a phallus is severely shaken; in this instant, boys are forced to confront the possibility that they, too, might 'lose' their penises.[16] As a response, they either 'repress' or 'disavow' what they have seen, both accepting and at the same time not accepting the absent organ (p. 353). In the usual course of events, boys are supposed to come to terms with their discovery, learn to control their fear of castration, and go on to develop 'normal' relations with women – in other words, the 'right feeling towards Women' that eluded Keats. For some, though, this resolution is only possible through the substitution of a fetishized object (such as the foot) in place of the missing phallus. The fetish is identified as:

> not a substitute for any chance penis, but for a particular and quite special penis that had been extremely important in early childhood but had later been lost. That is to say, it should normally have been given up, but the fetish is precisely designed to preserve it from extinction. To put it more plainly: the fetish is a substitute for the woman's (the mother's) penis that the little boy once believed in and . . . does not want to give up.
>
> (p. 352)

The fetish allows the castrated mother to be reconstituted as a phallic mother who no longer raises the spectre of castration in the young boy's mind. But the compromise is achieved at the price of an 'aversion' to the 'real female genitals' that is 'never absent in any fetishist' and which forms a '*stigma indelebile* of the repression that has taken place' (p. 353). With this in mind, when Keats asks Bailey to 'be charitable and put all this perversity [towards women] to my being disappointed since Boyhood' (*Letters*, I, 341), one also hears 'disappointed *in* Boyhood', because, as I will demonstrate, Keats's famous perturbation over women can be traced to his inability to assimilate the traumatic discovery of 'their [non-phallic] reality'.

Freud concludes that the fetish represents a 'triumph over the threat of castration', allows women to remain 'tolerable as sexual objects', but simultaneously reminds the fetishist of the truth, literally too terrible to contemplate, about female sexuality (pp. 353–4). Finally, foot fetishism is addressed specifically in the following terms: 'The foot or shoe owes its preference as a fetish . . . to the circumstance that the inquisitive boy peered at the woman's genitals from below, from her legs up' (p. 354). This 'insight' certainly illuminates a key 'shoe' story, *Cinderella*. Whatever else the glass slipper stands for, it affords the prince – an archetypally 'inquisitive boy' – an opportunity to peer up a large number of skirts as he helps would-be princesses try on the shoe. Now, as far as the prince is concerned, *Cinderella* is all about growing up, finding a 'right' feeling towards women, and getting married – even if this requires the assistance of a foot-focused fetish like the slipper. But the resolution arrived at by the prince is denied Keats, that other signally 'inquisitive boy'. If the prince, busily peering up skirts, is equally arrested by the fetishized object (the slipper) as by the thing it 'completes' (the female genitals), then his narrative successfully moves beyond this boyish stage into the grown-up's marriage bed and the realization of mature sexual desires. Keats, on the other hand, remains firmly in fetishistic mode, as his description of Diana's descent from the heavens in Book 1 of *Endymion* confirms:

> . . . once more I rais'd
> My sight right upward: but it was quite dazed
> By a bright something, sailing down apace,
> Making me quickly veil my eyes and face:
> Again I look'd, and, O ye deities,
> Who from Olympus watch our destinies!
> Whence that completed form of all completeness?
> (*Endymion*, I, 600–6)

Although this has not been remarked on, given the sight-lines that must logically prevail here, the Latmian shepherd boy quite literally looks up the skirt of a goddess. But – and this is precisely the point I want to discuss – his gaze is arrested by Diana's feet:

> Ah! see her hovering feet,
> More bluely vein'd, more soft, more whitely sweet
> Than those of sea-born Venus
> (*Endymion*, I, 624–6)

By focusing on Diana's feet, a fetishized substitute for the missing phallus, Keats hopes to avoid unpleasant thoughts of castration. His efforts seem not to have been wholly successful, however. In a recently rediscovered letter from 1818, Keats mentions a trip to the printers to 'geld' *Endymion*: 'I have been in Town two days gelding the first Book [*Endymion*] which is I think going to the Press today.'[17] Lewis Dearing suggests that *geld* occurs here in the archaic sense of excising offensive lines from a text:

16 *'Strange longings': Keats and feet*

> Influenced by his love of Chaucer, Spenser and by the Spenserians, Keats was fond of archaic and obsolete words and usages. *Geld* here may mean, as defined by the *OED*, simply 'to cut out portions of a book . . . especially objectionable or obscene passages'.
>
> (p. 16n)

But in view of the castration anxieties flickering beneath the surface of *Endymion*, particularly in Book 1, the first meaning of *geld* recorded by the *OED* – 'To deprive (a male) of generative power or virility, to castrate or emasculate' – seems equally appropriate. In fact, Keats's choice of words probably tells us less about his publisher's lack of enthusiasm for the young poet's philological experimentation, than reflects, parapraxically, a deep phallic anxiety to which *Endymion* returns again and again. Actually, within this context of castration, the reference to 'sea-born Venus' at I, 626 is extremely resonant. Venus is indeed 'sea-born' (her Greek name is 'Aphrogeneia', or 'sprung from the foam'), because Saturn castrated his father Coelus with a scythe, threw his elder's genitalia into the ocean, and Venus sizzled into the world.

By fetishizing Diana's foot into a substitute phallus, the goddess remains 'tolerable as a sexual object' in Keats's imagination. However, the accompanying aversion described by Freud also figures in Keats's depiction of Diana, as attested in the question: 'whence that completed form of all completeness?' (I, 606). This deeply ironic line deconstructs itself the moment it is uttered: for Keats, Diana is *anything* but complete. The text's gauche profession of sincerity (the image of completed completeness surely protests too much) does little more than confirm the difficulties facing Keats, caught between boyish and manly paradigms of desire and representation. As can be seen, the descriptive hierarchy governing the narration of Diana's descent draws into clear focus the predominantly boyish assumptions that underpin Keats's text:

>   . . . yet she had,
> Indeed, locks bright enough to make me mad;
> And they were simply gordian'd up and braided,
> Leaving, in naked comeliness, unshaded,
> Her pearl round ears, white neck, and orbed brow;
> The which were blended in, I know not how,
> With such a paradise of lips and eyes,
> Blush-tinted cheeks, half smiles, and faintest sighs,
> That, when I think thereon, my spirit clings
> And plays about its fancy, till the stings
> Of human neighbourhood envenom all.
> Unto what awful power shall I call?
> To what high fane? – Ah! see her hovering feet,
> More bluely vein'd, more soft, more whitely sweet

Than those of sea-born Venus, when she rose
From out her cradle shell.
(*Endymion*, I, 612–27)

Keats works himself up into raptures over Diana's 'soft hand', her maddening 'locks', the 'naked comeliness' of her 'pearl round ears', her 'orbed brow', the 'paradise of lips and eyes', her 'blush-tinted cheeks' – but is unable to proceed further towards Freud's 'longed-for sight of the female member' (p. 354), or even contemplate the realization of conventional manly desire. Rather, the exuberant commentary culminates (or, in Freud's terms, Keats's interest 'comes to a halt half-way', p. 354) with the goddess's 'hovering' *feet*: 'more bluely vein'd, more soft, more whitely sweet / Than those of sea-born Venus, when she rose / From out her cradle shell'.

We might pause over 'sweet', since this word maps a textual fault-line. Just as Keats's efforts at convincing us that Diana represents his ideal of womanhood give rise to awkwardness (completed completeness), Diana's 'sweet' feet vitiate his determination to respond to women in a 'manly' fashion. Consider the precise meaning of lines 624–7: here Keats emphasizes that Diana's feet are sweeter than 'sea-born' Venus' *when* she rose out of the ocean in a shell. This on first sight formulaic comparison produces an awkward conjunction of images. If 'sweet' is used in the sense of 'dainty', as seems to be Keats's intention, then Venus' feet present a problem. The goddess's extremities are wet from the sea and, one presumes, *salty*. Since 'salty' is a near antonym of 'sweet' (qualifying taste), the proximity of Diana's sweet (dainty) feet alongside Venus' salty ones is comical – surely not the effect Keats has in mind (although, in its cringe-worthiness, the image is certainly in keeping with boyish inexperience in matters of love – ask any inexperienced boy). The use of 'sweet' alongside an image of saltiness is not only bad; it is bad in a boyish way, and arises out of an infantile preoccupation with orality that is never absent when Keats uses the word 'sweet'.

Roland Barthes' elusive essay, *The Pleasure of the Text*, proposes that, as distinct from pleasure, desire can be characterized as 'expectation' since it is 'never satisfied', never completed.[18] Lack of completion is entirely characteristic of Keats's poetics, which, we could say, is anxious to be *seen* to be desiring the 'longed-for sight of the female member' (the goal of 'manly' narrative), without ever actually arriving at the 'uncanny and traumatic' spectacle. This is apparent in Diana's descent in Book 1 of *Endymion*, where the pleasure of completion, in visual terms, has been put off indefinitely. In Keats's new economy, feet have been substituted for the telos of manly desire (the 'longed-for sight'). Even where *Endymion* seems to move inexorably towards completion (one thinks of Endymion's 'union' with Diana towards the end of Book 1), closer scrutiny reveals the text folding back in on itself. The very instant in which the Latmian 'dared to press / Her very cheek' against his 'crownèd lip', he is transported with the goddess 'Into a warmer air':

> ... a moment more,
> Our feet were soft in flowers. There was store
> Of newest joys upon that alp.
>
> (*Endymion*, I, 664–6)

Once again, feet dominate the narrative, grounding not only the lovers in flowers, but Keats's erotic imagination in boyish exchange.

'Cold retreat'

The image of feet runs (pun intended) throughout *Endymion*. While it would distort facts to impart significance to each single instance (after all, when they are not flying or being transported by some other means, people have to use their feet to move around the text), the poem's more overtly fetishistic scenes destabilize apparently formulaic phrases such as 'lost in pleasure at her feet he sinks' (IV, 18), or descriptions of Diana as standing on 'light tiptoe divine' (II, 261). The cumulative effect is for *Endymion* to unfix normative modes of early nineteenth-century desire, disclosing ostensibly conventional love relationships as fetishistic, founded on aversion, anxiety, and physical apprehension.

The last example I want to discuss from Keats's 'apprentice' poem comes from Book 2, in the bower of Adonis. Here a cupid relates the story of Venus and Adonis to the shepherd boy:

> I need not any hearing tire
> By telling how the sea-born goddess pin'd
> For a mortal youth, and how she strove to bind
> Him all in all unto her doting self.
> Who would not be so prison'd? but, fond elf,
> He was content to let her amorous plea
> Faint through his careless arms; content to see
> An unseiz'd heaven dying at his feet;
> Content, O fool! to make a cold retreat,
> When on the pleasant grass such love, lovelorn,
> Lay sorrowing; when every tear was born
> Of diverse passion; when her lips and eyes
> Were clos'd in sullen moisture, and quick sighs
> Came vex'd and pettish through her nostrils small.
>
> (*Endymion*, II, 457–70)

The cupid's tale, like the story Keats tells Rice, describes a 'truth' about male psychology, in this case a fear of failure, of not measuring up to expectations. Adonis is 'content to see / An unseiz'd heaven dying at his feet; / Content ... to make a cold retreat' (ll. 463–5). His inability to engage with the surfeit of physicality registered in the description of a petulant and very obviously sexually frustrated Venus recalls Keats's confession that in the presence of women he was always 'in a hurry to be gone' (*Letters*, I, 341). The theme of 'cold retreat' (l. 465) is pursued throughout *Endymion*. Repeatedly, corporeality – the here and now – is declined in favour of substitutions; indeed, in terms of narrative, the poem moves from one dream-vision, reverie, and mimic temple to the next, leaving the forms of physical reality to be reproduced solely on the level of myth or statuary.

'Beauties, scarce discern'd'

In 1816, Keats composed a valentine ('Hadst thou liv'd in days of old'), for his brother George to send to Richard Woodhouse's cousin, Mary Frogley. Andrew Motion's recent biography of Keats detects a 'displaced sexual excitement' in this poem, concluding that 'where it is most direct it becomes voyeuristic'.[19] If the poem is voyeuristic it is also fetishistic, and possibly contains a hitherto unremarked image of feet in water to rival that found in the tale of strange longings told by Keats to Rice. The poem commences with a conventional treatment of Mary's beauty:

> Hadst thou liv'd in days of old,
> O what wonders had been told
> Of thy lovely countenance,
> And thy humid eyes that dance
> . . . .
> Of thy dark hair that extends
> Into many graceful bends:
> . . . .
>   . . . Add too, the sweetness
> Of thy honied voice; the neatness
> Of thine ankle lightly turn'd.
>   ('To [Mary Frogley]',
>   ll. 1–4, 13–14, 23–5)

These are formulaic images; I am more interested in the following passage:

> . . . those beauties, scarce discern'd,
> Kept with such sweet privacy,
> That they seldom meet the eye
> Of the little loves that fly
> Round about with eager pry.
> Saving when, with freshening lave,
> Thou dipp'st them in the taintless wave;
> Like twin water lilies, born
> In the coolness of the morn
>   ('To [Mary Frogley]', ll. 26–34)

Traditionally, 'those beauties' (l. 26) are taken as a reference to breasts. But coming as they do literally on the heels of Mary's 'lightly turn'd' ankles, one might conjecture whether by 'those beauties' Keats, at some subterranean level of consciousness, meant feet. At any rate, there are good reasons to doubt a description of breasts. Logically, 'dip' is more appropriate to feet or toes than breasts; indeed, it is difficult to conceive how Mary Frogley might have 'dipped' her breasts in water whilst maintaining her balance. Besides, one can hardly imagine Keats commenting so directly on Mary's breasts in a poem written for his brother George to send as a valentine.

There is other evidence to support a reading of feet over breasts. In Book 2 of *Endymion*, the shepherd boy indulges the following unwholesome fantasy of Diana:

> Within my breast there lives a choking flame –
> O let me cool it the zephyr-boughs among!
> A homeward fever parches up my tongue –
> O let me slake it at the running springs!
> . . . .
> Dost thou now *lave* thy feet and ankles white?
> O think how sweet to me the freshening sluice!
> (*Endymion*, II, 317–26; my emphasis)

The use of the unusual, poetic 'lave' in both Mary Frogley's valentine and *Endymion* (a noun in the former, a verb in the latter) suggests that the episodes were linked in Keats's mind. It is not unreasonable to surmise that each scene describes the same event: foot washing.

Miriam Allott cites Spenser's *Epithalamion* ('Her paps lyke lillies budded', l. 176), as a source for the disputed passage, and a traditional reading of the valentine discovers a venerable literary convention in the comparison of Mary's breasts with 'twin water lilies' (l. 33). But elsewhere in Keats, lilies are linked with *feet* – moreover feet in or by water. In *Hyperion*, Apollo stands 'Beside the osiers of a rivulet, / Full ankle-deep in lilies of the vale' (III, 34–5). So, even if Keats *thought* he was writing about breasts in Mary's valentine, he may really have had feet in mind. And if it *is* Mary Frogley's feet to which he alludes, then the cloying preciousness exhibited towards them ('scarce discern'd', 'kept with such sweet privacy', ll. 26–7) bears all the hall-marks of the boyish, fetishistic imagination.

Phallic mothers

In *The Fall of Hyperion*, too, the fetishized foot provides a point of entry into a libidinal economy in which 'normal' relations between Keats's male narrators and the women who share their poetic domain are disabled by phallic anxiety and genital aversion. We might consider the dreamer's confrontation with the goddess Moneta in Book 1 within this frame of reference. Although *The Fall of*

Hyperion is a later, purportedly more 'mature' work, we again find Keats worrying over women's 'reality' and trying to develop 'a right feeling' towards them. However, despite the unmistakable climate of personal crisis surrounding the early encounter with Moneta, the episode in fact represents Keats's attempt to 'absolutely get over' his wrong feelings.[20]

The dreamer emerges from his post-prandial slumber to find the surroundings of the 'mossy mound and arbour' transformed into the carved walls of an 'old sanctuary' (I, 60–2). Far off in the west of the building, he discerns steps leading up to an altar positioned at the foot of 'An image', eventually revealed as Saturn. This out-sized paternal projection activates a thousand phallic insecurities in Keats's narrator, who nevertheless feels compelled to approach the altar. At this point, the Oedipal triangulation is completed by Moneta, whose language, we are told, is 'as near as an immortal's sphered words / Could to a mother's soften' (I, 249–50). Keats describes the scene around her altar in the following terms:

> ... that lofty sacrificial fire,
> Sending forth Maian incense, spread around
> Forgetfulness of everything but bliss,
> And clouded all the altar with soft smoke,
> From whose white fragrant curtains thus I heard
> Language pronounc'd: 'If thou canst not ascend
> These steps, die on that marble where thou art'.
> (*The Fall of Hyperion*, I, 102–8)

The altar, then, is 'clouded' from view by 'soft smoke' forming 'fragrant curtains' around it (I, 105–6). This image is yet another guise of the maternal skirts, last seen in Diana's descent in *Endymion*; the skirts are fetishized here for reasons that Freud makes clear: 'Pieces of clothing, which are so often chosen as a fetish, crystallize the moment of undressing, the last moment in which the woman could still be regarded as phallic' (pp. 354–5). At line 106, the poetic curtain metaphor makes the association of cloud or smoke with fabric apparent; but the link is also made elsewhere more colloquially. We discover it, for instance, in *The Cap and Bells; or, The Jealousies*, in the injunction to see at line 553: 'See, past the skirts of yon white cloud they go'. Comparison with *The Cap and Bells* is doubly rewarding in the light of *Endymion*. The line just quoted refers to Princess Bellanaine's airborne journey from Pigmio to the faery city of Emperor Elfinan; as the 'fluttering embassy' bear Bellanaine to the ground, her descent, like Diana's, receives lavish attention:

> Gentlemen pensioners next; and after them,
> A troop of winged janizaries flew;
> Then slaves, as presents bearing many a gem;
> Then twelve physicians fluttering two and two;
> And next a chaplain in a cassock new;

> Then lords in waiting; then (what head not reels
> For pleasure?) the fair Princess in full view,
> Borne upon wings, – and very pleased she feels
> To have such splendour dance attendance at her heels.
> (*The Cap and Bells; or, The Jealousies*, ll. 586–94)

This passage is little more than a bawdy reworking of Diana's descent in *Endymion*, with the 'joke' made more explicitly this time. As the princess floats earthwards, we watch with the boyishly inquisitive members of the crowd below, whose necks crane to look up her skirts: '(What head not reels / For pleasure?) the fair Princess in full view' (ll. 591–2). 'Full view' is misleading, however. As we should expect of Keats by this stage, the collective gaze is not permitted to proceed to 'the longed-for sight', but must remain content to 'dance attendance at [Bellanaine's] heels'.

I want to return to *The Fall of Hyperion* via Keats's mother. As Diane Long Hoeveler reminds us, Frances Keats, who died in 1810 when Keats was fourteen, is virtually absent from her son's letters and poems.[21] Robert Gittings supposes that this silence 'suggests some shattering knowledge, with which, at various times in his life, [Keats] can be seen dimly struggling to come to terms'.[22] It is tempting to read this 'shattering knowledge' as the distantly recalled and fervently disavowed moment of anatomical discovery discussed by Freud in 1927, allowing the origins of Keats's fetishistic imagination to be traced to a traumatic maternal encounter. Indeed, while little is known about Keats's relationship with his mother, there is anecdotal evidence to indicate that she was strongly linked with the first stirrings of fetishism in his mind. Keats's friend, the painter Benjamin Robert Haydon, relates an incident from Keats's childhood, in which the poet, aged about five:

> . . . once got hold of a naked sword and shutting the [front] door swore nobody should go out. His mother wanted to do so but he threatened her so furiously she began to cry, and was obliged to wait till somebody through the window saw her position and came to her rescue.[23]

Whether or not this episode actually took place, and bearing in mind that the narrative is Haydon's, not Keats's, the account is suggestive. It figures Keats as an exaggeratedly phallic young boy (holding an out-sized, grown-up's sword), trying to conceal his mother from view (he 'swore nobody should go out'), but who is seen anyway from outside ('somebody through the window saw her position'). Keats's response to the discovery of women's 'reality' is twofold. First he wards off thoughts of castration and aggressively reaffirms his own phallic status by waving about the sword. At the same time he tries to repress or 'disavow' his discovery by preventing his mother from leaving her house. But if one symbol of the female genitals, the door, is prevented from signifying (shut and barred), another, the window, reveals the reality of women's 'positions' to those inclined to see them.

Later in life, Keats was still working through his relationship with his mother as part of his endeavour to rectify the 'wrong' feelings he held about women. Moneta, who seems to represent the mother at some level, becomes part of this process in *The Fall of Hyperion*. We left the dreamer about to ascend the steps to Moneta's altar:

> Prodigious seem'd the toil; the leaves were yet
> Burning, – when suddenly a palsied chill
> Struck from the paved level up my limbs,
> And was ascending quick to put cold grasp
> Upon those streams that pulse beside the throat:
> I shriek'd; and the sharp anguish of my shriek
> Stung my own ears – I strove hard to escape
> The numbness; strove to gain the lowest step.
> Slow, heavy, deadly was my pace: the cold
> Grew stifling, suffocating, at the heart;
> And when I clasp'd my hands I felt them not.
> One minute before death, my iced foot touch'd
> The lowest stair; and as it touch'd, life seem'd
> To pour in at the toes: I mounted up . . .
> (*The Fall of Hyperion*, I, 121–34)

With great exertion the dreamer reaches the altar, finds himself before Moneta, and is instantly immobilized with fear:

> . . . I had a terror of her robes,
> And chiefly of the veils, that from her brow
> Hung pale, and curtain'd her in mysteries
> That made my heart too small to hold its blood.
> (*The Fall of Hyperion*, I, 251–4)

His terror derives from thoughts of the castrated phallus concealed beneath Moneta's robes and veils. The imagery at line 254 is particularly revealing of the nature of the dreamer's predicament. The heart that becomes 'too small to hold its blood' could, of course, be read in two ways: either the heart is simply unable to cope with the sheer volume of blood pumping through it; or, in an opposite sense, Keats is describing a moment of *de*-tumescence, in which the heart shrinks until it is no longer able to pump vigorously, or even 'hold its blood'. A moment of supreme dysthymic apprehension would be entirely appropriate to the wider tenor of timidity and tremulousness. What is more, given the phallic anxieties that prevail at this point, it is telling that in line 250, Keats should make an unequivocal association between Moneta's 'sphered words' and the language of motherhood. This identification reconstructs around the altar what Freud calls the original 'uncanny and traumatic' revelation of anatomical difference. That is to say, Keats seems determined to manoeuvre his narrator into a position that allows him, vicariously, to renegotiate the original discovery that first determined the boyish, fetishistic parameters of his poetic imagination.

Accordingly, at line 256, Moneta casts aside her maternal veils. But if her intention is to force the 'Boyish imagination' to accept the 'reality' about women, she is singularly unsuccessful. The dreamer immediately and resolutely transfers his gaze to her feet: '"Shade of Memory!" / Cried I, with act adorant at her feet' (I, 282–3). This 'Shade of Memory' is evidently that of the 'uncanny and traumatic' spectacle identified by Freud; but Keats remains unable, or ultimately unwilling, to assimilate it. His determinedly fetishistic act of focusing on Moneta's feet refigures the goddess as a phallic mother. Entirely characteristic of Keats's immature libidinal economy, aversion and boyish desire coalesce to prompt yet another retreat into the fetish.

'Tiptoe, amorous cavaliers'

If 'castrated' women present one kind of threat to Keats's fragile sense of masculinity, then 'manly' men present another that the poet struggles to resolve. On his way to the altar steps in *The Fall of Hyperion*, Keats's dreamer pauses underneath the massive image of Saturn, whereupon Moneta remarks that he is 'safe beneath this statue's knees' (I, 181). In view of the fact that the dreamer stands, literally, in the shadow of the titanically dimensioned paternal phallus, Moneta's speech is a piece of consummate irony. For Keats, whose letters are punctuated by concerns about manliness, worries that the public perceived him as effeminate, and nervous asides about his small stature, it is difficult to conceive of a more disorienting space.

Keats's diminutive proportions were a constant source of embarrassment. In June 1818, he remarked to the Jeffrey sisters, Marian and Sarah: 'I being somewhat stunted am taken for nothing' (*Letters*, I, 291). While the context of this aside in the letter suggests that it was written in jest, the adage that some things in life are so serious they can *only* be joked about is apposite. From the outset of his career, Keats lamented what he considered his exclusion, due to shortness, from the codes and forms of 'manly' courtship. This sentiment is audible in an often-quoted early sonnet, 'To – ['Had I a man's fair form']':

> Had I a man's fair form, then might my sighs
> Be echoed swiftly through that ivory shell
> Thine ear, and find thy gentle heart.
> ('Had I a man's fair form', ll. 1–3)

In 'sighs', Wolfson detects a rueful pun on *size*, which further reinforces Keats's sense of disfellowship from 'grown-up' society.[24]

Alongside Keats's bashfulness about his height, we find occasional moments of ebullient, inviolable confidence, such as his conviction that he would be counted 'among the English poets' (*Letters*, I, 394) after his death when there was little evidence to suggest it at the time. Such claims could be said to form a megalomaniacal counter to more familiar moments of low self-esteem. Keats's grand plan in 1817 to compose a huge poem (*Endymion*) that would be '4000 Lines' long (*Letters*, I, 170), is a case in point. The project surrenders its phallic insecurities easily, and is another counter-measure against deep-seated feelings of inadequacy – if Keats felt that his stature disadvantaged him in female company ('I do think better of womankind than to suppose they care whether John Keats five foot hight likes them or not', *Letters*, I, 342), then *Endymion* would prove his poetic rather than physical prowess. Additionally, the exercise would allow him to compete with England's great historical poets, who, Keats points out in an instance of unequivocal phallic anxiety, never wrote short pieces (*Letters*, I, 170). To confirm *Endymion*'s phallic preoccupations, we need only look at the poem's motto: 'the *stretched* metre of an antique song' (my emphasis), inscribed to the memory of another 'boy' poet with low self-regard, Thomas Chatterton. Byron immediately recognized the nature of the anxieties voiced in the motto, denouncing the '*outstretched* poesy of this miserable Self-polluter of the human Mind' (Byron's emphasis) to the publisher John Murray.[25]

Keats seems to have considered himself in competition with a certain sort of man. We know, for example, from his letters that he nurtured a sense of inadequacy towards the older, outgoing, sexually confident (and *mature*) Charles Brown, and suspected his fiancée Fanny Brawne of being secretly attracted to his friend.[26] Psychologically, his feeling of shortcoming in the vicinity of other men is co-identical with the crisis experienced by the dreamer beneath Saturn's knees in the second *Hyperion*. And this brings me to my final point. I want to suggest that just as Keats's interest in female feet points to key processes conditioning and inflecting his representation of women, 'male' feet are equally disclosing. Has it ever occurred to anyone that men in Keats are frequently introduced feet first, so to speak? The first time we meet Saturn in *The Fall of Hyperion*, we are directed to his massive feet. Similarly, Saturn's presence in the first *Hyperion* is initially registered by the 'large foot-marks' he leaves imprinted in the sand (I, 15). So, too, the virile suitors in *The Eve of St Agnes* are introduced as 'tiptoe, amorous' cavaliers (l. 60). For what may well be therapeutic reasons, Keats delights in deflating these iconically *manly* men. Saturn's huge footprints lead to an 'unsceptred', emasculated Saturn, who sits with 'bow'd head' in defeat (I, 19–20); while in stanza 7 of *The Eve of St Agnes*, Madeline proves completely, even comically, impervious to the efforts of the tiptoe suitors to impress her. Oblivious to their posturings, she is lost instead in contemplation of Porphyro, that most Keatsian of heroes: effeminate, naïve, voyeuristic, and reluctant to engage directly with female corporeality.

I would like to expand this last point briefly, since I believe that the character of Porphyro embodies many of the psychological processes that animate Keats himself. This is particularly true with regard to Porphyro's desire for a 'cold retreat' from the realm of the corporeal. For despite Hagstrum's view that 'Keats delights in consummation', even the notoriously 'explicit' description of Porphyro and Madeline's love-making in stanza 36, which so perturbed Keats's publisher, is narrated around the act of absenting oneself from the physical world: 'Into her dream he melted, as the rose / Blendeth its odour with the violet' (ll. 320–1). With this retreat, Porphyro reflects Keats's own discomfiture in the presence of women ('When I am among women . . . I am in a hurry to be gone', *Letters*, I, 341). One could say that the matrix of personality surviving in the letters and poetry that we know as John Keats, and Porphyro his poetic creation, are virtually indistinguishable in stanzas 26–30. There the disengaged Keatsian narrator watches over the sleeping, non-threatening Madeline, barely able to resist the pervasive languidity and stay awake himself, leaving the task of seduction to his alter ego, his manly *Doppelgänger*, who inhabits Madeline's dream-vision.

Even when Madeline wakes up, Porphyro conspires to prolong the illusion of dreaming, or at any rate soften the transition into the waking world. He overburdens the scene with piles of dream-like foods: candied apple, quince, plum, jellies, lucent syrups – a totally impractical, indigestible feast that Marjorie Levinson suggests seems never to have been meant for eating.[27] Consisting 'entirely of children's foods' as Levinson notes (p. 121), the feast is a richly signifying emblem of immaturity. Ultimately, though, the banquet does little more than defer the moment when Porphyro must perform the altogether trickier feat of maintaining Madeline's interest in the 'real' world. To be sure, St Agnes's charmed maid experiences a moment of 'painful change' in stanza 34, and is especially struck by the contrast between the Porphyro of her dreams (the manly romance-hero), and the rather disappointing Porphyro sitting beside her on her bed: 'How changed thou art! How pallid, chill, and drear!' (l. 311). Perhaps to herself Madeline muses, 'How *short*!' But in so far as Porphyro actually succeeds in winning Madeline's heart (and survives to boot, unlike Porphyro's similarly unmanly cousin, Lorenzo – the 'hero' of an immature poem that even Keats thought contained 'too much inexperience of li[f]e', *Letters*, II, 174), *The Eve of St Agnes* is a piece of poetic therapy for Keats, and possibly his healthiest poem.

2 'Full-grown lambs'
Immaturity and 'To Autumn'

It is a commonplace of Keats criticism to present the poet as struggling against both a debilitating sense of his own immaturity and the wider public perception of him as 'immature'. Keats's doleful suspicion that he was merely a 'weaver boy' in the eyes of reviewers and other 'literary fashionables' was confirmed by Byron's caustic reference to his '*p—ss a bed*' poetry, and by John Gibson Lockhart's conclusion that Keats was only 'a boy of pretty abilities'.[1] In 1820, the *Guardian* ironically praised his 'juvenile industry', while the *London Magazine* condemned his 'boyish petulance'.[2] Throughout his poetic career, Keats contended with reviewers who configured him as 'effeminate' or 'callow', and who routinely exhorted him to 'grow up'. But while Keats's relationship with immaturity and 'juvenile industry' may have been fraught, it was by no means wholly disabling. Marjorie Levinson has shown with customary dexterity how Keats used his cultural marginality, stylistic vulgarity, and 'adolescent' sexuality to subvert authoritarian values extolled by '*soi disant* guardians of public taste' like Lockhart and J. W. Croker.[3] Indeed, Keats's work often teeters self-consciously on the edge of puerility, such 'teeterings' becoming the condition for contestations of various kinds. But – and this is my point – 'To Autumn' is usually seen as being differently preoccupied. For Levinson, the ode is 'probably the only one of Keats's poems where the self-consciousness – the class and personality line – gets overwritten' (p. 30). Helen Vendler finds repeated 'mitigations, easings, and softenings' that allow us to apprehend Keats's 'less combative attitude',[4] while Michael O'Neill asserts that the ode is empty of 'gestures of protest' and 'assertions of self'.[5] We can detect a clear desire to redeem a poem that is possibly (on first reading at least) Keats's most powerfully and self-possessedly canonical from the unrest discernible elsewhere in his oeuvre, unrest deriving from tensions generated by an equivocal stance towards maturity. Readers have traditionally been reluctant to permit these tensions to problematize 'To Autumn'. We could, indeed, go so far as to say that there is a will to recognize the ode as a 'perfect' work of serene contemplation and unshakable maturity (the strained sense of a 'willed' recognition is deliberate).

The powerful logic of maturity that is understood to reside in the poem is either discovered within its thematic structure and narrative (Walter Jackson

Bate suggests that the ode aspires to 'resolution';[6] Andrew Motion argues that any equivocation in the poem is curtailed, finally, in the fact that 'autumn is about to turn into winter'[7]); or it is identified in the artistic processes of growth and development assumed to have produced the poem (thus we have Keats's 'finest ode' in Helen Vendler's words; and the 'most perfect of [Keats's] poems and perhaps the most perfect in the English language', in Morse Peckham's view).[8] New historicist readings, too, seemingly unconcerned with allegories of human growth and dissipation, appear loathe to dispense with maturity as a measuring stick of the poem's accomplishment. Nicholas Roe's analysis of the ode in *John Keats and the Culture of Dissent* (1997) could be said to have swapped artistic maturity for *political* maturity. In Roe's critique, 'To Autumn' is read as codifying a 'grown-up', covert awareness of potential insurrection, where contestation is lodged in semantic groupings like 'close bosom-friend' and 'clammy cells', phrases supposedly redolent of intrigue and its bed-fellow – 'barred' incarceration.

It is my contention that *even* 'To Autumn', a work we have come to regard as having achieved a supreme maturity, in fact dramatizes – possibly more urgently than anywhere else in Keats – a fundamentally ambivalent relationship with growth and maturation. Moreover, this ambivalence is intimately bound up with political opposition.[9] To be sure, previous interpretations have registered a peripheral awareness of the ode's unease with its own mature imagery. In *John Keats's Dream of Truth* (1969), for instance, John Jones noted that the fields of autumn call up the 'green fields' of spring.[10] Keats's dual focus was detected, too, for that matter, by his contemporary readers. A critic for the *Monthly Review* sensed that the volume in which 'To Autumn' first appeared, *Lamia, Isabella, The Eve of St Agnes, and Other Poems* (1820), was 'involved in ambiguity' (immediately following this insight, the *Monthly* reprinted the ode in its entirety).[11] But the extent to which – and the psychological reasons why – Keats contrives, systematically and purposefully, to smuggle a subversive and defiant counter-discourse of immaturity into the 'core' of ripe, mature thoughts and a mature logic, has not been delineated. Geoffrey Hartman argues that 'consciousness almost disappears in the poem'; yet it seems to me that 'To Autumn' is engaged in a profound crisis of consciousness and personality.[12] The outwardly calm landscape of 'To Autumn' is a field of struggle on which Keats asserts the legitimacy of 'juvenile industry' and 'boyish' subjectivity against his critics' adult reprimands. In this chapter, I examine a series of disturbances in Keats's most famous and apparently coherent comment on 'ripeness', 'timeliness', and old age. These disturbances, I argue, ultimately call the poem's canonicity, specifically as an allegorical poem on ageing and closure, into question. I want to suggest that troubled and troubling phrases in 'To Autumn' such as 'full-grown lambs', which provides this chapter's title – phrases that insist on their links with youth in the midst of maturity – interrupt the poem's celebratedly seamless narrative, contesting the sovereignty of autumn and opening a perspective onto a 'boyish' or 'adolescent' aesthetic that suffuses Keats's whole work. Most exciting of all, at the same time as the season's authority is imperilled, the cultural authority of reviewers like Lockhart and Croker is unfixed by the ode's immature aesthetic. Once we begin to appreciate Keats's enduring fascination with the 'pleasant wonders' of youth (*Letters*, I, 281), the persistent myth of Keats's poetic career as a linear progression from the juvenile products of apprenticeship with Leigh Hunt to the ripe fruits of the mature odes can be exploded. In 'To Autumn', Keats is engaged in no less radical a process than undermining his own (once hard fought for and always disputed) authority as a mature poet. Indeed, this process could be said to characterize the poet's later work; at any rate the ode's emphasis on youth, and its iconoclastic disavowal of the mature values demanded by conservative reviewers, looks forward to the schoolboy humour of *The Cap and Bells; or, The Jealousies*, rather than back to Keats's desperate efforts at writing poems in the 'grown-up' style of Milton.

Beldames and Belle Dames

That Keats harboured a vulnerability to the charge of physical immaturity is apparent throughout his correspondence. In March 1819 he wrote to Joseph Severn, acquiescing to the painter's wish that his miniature portrait of Keats should appear in the Royal Academy exhibition. The anxieties generated for Keats by the exhibition appear transparently in the following passage:

> What good can it do to any future picture – Even a large picture is lost in that canting place – what a drop of water in the ocean is a Miniature. Those who might chance to see it for the most part if they had ever heard of either of us – and know what we were and of what years would laugh at the puff of the one and the vanity of the other.[13]
>
> (*Letters*, II, 48)

Keats is obviously unsettled at the prospect of his diminutive likeness being displayed among the exhibition's giant canvasses. His scepticism was perhaps justified: Severn's painting depicts Keats with large child-like eyes and childishly small hands. In addition, Keats fears that if his (and Severn's) young age were known, he would be the object of further ridicule. It is telling that the only noun Keats capitalizes in the above excerpt is 'Miniature', as if he strains to lift the word above itself. In any event, the phonetic proximity of 'miniature' to 'immature' serves to alert us to the kind of anxieties that are in operation. Severn's 'Miniature' of a young Keats is dismissed by the poet as a 'drop of water in the ocean'. Another water image, from a more famous letter to Reynolds dated 3 May 1818, elaborates his anxieties about intellectual, as opposed to physical, immaturity. Keats begins to expound enthusiastically to Reynolds on the importance of 'widening speculation' and developing intellect to dissolve any 'Bias' that could lead to prejudice 'when the Mind is in its infancy' (*Letters*, I, 277); but when Keats overhears himself discoursing on 'knowledge' in this grown-up manner, he suddenly loses confidence, afraid that his ideas sound half-baked:

> An extensive knowledge is needful to thinking people – it takes away the heat and fever; and helps, by widening speculation, to ease the Burden of the Mystery . . . (you will forgive me for thus privately treading out [of] my depth and take it for treading as schoolboys tread the water).
>
> (*Letters*, I, 277)

Despite concerns about appearing immature, or 'smokeable', as he puts it elsewhere in his letters, Keats was fascinated by the prospect of prolonging a youthful or adolescent state of intellect – something he explores in the 'Mansion of Many Apartments' letter, which compares the development of the mind to a passage through a series of rooms. The first room he terms the 'infant or thoughtless Chamber, in which we remain as long as we do not think'. The second – and the most seductive for Keats – is the 'Chamber of Maiden-Thought':

> [W]e no sooner get into the second Chamber . . . than we become intoxicated with the light and the atmosphere, we see nothing but pleasant wonders, and think of delaying there for ever in delight.
>
> (*Letters*, II, 281)

Fantasies of 'delaying . . . for ever' in this adolescent realm of wonderment notwithstanding, Keats sadly notes that the grown-up world of 'Misery and Heartbreak, Pain, Sickness and oppression' eventually impinges. The Chamber of Maiden-Thought 'becomes gradually darken'd' and the maturing intellect reluctantly leaves it to venture into the 'dark passages' beyond, signalling the third phase of the mind's development towards full maturity. Although Keats thought that Wordsworth had come to this point, he did not believe he had himself reached these passages yet. This particular milestone is projected into a jeopardized, conditional future: 'Now if we live, and go on thinking, we too shall explore them' (*Letters*, I, 281).

Keats 'returns' to the Chamber of Maiden-Thought in the poem that most vocally insists on and celebrates the validity of immature love, *The Eve of St Agnes* (composed in early 1819). The phrase itself is tantalizingly invoked in stanza 21 by the 'maiden's chamber', where Madeline – whose name incorporates all the letters of 'maiden', reinforcing her identification with youth – sleeps and dreams. The critical consensus has always been wary of interpreting Madeline's chamber allegorically; but read with one eye open to issues of immaturity, the bedroom proves to be disclosing in more ways than are immediately obvious. To explain what I mean, I should like to turn briefly to the figure of Porphyro. This archetypal 'young lover' enacts a youthful incursion into the petrified, grown-up world of 'Old Angela', the 'ancient Beadsman', 'old Lord Maurice', and the sexually knowing 'tiptoe cavaliers' (what is more, Porphyro gets the better of them all). With the aid of 'Angela the Old', he prepares to spy on Madeline, secreting himself, with all the onanistic overtones that properly accrue to this term, in the 'maiden's chamber' (we will see more images of adolescent effluence in the 'o'er-brim[ming] clammy cells' of 'To Autumn'):

> Safe at last,
> Through many a dusky gallery, they gain
> The maiden's chamber.
> (*The Eve of St Agnes*, ll. 185–7)

Like the 'Chamber of Maiden-Thought', Madeline's bedroom is a sensual and intoxicating locale where one can view 'pleasant wonders', represented within the terms of the poem by the spectacle of Madeline's slow strip ('by degrees', l. 229); and Keats's hero is reluctant to leave it (just as the 'Mansion of Many Apartments' letter prophesies). This poetic reification of the Chamber of Maiden-Thought, and the philosophy accompanying it in the letter, suggests that while Keats worried about being perceived as immature and inexperienced, at the same time and in major poems – moreover, poems ostensibly written with the intention of giving critics less to object to – he develops an adolescent aesthetic that celebrates youthfulness, and youthful love in particular.[14]

This aesthetic does not always produce characters as congenial as Madeline and Porphyro. In Keats's most apprehensive moments, a morbid preoccupation with exploring the tensions between maturity and immaturity, combined with an erotic poetics within which Keats's agency is often severely limited, ultimately produces such hybrid creatures of innocence and experience as Lamia ('Not one hour old, yet of scienital brain / To unperplex bliss from its neighbour pain', *Lamia*, I, 191–2), and La Belle Dame, a 'fairy's *child*' (l. 14; my emphasis), who nevertheless bears the mark of age in her name ('beldame': an aged woman).[15] Barbara Johnson's exhilarating analysis of 'La Belle Dame sans Merci' demonstrates how key ambiguities in the poem, centred on line 19 ('She look'd at me as she did love' – where 'as' could mean 'while' or 'as if'), provoke powerfully antagonistic readings of the Lady as polarized allegories of innocence or experience.[16] Within Keats's equivocal psychodynamics, the Lady is either a pure and sincere lover, cruelly abandoned by an hysterical male unable to cope with the forces he has aroused, or a more traditional incarnation of the knowing seductress who deceives a naïve and psychically vulnerable knight-at-arms (a miniature knight who is never capitalized, although La Belle Dame *is*).[17] While Johnson's critique is stimulating, I would suggest that these alternative readings need not be mutually negating. The rival portraits can, in fact, be (and in a sense already are) conflated into one supremely unsettling woman embodying Keats's ambivalent attitudes towards maturity and its adolescent antitype.

It is helpful here to recall that Old Angela in *The Eve of St Agnes* is also identified as a 'beldame' (l. 90). As well as denoting, with depreciative sense, a 'loathsome old woman', the term was also used, the *OED* records, to address nurses in the sixteenth century. This beldame ministers to Porphyro's sexual longings for Madeline. Keeping this in mind and turning back to La Belle Dame (sans Merci) – it is possible to see an experienced 'beldame' side of the Lady's character pimping to a corresponding innocent and immature 'Belle Dame' side. That is to say, the beldame brings the lustful knight-at-arms to La Belle Dame's grot in a reworked version of Old Angela leading Porphyro 'in close secrecy, / Even to Madeline's chamber' (ll. 163–4).[18] This time, age (represented by the Lady's beldame qualities), appears to win out over youth (the knight): in a near reversal of events in Madeline's bedroom, the knight-at-arms – who is as bad at being a knight as the 'pallid' Porphyro was at being a Romance hero – sleeps and dreams while the scene is observed and voyeuristically 'consumed' by his female counterpart.

The co-existence of age and experience with youth and innocence in 'La Belle Dame sans Merci' is what unsettles both the knight and Keats most severely. As a matter of fact, older people – ranging from austere poetic characters like Moneta in *The Fall of Hyperion*, to acquaintances such as Keats's financially astute guardian Mr Abbey, and the sexually accomplished Charles Brown – nearly always mobilize unease in Keats.[19] When he composed 'To Autumn', however, he seems to have found a way in which this dual presence could be used to unsettle other people, as we shall discover.

'Involved in ambiguity'

'To Autumn' is traditionally regarded as Keats's paean to maturity – artistic maturity, in respect of the poet's coming to full powers, and maturity embodied in the allegorical passage from spring through to autumn, into an implied, if unnamed, winter. Anne Mellor, in common with several other commentators, considers 'To Autumn' to be 'Keats's great Ode'.[20] For a number of Keats's (more enlightened, Mellor would say) contemporary reviewers, the volume in which the ode (or rather 'Ode') appeared also marked a 'gigantic stride' and signalled the poet's newly achieved 'calm power'.[21] The ode has remained a poem of growth, resignation, and acceptance: 'unequivocal acceptance', in Jack Stillinger's words.[22] As I suggested at the beginning of this chapter, even recent new historicist critiques of the poem, seemingly unconcerned with allegories of human youth and age, could be said to swap one version of maturity for another. Nicholas Roe finds in 'To Autumn' not chronological or artistic maturity, but *political* maturity, shrewdly fugitive (in view of the troubled times), and all but concealed in apparently innocent, yet precisely for this reason *doubly* mature, words and phrases suggestive of revolution and intrigue. These include such references as 'close bosom-friend of the maturing sun' (l. 2), 'clammy cells' (l. 11), and fecund locutions (for literary critics) like 'conspiring'. In these strong and undeniably exciting readings, 'To Autumn', whether through conscious subterfuge on the part of

Keats, or by less directed means, is assumed to reflect and comment – maturely – on the turbulent politics of the period. Yet it is in these outwardly 'mature' and apparently proof-laden phrases where the deepest fractures appear in the poem's logic. The autumnal surfaces of the poem may shine in the warmth of the maturing sun, but this is truly a *Schein* or 'apparent' autumn, since through a series of semantic and grammatical disturbances, in tautologies, oxymorons and verbal ambiguities, Keats's autumn emerges as an ironic and subversive antitype of the conventionally 'mature' season. In the same way that Porphyro represents a youthful challenge to the adult world of 'Old Angela', the 'ancient Beadsman', and 'old Lord Maurice', references to 'clammy cells' and 'close bosom-friends' resist the mature rhythms and seemingly inexorable cadences of autumn.

Several reviewers, as we have seen, discerned signs of 'development' in the *Lamia* volume of 1820 where 'To Autumn' first appeared. The *Eclectic Review* found 'intellectual growth', and printed all three stanzas of 'To Autumn' as proof.[23] In the *Indicator*, Leigh Hunt declared that Keats 'takes his seat with the oldest and best of our living poets'.[24] But in less partial quarters a lingering doubt remained. Even the *Eclectic* could not avoid noticing something immature about Keats that was not contingent upon his actual age: 'Mr Keats, it will be sufficiently evident, is a young man – whatever be his age, we must consider him as still but a young man.' The reviewer, probably Josiah Conder, worried that Keats's poetics was dangerously close to being 'childish' in places, and he found ample evidence of 'school boy taste'.[25] Keats's reaction to, or rather anticipation of, such attitudes was to assure his friends, and particularly his publisher, that the new volume was designed to placate his critics. Individual works, however, rather suggest that Keats resented the fact that appeasement was necessary in the first place. For instance, in *The Eve of St Agnes* – one of the 1820 volume's title pieces – we could view Porphyro's cautious, but nevertheless headstrong, windings through the dark passages of the castle in which 'old Lord Maurice', 'dwarfish Hildebrand', and the 'whole blood-thirsty race' reside, as an attempt to cock a snook at, while eluding, the crusty reviewers of *Blackwood's* and the *Quarterly* in their exclusive and excluding fortresses of literary taste. As I will outline, too, the hidden engagements and youthful resistances of 'To Autumn' begin to look more and more like calculated and thoroughgoing acts of poetic defiance against Keats's critical foes, rather than appeasement. And not just critical foes: 'To Autumn' also works against the solidified canons of posterity, the poetic afterlife that welcomes mature work but is less open-armed, as Keats realized, to 'juvenile industry' (which is consigned to a category of its own: 'juvenilia').

A writer for the *Monthly Review* suspected that *Lamia, Isabella, The Eve of St Agnes, and Other Poems* was 'involved in ambiguity', a hunch which the first few words of 'To Autumn' would seem to confirm: 'Season of mists and mellow fruitfulness'. Mists are, after all, the very condition of ambiguity. They confuse and obfuscate; they send people the wrong way. (Keats commented to Reynolds a day or so after composing 'To Autumn': 'I am all in a mist; I scarcely know what's what', *Letters*, II, 167). In the same letter, Keats records having an 'unsteady & vagarish disposition'. A similar unsteadiness may be found in the ode, unbalancing the poem's famous equilibrium and constituting a contrary energy to the (at first glance) 'steady' autumn we observe crossing a brook in line 20. Indeed, we might say the poem constantly teeters, even where it appears to be most composed, since many of the images that in orthodox readings make up the ode's renowned maturity are *doubly* composed, harbouring reversed images of immaturity within them.

The first 'problem' that disrupts views of 'To Autumn' as a poem of and about maturity occurs in line 2. We are told that autumn is the 'close bosom-friend of the maturing sun'. The phrase is plurally arresting, containing at least two, possibly three, anomalous elements. To begin with, '*close* bosom-friend' (my emphasis) is tautological, since 'bosom-friends' are by definition 'close'. The amplified sense of proximity in this double image of closeness (collating a 'close friend' and a 'bosom friend') suggests a different kind of intimacy from that indulged in by Roe's political schemers: namely, the intimacy enjoyed by infants lying on their mother's breast (lying close to the bosom). Which is to say that Keats is detained by mother/son imagery. The next, related disturbance in the ode's supposedly seamless narrative on the theme of ripeness occurs with 'maturing sun'. Here we are faced with a decision: whether to read 'maturing' as verb or adjective, a choice that results in either a mature sun that matures crops, or an immature sun that is itself still engaged in a process of maturing and getting older. Add to this the third problem – the homophonic incorporation of 'son' in 'sun' – and we discover in the line a son who is maturing, but still preoccupied by memories of lying on the maternal breast (Keats lost his mother at the age of fourteen, a loss which was to plunge him into chronic debt, a threatened Chancery Bill, and financial dependency).[26] Keats appears to be nostalgic for the 'close bosom' relationship he has lost; we have already seen how he writes plaintively about the prospect of leaving the second stage of intellectual maturation, at which point the 'weariness, the fever, and the fret' of the adult world break in upon one, where 'but to think is to be full of sorrow' ('Ode to a Nightingale'). Indeed, in 'Ode to a Nightingale', a poem in close dialogue with – a close bosom-friend of – 'To Autumn', the ultimate logic of maturity is presented in wholly uncompromising terms: 'youth grows pale, and spectre thin, and dies' (l. 26). Ripening is not a phenomenon Keats feels should be met with equanimity or resignation. It becomes apparent, at any rate, that the idea of growing up is more complex for Keats than inherited readings of 'To Autumn' allow.

Correspondence between Keats and his sister Fanny frames many of these predicaments. In a letter of 10 September 1817, Keats self-consciously constructs himself as a mature intellect eager to promote Fanny's own educational development. But he is clearly uncomfortable in the role thus fashioned for himself; moreover, he frequently gives his unease away. Two-thirds of the way through the letter, in which Keats has already deprecated his writings as childish 'scribblings', attention is turned to the early inculcation of the French language in English school pupils:

> I wish the Italian would supersede french in every School throughout the Country for that is full of real Poetry and Romance . . . Italian indeed would sound most musically from Lips which had b[e]gan to pronounce it as early as french is cramme'd down our Mouths, as if we were young Jack daws at the mercy of an overfeeding Schoolboy.
>
> (*Letters*, I, 155)

Like 'maturing sun' in 'To Autumn', 'overfeeding Schoolboy' at the end of this passage is unstable, supremely vulnerable to an inversion of sense. Keats is either the 'young Jack daw' being force-fed French (overfeeding on French), or the 'Schoolboy' who *does* the overfeeding (that is, a teacher who is himself still a pupil). Or both, because as with 'close bosom-friend' the key idea in each of these readings – youth – is doubly present. Furthermore, both available images of immaturity are folded back onto Keats himself.[27] As a matter of fact, the passage quoted above seems to me precisely to prefigure Keats's uncertainty with the 'maturing sun' in his ode. There, as we have just seen, the sun aspires to the role of 'mature' maturer of young plants and crops; but the possibility that the sun, too, is still maturing (is not yet fully grown) always threatens to undercut its authority, and that of Keats's mature rhetoric. Similarly, while that other maturing son, Keats, begins his letter to Fanny with a desire to help his sister ripen intellectually, he finishes it by confirming his own shaky mandate in this respect.

In the ode, Keats reveals himself as a 'maturing s[o]n', uneasy that the 'pleasant wonders' of the second stage of intellectual development are coming to an end; unsettled at the onset of maturity with its pains and new responsibilities. This might explain why the sun has to 'conspire' sinisterly with autumn to 'bend with apples the moss'd cottage-trees', 'swell the gourd', and 'fill all fruit with ripeness to the core'. Keats's profound discomfort at the notion of 'ripeness' is palpable: 'to the core' usually collocates backwards with 'rotten', where 'rottenness' is the disgusting corollary of 'ripeness'. It is as though Keats expresses dismay at the inevitability of growing up. Even in the very process of ripening he looks forward to a second youth where the sun that will 'swell the gourd' (a clear image of pregnancy) will also 'set budding more, / And still more, later flowers for the bees' (ll. 8–9). This desire is expressed prosaically in a letter to Rice of February 1820: 'The simple flowers of our sp[r]ing are what I want to see *again*' (*Letters*, II, 260; my emphasis). It is, then, not only the bees that hope 'warm days will never cease' (l. 10). Keats, too, is reluctant to bid adieu to the spring and summer, contriving a second period of immature growth – a second spring – in his ode, complete with budding flowers, in the midst of autumn and autumnal imagery.

At the end of stanza 1, Keats imagines the bees' 'clammy cells' as 'o'erbrimm'd' (l. 11). At face value, this image simply acknowledges autumn's fruitfulness. It has also been seen as a knowing reference to the damp prison cells in which many liberals and radicals – including Leigh Hunt, who was to become Keats's own close friend and mentor – were imprisoned, especially during the suspension of habeas corpus. But it is equally comprehensible read as a reference to youthful 'fruitfulness', and links to other instances where Keats celebrates adolescent effusiveness. Two of these occur in *The Eve of St Agnes*, at the point at which Porphyro secretes himself in the 'maiden's chamber' (a youthful secretion anticipating the o'er-brimming 'clammy cells' and 'last oozings' of autumn), and with the 'solution sweet' that literally stains stanza 36.[28] Marjorie Levinson is not the first commentator to recognize Keats's onanistic preoccupations: Byron, for example, asserted that Keats was always 'f—gg—g his *Imagination*', denouncing him as a 'miserable Self-polluter of the human Mind' to the publisher John Murray.[29] In the *Eclectic Review*, Josiah Conder was less direct but equally meaningful when he warned the poet not to indulge in 'wasteful efflorescence' in his works;[30] while Keats's one-time friend, the *European Magazine* reviewer George Felton Mathew, smuttily referred to Keats as a 'proud egotist of diseased feelings and perverted principles' who was given to 'pouring forth his splendours' in verse.[31] All these commentators make a valid point. The sticky cells, 'later flowers', and hopeful bees of stanza 1 invite us to scrutinize Keats's purported willingness to embrace the seasonal maturity and allegorical finality signalled by the approach of autumn.

Keats's efforts to derail autumn's progress appear even more explicitly in stanza 2, which is constructed around a series of images that seem to have been selected with the express purpose of undercutting the season's authority and prolonging a period of immature wonder. Autumn is pictured 'sitting careless on a granary floor' (l. 14), hair 'soft-lifted' (l. 15) by the wind in one of those jejune 'Cockney' constructions that reviewers like Croker and Lockhart rejected as emblematic of Keats's offensively immature 'jargon'.[32] (The expediency of halting Autumn's labours in the granary is clear: granary floors are unsettling loci, strewn with what Keats would regard, appalled with Geoffrey Hill, as 'the husks of what was rich seed', 'Merlin', line 2.)[33] Or Autumn lies 'drows'd with the fume of poppies' on a 'half-reap'd' furrow (ll. 16–17), the reaper's hook sparing the 'next swath and all its twined flowers' (l. 18).[34] Alternatively, Autumn watches on with 'patient look' as the 'last oozings' of summer are squeezed out of the cider-press (l. 22). One would have to be patient indeed, since while it is possible to watch a last 'oozing', 'oozings', with its deferring plural, implies that there will always be another drop to issue from the press. 'Lastness' in Keats's poem begins to appear as a progressive, unended condition. Think again of the cider-press – intimately associated with intoxication, it recalls, together with the narcotic 'fume of poppies', the letter of 3 May 1818 where Keats describes to Reynolds the second stage of the mind's development: 'We become intoxicated with the light and the atmosphere, we see nothing but pleasant wonders, and think of delaying there for ever in delight.' As in the Chamber of Maiden-Thought, then, the climate in the second stanza of 'To Autumn' is one of delay, postponement, and arrested development.

By the third stanza, the 'songs of spring' have given way to the music of autumn with its 'wailful choir' of small gnats (l. 27). So far I have endeavoured to show that the spots in 'To Autumn' where Keats's ambivalence towards maturity is most pronounced are marked by episodes of semantic disjuncture. It is no different in the final stanza. 'Small gnats' is oddly observed and virtually tautological, just like 'close bosom-friend'. Gnats *are* small. Talking about 'small gnats' is akin to referring to 'tall skyscrapers'. The qualifier is troublesomely superfluous; it seems present only for the purpose of drawing attention to itself and indicating how the poem is to be read (the text can be said to illuminate its own reading at this point). Looked at from another angle, 'small gnats' also registers Keats's desire to store images of smallness and youth against the ruinous approach of maturity in the guise of autumn and winter, an approach that the choir of gnats bewails. Youth's transforming presence in the stanza is confirmed by Christopher Ricks, who with characteristic inventiveness discovers 'Keats's greatest blush' in the lines 'barred clouds bloom the soft-dying day, / And touch the stubble-plains with rosy hue' (ll. 25–6). Blushes, of course, are intimately associated with adolescence.[35] The idea that Keats's verse blushes at this point is singular; but the choice of 'bloom', a term that in a non-transferred sense is conventionally linked to flowering plants (which have usually wilted and died by autumn), also allows an additional flicker of unseasonal subversion to discompose autumn's authority. Even (or especially) here, where the day is slipping away and 'soft-dying', Keats clings to the outward forms of spring and summer rather than take solace in those of autumn. In this respect, Keats's poem has more in common with Dylan Thomas's 'Do Not Go Gentle into that Good Night', which exhorts an aged father to 'rage, rage against the dying of the light' – that is, to *resist* closure – than with canonical poems of dignified acceptance such as, say, Tennyson's 'Crossing the Bar'.

These adolescent 'survivals', this assortment of immature representations, is further buttressed by the 'full-grown lambs' that 'loud bleat from hilly bourn' (l. 30). This is at best a curious, and at worst a scandalously contradictory, image to find in a 'perfect' poem, since, as Helen Vendler herself notes, a full-grown lamb is no longer a lamb, but a sheep.[36] The phrase is a 'fleecy oxymoron' in Andrew Motion's playful (not to mention Keatsian) description.[37] The 'jolt' in signification caused by the 'full-grown lambs' can perhaps be ascribed to the fact that Keats relishes an unseasonal association with lambs and the time of year when they are usually born (on 'hilly bourns'). In other words, although the presence of sheep should be proof positive that spring has departed, the mature image is sabotaged by the invocation of lambs and the lambing season. The multitude of unstable signs in 'To Autumn' leads us incrementally, but cumulatively, to the conclusion that it is Keats himself who aspires to be a 'full-grown lamb'. The aptness of the phrase seems to have been noticed by one of Keats's contemporary reviewers:

admonishing Keats for a showy 'parade' of his fascination with all things classical in *Lamia, Isabella, The Eve of St Agnes, and Other Poems*, Josiah Conder concluded that such tastelessness' indicated the author had a long way to go before he became a 'full-grown scholar'.[38] The nearness of 'full-grown scholar' to 'full-grown lambs' suggests that Conder was both exercised by the image in the ode, and able to recognize its appositeness applied to Keats himself.

Perversely for a poem that ostensibly sets out to celebrate autumn, 'To Autumn' participates, or aspires to participate, in the *jouissance* of spring, in the sexy 'pleasant wonders' of youth. Keats's autumn is thoroughly ambivalent; it is involved in ambiguity at every level. Was Keats disturbed by the thought that in his bid to write a canonical poem about autumnal closure, a poem that would place him 'among the English Poets after [his] death' (*Letters*, I, 394), he had actually composed a poem on the joys of spring and new beginnings? Was he perturbed that he had announced, however obliquely, his preference for being a lamb rather than a sheep? Keats undoubtedly realized that the notion of 'lamb-likeness' was double-edged, particularly as far as the public's perception of him was concerned. In 'Ode on Indolence', composed in late May or early June of that year, he declared he did not want public praise if the price was to be regarded as 'A pet-lamb in a sentimental farce' (l. 54), appreciating that by playing the 'full-grown lamb' in his life and works he risked being perceived by 'literary fashionables' and personal acquaintances alike as ridiculously immature. But these anxieties notwithstanding, the 'full-grown lambs' in 'To Autumn' mark the troubled juncture of conflicting seasonal (and allegorical) energies, and indicate the nature of Keats's ambivalent engagement with his text. Keats looks 'to' autumn, but it never quite seems to arrive – at least not unambiguously. It is perhaps not without significance that the ode takes the form of an address 'to' autumn, rather than a contemplation 'on' it. Just as the ode *to* a nightingale directly confronts and refuses the bird's offer of closure in the form of aseasonal, 'full-throated' ease – doubly attractive to Keats, whose own sore throats announced the beginning of the end – the ode *to* autumn challenges and defers (even if it cannot refuse) the 'natural' mature closure of the season.

To conclude this section, two days after composing his ode, Keats told Reynolds: 'I always somehow associate Chatterton with autumn' (*Letters*, II, 167). This is an odd connection to make. Autumn is traditionally identified with age and maturity whereas, in popular cultural fictions, Chatterton, the 'marvellous boy', stood for a potent myth of precocious, doomed youth, a myth that was proclaimed everywhere from 'tribute' poems to commemorative tea-towels. In Keats's configuration, 'Chatterton' is an oddly motivated sign where youthful naïvety and age intersect. Keats justifies his Chatterton/autumn link by explaining that Chatterton was 'the purest writer in the English Language'. 'Purest' relates in an obvious sense to Keats's remark on the 'chaste' autumn weather of 1819 (*Letters*, II, 167); but in a letter to his brother and sister-in-law, he elaborated on why he liked Chatterton's diction so much: 'The Language had existed long enough to be entirely uncorrupted of Chaucer's gallicisms and still the old words are used . . . I prefer the native music of [Chatterton's language] to Milton's cut by feet' (*Letters*, II, 212). The chronology here is curious: within contemporary discourses of linguistic primitivism – from Adam Smith's essay on 'The Origin of Language' to Wordsworth's 1802 Preface to *Lyrical Ballads* – it is earlier, not later stages of language that are supposed to be 'pure' and 'uncorrupted'. The best languages are precisely those that have *not* existed long enough. However, although Chatterton's language has 'existed long enough' to lose its 'gallicisms', it still uses 'the old words' – by which Keats means the *young* words: words that were spoken in the language's infancy. It is as though for Keats the 'music' of Chatterton's language represents, simultaneously, the songs of autumn *and* spring, youth *and* maturity. Bob Dylan's contradictory, but perfectly comprehensible, line from a 1964 song, 'My Back Pages', sheds light on this conundrum: 'Ah, but I was so much older then, / I'm younger than that now.' This repeated refrain asserts the efficacy of a second youth; it advocates growing wise by growing younger, like King Lear, joyously reversing the superannuations of age. Chatterton's idiom is similarly Lear- or Merlin-like for Keats: it lives backwards, getting younger as it gets older, encapsulating the energies in 'To Autumn' I have been describing.

Apple pies

Retrieving an 'immature' counter-discourse from 'To Autumn' requires reading several lines, phrases, and even single words, 'against' themselves. It might seem to be asking a great deal of individual terms to bear the weight of a whole critique; one can always object that words mean just what they say. But words never *just* mean that: delimitations of this kind are the form-destroyers of all criticism. 'To Autumn' is perhaps Keats's most tricksical, elusive poem. After all, it has managed to install itself into the most central, enduring canon of English literature (where male authors ponder the mysteries of age and death); and it does so chiefly by portraying itself as the mature work of a matured poet writing about maturity.

Certainly, with the greatly anthologized 'To Autumn', Keats's conviction that he would be 'among the English Poets after [his] death' has turned out to be prescient. The ode has even been used in a national television advertising campaign (for apple pies), something that has so far eluded even Milton, the *über* grown-up literary precursor against whom Keats habitually and nervously measured himself.[39] As a matter of fact, the well-known advertisement for Mr Kipling's pies that appeared in the 1980s, featuring a voice-over of 'To Autumn', constitutes one of the best commentaries on Keats's ode. It penetrates, almost certainly without realizing it is doing so, the poem's veiled comments on Keats's allegorical life – comments that are themselves obscured by the season's 'mists', and thus missed. Shot in a laden orchard and bathed in golden light, the advertisement evokes the hazy mellow fruitfulness of stanza 1. The focus quickly moves, however, to a pair of children who are about to be given apple pies (manufactured for childish palettes), and the meticulously constructed autumnal iconography shifts into the background. A benevolent old man in the autumn of his years – the personification of autumn, that is – carries the pies over on a plate; but he is simply the means of delivering the pies to the children. The camera is interested only in the image of smiling youth – youth that is about to gorge itself on the immature pleasures of sugary pies. Just as the (now) archetypal 'autumnness' of Keats's poem is upstaged in the advertisement by the presence of 'happy, happy' youth – who will remain 'for ever young' in a celluloid version of the immortality attained by the lovers on the Grecian urn's relief – Keats, too, smuggles a counter-discourse of abiding immaturity into the midst of his ode's mature thoughts and mature ethos. In a poem supposedly about death and completion, Keats succeeds in writing verses that are, in more ways than one, 'fit to live' (published Preface to *Endymion*) – verses that are precisely about living, and hardly at all about death.

'To Autumn' is a poem that strives for canonicity, a poem that insists it is of 'such completion' to warrant 'passing the press', even as the 'youngster' *Endymion* was not (published Preface). But in the canons of English literature 'To Autumn' is a Trojan horse. It quietly subverts the mature values it ostensibly buys into and appears to eulogize. Read alongside a more unproblematically conceived and executed poem on maturity and finality such as Tennyson's 'Crossing the Bar', a poem whose only link with youth is the lamb-like meekness that accompanies Tennyson into the abyss, 'To Autumn' now sounds distinctly ambivalent in its professions of resignation and completion. The *Monthly Review*'s critic was right to suspect equivocation on Keats's part. Historically, readers have responded to – have willingly been subsumed in – the ode's steady autumnal music, to the extent that critical discourse on 'To Autumn' frequently adopts the calm tone, register, and balanced cadences thought to characterize the poem itself (witness the 'rhythm of a steady rising and setting' in Vendler's own finely, and finally, balanced prose).[40] But it is the 'songs of spring' we should be listening to – and this despite the poem's mischievous and thoroughly disingenuous injunction to 'Think not of them' (l. 24). The songs of youth have not departed. To the question 'Ay, where are they?', the answer is, in odd and difficult-to-reconcile phrases like 'maturing sun', 'close bosom-friend', 'small gnats', and 'full-grown lambs' – in lines and terms that produce ripples in the poem's famous coherency. It is Keats's joyous commitment to the 'pleasant wonders' of youth and immaturity, moreover in the face of reviewing censure and private qualms, not his supposed resignation to age and dissolution, that makes 'To Autumn' his most accomplished poem.

Creeping birds and industrious bees

Boyishness for Keats could be an intensely and calculatedly political standpoint. But it also presented itself as an appealing realm of retreat, the allure of which at times threatened – paradoxically enough – to imperil the project of boyish subterfuge I have been outlining. This essential duality can be apprehended in a supremely ambiguous phrase like 'close bosom-friend', which is capable of signalling both conspiratorial poetics *and* a retreat to the maternal breast; 'mature' political consciousness in the new historicist sense, *and* a desire to step back from adult responsibilities.[41] In this final section, I'd like to propose that in addition to its various other preoccupations, 'To Autumn' nervously debates the merits of grown-up political engagement versus childish withdrawal from political life. To put it another way, I believe that in the ode Keats can be observed trying to determine whether he has written a 'grown-up' poem, or not (or both).

To explore this idea further, I want to draw into focus a neglected sonnet by one of Keats's acquaintances and poetic rivals, Barry Cornwall (pseudonym of Bryan Waller Procter). The poem in question, 'Spring', is little known today, but was familiar enough in 1820. It first appeared as part of a sequence entitled 'The Seasons' in Leigh Hunt's *Literary Pocket-Book* for 1820 (published at the end of 1819). It was reprinted in *A Sicilian Story; with Diego Montilla, and Other Poems* (1820), one of two volumes Cornwall sent as a homage to Keats (who received them by 27 February 1820; see *Letters*, II, 267–8); and it appeared again in the second edition of *A Sicilian Story*, also in 1820:

Spring

It is not that sweet herbs and flowers alone
   Start up, like spirits that have lain asleep
   In their great mother's iced bosom deep
For months; or that the birds, more joyous grown,
Catch once again their silver summer tone,
   And they who late from bough to bough did creep,
   Now trim their plumes upon some sunny steep,
And seem to sing of Winter overthrown.
No – with an equal march the immortal mind,
As tho' it never could be left behind,   10
   Keeps pace with every movement of the year;
      And (for high truths are born in happiness)
As the warm heart expands, the eye grows clear,
   And sees beyond the slave's or bigot's guess.[42]

Cornwall's sonnet, stylistically reminiscent of Keats (especially in line 12), strongly associates spring with the mother/child relationship. In the first three lines, the 'children' of spring (the sweet herbs and flowers) have lain asleep in their mother's bosom. Both Cornwall, who Hunt said reminded him of 'the young poet Keats', and Keats appear to understand a code that links bosom friends with immaturity and spring.[43] Just as the relationship between Keats's autumn and the 'maturing sun'/son is figured around the protective bond of mother and infant (in line 2, autumn is the 'close bosom-friend' of the maturing son), Cornwall's spring herbs and flowers lie asleep safe 'in their great mother's iced bosom deep' (l. 3). Like Keats's autumn, Cornwall's winter does not signify death, but is rather the precondition for the continuance of youth. But despite the presence of the maternal breast in both works, there are significant differences in the manner in which the theme of immaturity is developed in each. Where Keats is always seduced by the comforts of the breast, Cornwall seems resolved to leave its pillowy refuge.

Keats composed 'To Autumn' some time around 19 September 1819. It is possible he knew Cornwall's sonnet 'Spring' before that date, although he claims not to have read anything by his rival until late February 1820.[44] When Keats does mention Cornwall's volumes in a letter to John Hamilton Reynolds, he is not particularly complimentary:

> I confess they tease me – they are composed of Amiability the Seasons, the Leaves, the Moon &c. upon which he rings (according to Hunt's expression) triple bob majors. However that is nothing – I think he likes poetry for its own sake, not his.
>
> (*Letters*, II, 268)

Immediately after making these barbed comments, Keats, recovering from a setback in his health, informed Reynolds of his plans to continue with *The Cap and Bells; or, The Jealousies*. In doing so, he made a curious error of spelling: 'I shall soon bee [*sic*] well enough to proceed with my fairies.' I do not think I am entering the realm of make-believe myself by proposing that Cornwall's sonnets on 'The Seasons' – notably 'Spring', which Keats had just been reading in the copy of *A Sicilian Story* sent to him by Cornwall – called to mind the ode 'To Autumn', with its ambiguous bees (boyishly over-effusive, yet intimately linked with political incarceration), producing a parapractic 'slip' in Keats's letter. At some level of consciousness, Keats recognized a shared project in his and Cornwall's poems, which went beyond the authors' mutual preoccupation with maternal fantasies to extend into political realms. Irrespective of the issue of chronological precedence (which I have explored elsewhere), Keats's 'To Autumn', I would suggest, can be heard communing with Cornwall's 'Spring', whose spiky and *mature* political energies complicate the famous ode.

For Keats, just as for Cornwall, thinking about politics in any concerted sense involved entering a 'grown-up' world where the wrong affiliations, the wrong kind of close bosom-friends, could lead to incarceration – or worse. Whether one adopts Jerome McGann's or Nicholas Roe's line on 'To Autumn' (as either a poem that displaces/eludes history, or one that subtly but subversively acknowledges it), the ode, composed in a post-Peterloo atmosphere of watchful caution, is to some degree equivocal about its standing to political activism. But while 'Spring' also exhibits some coyness about the exact nature of its ideological polemic, Cornwall is less guarded, less undecided than Keats. The sonnet's 'conceit' is that just as flowers do not die in winter, but lie waiting to 'start up' again in spring (l. 2), so, too, is the human mind with its radical consciousness 'immortal' and able to keep pace with 'every movement of the year' (ll. 9–11). References to 'starting up' and the 'immortal mind' prompt one to suspect that Cornwall's winter (l. 8) is a political season (tellingly 'overthrown'). It possibly alludes specifically to the grim winter of 1817, during which habeas corpus had been suspended.[45] The spring of 1819, on the other hand, was a period of watchful optimism, marked by radical consciousness-raising and popular marches for electoral reform. This contextual frame allows us to see additional significance in Cornwall's sonnet. Consider lines 9–11:

> . . . with an equal march the immortal mind,
> As though it never could be left behind,
>   Keeps pace with every movement of the year.

'Equal march' hints at the marches and rallies held in industrial towns across the north of England between 1816 and 1819. We can also detect political hue in statements like 'high truths are born in happiness' (l. 12), and in references to eyes growing clear and seeing 'beyond the slave's or bigot's guess' (ll. 13–14). Even lines 5–7, describing birds that 'late from bough to bough did creep', begin to resonate suggestively. It is tempting to view Cornwall's 'birds' as political activists, who by creeping about were able to defy the Seditious Meetings Act (in force from the beginning of 1817 until 24 July 1818). The birds also 'seem to sing of Winter overthrown' (l. 8), the reference to 'overthrowing' transforming the line from a seasonal cliché to an audaciously blatant allusion to the toppling of an unpopular political regime. We could go further, interpreting the plumes trimmed by the birds literally – and literarily – as the trimmed quills of pens, conjuring up the untiring efforts of radical editors and essayists to assail Lord Liverpool's despised regime from oppositional pamphlets and the pages of publications like the *Black Dwarf*, the *Cap of Liberty*, and the *Political Register*.

If Keats's 'To Autumn' – either eliding, or cautiously alluding to, the massacre of workers and reformers on Manchester's St Peter's Field in August 1819 – is ambivalent about maturely embracing or immaturely retreating from political involvement, Cornwall's 'Spring' is more self-assured when it comes to urging 'grown-up' action. Then again, as I have already intimated, Cornwall's sonnet depicts a pre-Peterloo political landscape and almost certainly refers to the altogether more hopeful spring of 1819, when a series of best-selling radical tracts, tours by celebrated orators like Henry Hunt, popular marches, and the memory of recent successful defences against charges of sedition and libel (cases that made celebrities of T. J. Wooler, W. Hone, and R. Carlile), raised expectations of reform. Composed from a far darker, post-Peterloo perspective, it is hardly surprising that 'To Autumn' ruminates on the relative prudence of political steadfastness/retreat in full consciousness of the brutal response that activism could elicit, and had already elicited in Manchester.

'Full-grown lambs': immaturity and 'To Autumn'

As well as conversing with each other, 'Spring' and 'To Autumn' engage dialectically with an earlier work of notable ambiguity, Andrew Marvell's 'The Garden' (together with Milton, Marvell was Cromwell's Latin secretary).[46] Marvell's poem struggles to contain tensions between overt and covert themes that bear striking resemblances to those energizing Keats's and Cornwall's work. Just like Marvell's 'Upon Appleton House', 'The Garden' debates the personal ethics of withdrawing from public affairs to seek refuge in an Edenic pastoral space. The dilemma addressed in 'The Garden' anticipates that pondered by Keats and Cornwall – whether to face up, maturely, to political responsibilities, or to evade one's duty as a liberal through indulgent retirement. The allure of retreat is stated (and immediately complicated) in stanza 5 of Marvell's poem, which evokes the first stanza of 'To Autumn', as well as conjuring images from 'Ode to a Nightingale':

> What wondrous life in this I lead!
> Ripe apples drop about my head;
> The luscious clusters of the vine
> Upon my mouth do crush their wine,
> The nectarene, and curious peach,
> Into my hands themselves do reach;
> Stumbling on melons, as I pass,
> Ensnared with flowers, I fall on grass.[47]
> ('The Garden', ll. 33–40)

Here, the timeless comfort of pastoral is disrupted by melons that cause one to stumble, and flowers that ensnare. The very notion of disconnecting oneself from the world of political tangibilities is illusory, Marvell concedes, since even in the calm of an autumn garden, ripe fruit can trip people up and flowers can 'ensnare' (a word loaded with clear political connotations of intrigue and entrapment).

Keats and Cornwall respond to the dilemma set by Marvell in different ways. For Keats, the maternal breast – representing the ultimate retreat – is always, finally, seductive, even if political realities threaten to invade the boy's immature fantasies. Compare the reference to 'barred clouds' blooming the stubble-plains in stanza 3 of 'To Autumn' – which superimposes an image of incarceration over apparently open ground – to the ensnaring flowers in Marvell's pastoral idyll. Cornwall's emphasis, conversely, shifts towards 'start[ing] up' and leaving the 'great mother's iced bosom', on renewed action and decisiveness. Little wonder, then, that Hunt was pleased to include 'Spring', an otherwise indifferent poem, in the *Literary Pocket-Book* for 1820, printing it alongside passages from his own politically charged 'Calendar of Nature'.

Cornwall's dialogue with Marvell is especially close (and close-bosomed). Where the older poet offers a tempting image of refuge in which 'the mind, from pleasures less, / Withdraws into its happiness' (ll. 41–2), Cornwall responds: 'No – with an equal march the immortal mind / . . . keeps pace with every movement of the year' (ll. 9–11), insisting on the necessity of keeping a firm hold on political realities. The bird that sits in the 'boughs' in stanza 7 of 'The Garden', 'comb[ing]' its silver wings' and 'wav[ing]' in its plumes the various light', 'till prepared for longer flight', is given more purpose in 'Spring', where the birds, as we have already observed, 'trim their plumes . . . / And seem to sing of Winter overthrown' ('overthrown' invests 'trim' with connotations not only of preparing to write, but also perhaps of preparing a weapon for firing). Cornwall is clearly anxious that his poem's political message should be recognized in the right quarters: the first line of 'Spring' – 'It is not that sweet herbs and flowers alone' – unmistakably echoes the last line of Marvell's poem:

> . . . the industrious bee
> Computes its time as well as we.
> How could such sweet and wholesome hours
> Be reckoned but with herbs and flowers!
>   ('The Garden', ll. 69–72)

The equivocal 'but' in the concluding line of 'The Garden', carrying with it the sense of 'only' *and* 'except', is addressed and clarified by Cornwall, who replies: 'It is not . . . sweet herbs and flowers *alone*' (my emphasis). The significance of this final word for Cornwall is that it is *not* only flora which is, or should be, awakened by spring, but also the visionary consciousness of the radical mind.

'The Garden' stands as an emblematically ambiguous poem for Keats and Cornwall, from which 'To Autumn' and 'Spring' both draw, and against which they measure, their own strategies of equivocation. The principal divergence, however, is that while Cornwall is ready to shut down the ambiguity of Marvell's final line with a call to political activity – while Cornwall is ready to grow up, so to speak – Keats absorbs 'The Garden's thoughts on retirement and disengagement into his immature aesthetic. This can be most clearly apprehended in the no less busy, but distinctly immature versions of Marvell's 'industrious bee' (l. 69) that reappear in lines 9–11 of 'To Autumn': the adolescent bees who 'o'er-brim' their 'clammy cells' in joyous, onanistic, 'juvenile industry'. We might say that where Cornwall's response to the dilemma posed by 'The Garden' is to decide in favour of 'grown-up' action, Keats is always attracted to the idea of remaining in Marvell's pastoral realms of wonder and superabundance.

3 'Give me that voice again'
Keats and puberphonia

There is a general readiness among readers to appreciate Keats as the poet who, after the badness of the early poems, spectacularly and precociously 'finds his voice'. In Marlon Ross's version of the familiar narrative, Keats 'transvalues poetic aspiration into the gaining of a mature voice'.[1] Ross is sensitive, certainly, to a key desire in Keats: the desire, at some level of consciousness, to develop a manly register and acquire what an early work, *I Stood Tip-toe*, refers to admiringly as the 'mighty voice' of Apollo (l. 56).[2] But also discernible in the poetry is a strong counter-impulse aimed at prolonging a period of what, in *Sleep and Poetry*, Keats calls '*whining* boyhood'. In *Coming of Age as a Poet: Milton, Keats, Eliot, Plath* (2003), Helen Vendler asserts that a young writer's 'search for an adult style' is 'inexpressibly urgent', paralleling on an aesthetic plane 'the individual's psychological search for identity'.[3] While I concur with Vendler that style is closely bound up with psychological identity, this chapter proposes that Keats's work repeatedly dramatizes a *reluctance* to participate in the ritual finding of voice. Indeed, the idea of developing adult vocality triggers acute physical and psychological discomfiture in Keats, which is sublimated poetically and can thus be 'read'. Like many adolescent boys whose voices begin to break – or, to give the phenomenon its medical term, undergo 'vocal maturation' – Keats does not greet the onset of deeper, 'ponderous syllables' (*Hyperion*, II, 305) with unambiguous delight. Even where the prospect of physical development might be expected to appeal to him (in episodes of amorous rendezvous, for example), we typically confront strategies aimed, consciously or otherwise, at protracting and preserving boyish intonations. Garrett Stewart has observed, nicely, of Keats that 'his words often become his theme'.[4] In what follows, I want to show that Keats's theme is often not just his words, but his *voice*.

Out of several early Keats poems intimately concerned with (breaking) voices, the one most obviously so detained is 'On First Looking into Chapman's Homer' (1816). This is not simply where Keats first hears Homer, but also, according to traditional criticism, where we first hear Keats himself 'speak out loud and bold' (l. 8):

> Much have I travell'd in the realms of gold,
>   And many goodly states and kingdoms seen;
>   Round many western islands have I been
> Which bards in fealty to Apollo hold.
> Oft of one wide expanse had I been told
>   That deep-brow'd Homer ruled as his demesne;
>   Yet did I never breathe its pure serene
> Till I heard Chapman speak out loud and bold:
> Then felt I like some watcher of the skies
>   When a new planet swims into his ken;   10
> Or like stout Cortez when with eagle eyes
>   He star'd at the Pacific – and all his men
> Look'd at each other with a wild surmise –
>   Silent, upon a peak in Darien.

Critical orthodoxy, indeed, presents the sonnet as a defining moment, a milestone in artistic development. For John Barnard, it is Keats's 'first real poem'; while Andrew Motion refers to the sonnet's 'exceptional and suddenly found maturity'.[5] Helen Vendler, in a chapter entitled 'Perfecting the Sonnet', thinks of it as the place where Keats 'finds his voice'.[6] We tend, then, and are encouraged, to see in the sonnet a poet who is engaged in the ritual act of finding, or who has just found, his grown-up voice.[7] Yet, considered logically, 'speaking out' *as an act of boldness* is not something easily associated with the matured voice of a matured man. On the contrary, speaking out (of turn) can only be staged with the wavering voice of the boy, for whom such acts of presumption actually *require* a degree of boldness. Despite the assurance with which Barnard and Motion point to signs of maturity in 'On First Looking into Chapman's Homer', I would contend that the boyish accents of Keats's earliest poems remain audible. They are perhaps most evident in the 'Cockney' rhyme of 'demesne'/'serene'; but can also be heard in the overwrought proclamations of the boy who has been allowed to stay up too late: 'Then felt I like some watcher of the skies / When a new planet swims into his ken' (ll. 9–10). To be sure, the poetic voice in this justly famous sonnet is breaking; but crucially has not yet broken. The poem as a whole constitutes a pubescent wavering between vocal registers: if the opening lines are impressively and precociously stentorian, they are balanced by the excitable bleatings of lines 7–10.

Unexpected pitch breaks and vocal 'wobble' record yet another aspect of Keats's psychologically deep-seated reluctance to leave the sanctuary of the 'Chamber of Maiden-Thought'. Such, however, is the complexity of the poet's relationship with the often mutually contradictory logic(s) of immaturity, that it is possible, too, to pinpoint instances where a boyish poetics (in which the always-just-breaking voice is granted primacy), is self-consciously willed into existence. In addition, then, to scrutinizing cases where aversion to vocal maturation has left indelible traces in condensed or sublimated form, I am interesting in outlining a second category of boyish response in which Keats actively seeks to postpone the arrival of his adult register and prolong his boyish voice. Consider, in this respect, the poet's last volume, *Lamia, Isabella, The Eve of St Agnes, and Other Poems* (1820). Despite critical exhortations that he eschew 'school boy taste' and finally grow up, Keats persisted in using what Establishment reviewers like Josiah Conder denounced as a prattling idiom that was (still) 'very childish'.[8] Jerome McGann's judgement that the 'politically reactionary' 1820 volume was designed to ingratiate its author with readers and reviewers alike, overlooks, then, an important aspect of Keats's uniquely conceived challenge to literary authority.[9] In choosing to preserve inflections identified by reviewers as 'childish' – moreover, at the same time as systematically eradicating the *über*-adult strains of Milton's voice ('Miltonic intonation') from his poetry, notably *The Fall of Hyperion*[10] – Keats is making an emphatically political decision. The cost was his poetic reputation and any hopes of success in his lifetime. This circumstance in itself requires of us that we address a common misconception about Keats's boyishness: namely, that it always represents artistic or aesthetic lack of judgement, a signal failure of taste.

At various points in Keats's writing, in key letters, early verse, and in the published Preface to *Endymion* – which positions the poem as a production of the troubled intermediate 'space of life' between the 'imagination of a boy' and the 'mature imagination of a man' (*Poems*, p. 102) – Keats presents himself in terms that evoke Malvolio's speech in Act I, Scene v of *Twelfth Night*:

> *Olivia*: Of what personage and years is he?
> *Malvolio*: Not yet old enough for a man, nor young enough for a boy; as a squash is before 'tis a peascod, or a codling when 'tis almost an apple. 'Tis with him in standing water between boy and man. He is very well-favoured, and he speaks very shrewishly. One would think his mother's milk were scarce out of him.[11]

The conceptual interpretations that follow may leave the reader, too, in something of a 'standing water', transitional state of undecidedness. This 'effect', I would argue, is the typical product of any strong reading of a familiar text, and (like Leavis's 'Yes, but' model of the ideal response in a critical exchange) it can never envisage a *wholly* convinced reader of any critical argument which is truly interesting (or, for that matter, a wholly convinced writer).[12] Indeed, the very strength of the reading is inseparable from the production of this Heisenbergian 'uncertainty' effect in the reader (and not *too* far from Keats's own theorization of Negative Capability, the state of 'being in uncertainties, Mysteries, doubts, without any irritable reaching after fact & reason'; *Letters*, I, 193). To go back, therefore, to what I was saying in my Preface – and to what Keats says in his original Preface to *Endymion* – the important thing is that criticism (like art) should provoke 'conversation' or even 'bickerings' (*Poems*, p. 739). It seems to me that resourceful exchange – creative colloquy –

between critic and reader is a subtler and, ultimately, more beneficial, relationship than one in which a critic attempts to convince the person reading his or her argument, and thus close down interpretive possibilities by ending the 'Yes, but' catenation of critical exchange.

'Give me that voice again'

'Persistent puberphonia' in male adolescent subjects may be defined as the 'failure to develop characteristic low-pitched phonation'.[13] Both organic and psychological factors can give rise to the condition. A key psychological feature in the aetiology of puberphonia, Margaret Fawcus's clinical study of vocal disorders elucidates, is the 'fear of assuming a full share of adult responsibility' (p. 215). There is certainly good evidence in the poems and letters to support the idea that Keats was reluctant to assume adult responsibility. There is also much to suggest, as we have seen in earlier chapters, that he was profoundly apprehensive about the physical aspects of maturation, the 'growing up-ness' of growing up, if you like. Vocal development is one of the more public manifestations or proofs of physical maturity, of course, and Keats seems to have regarded it with especial scepticism. Some of his most profound misgivings are dramatized in the early work, *Calidore*, composed in the spring of 1816, and included in *Poems* (1817). John Barnard counts the poem among 'the worst moments in Keats's first volume'.[14] Arguably, he is right. None the less, if the poem is one of the volume's worst moments, it is also one of its most disclosing.

Calidore was envisaged as a *rite de passage*, which is how it is usually read – although, tellingly perhaps, Keats left the poem uncompleted – a *rite de passage* both at the level of male narrative, Calidore's story, and in terms of what the poem represented in Keats's tiny oeuvre in 1816.[15] At the beginning of the tale, 'Young Calidore' is described in appropriately childish vocabulary as 'paddling' his boat, rather than, say, manfully shouldering the oars, across a lake (l. 1). The would-be knight puts ashore at a little island, which is dominated by a single phallic emblem:

> The lonely turret, shatter'd, and outworn,
> Stands venerably proud; too proud to mourn
> Its long lost grandeur: fir trees grow around,
> Aye dropping their hard fruit upon the ground.
> (*Calidore*, ll. 38–41)

Phallic, yes. But these lines project a distinctly forlorn image of masculine power: 'shatter'd, and outworn', 'too proud to mourn / Its long lost grandeur'. Calidore appears to be insensible to the warning signs; insensible, in fact, to all forms and symbolic functions of masculine authority as he wanders around the leafy glades exploring the island's 'pleasant things' (l. 53), which sound suspiciously like the 'pleasant wonders' of the interstitial 'Chamber of

Maiden-Thought' (*Letters*, I, 281). Calidore immerses himself in the boyish pleasures of the island as, not for the last time in the poem, agents of mature masculinity are forced to rouse the young knight from his childish reveries. Sure enough, at line 54, Calidore's 'glad senses':

> . . . caught
> A trumpet's silver voice. Ah! it was fraught
> With many joys for him.
> (*Calidore*, ll. 54–6)

The trumpet announces the poem's specific concern with voice. Equally arresting is this passage's enshrinement of conflicting attitudes towards vocal development. The point needs elaborating. 'Fraught / With many joys for him', it strikes me, is decidedly and decisively odd. To start with, the qualifying 'for him' is virtually superfluous within the immediate signifying field. Who else, other than Calidore, could the trumpet's joys be meant for? Indeed, the inclusion of 'for him' introduces a potentially troubling element into the poem: namely, the notion that the trumpet's 'silver voice' is not 'fraught with many joys' for other men in the same way that it is for Calidore. And how, exactly, is the trumpet's voice *fraught* with joys? How, that is, is Keats using, or to phrase it slightly differently, how does he *think* he is using, 'fraught'? Is the word supposed to signify 'attended with' (*OED*, sense 3a); or '"big" with the . . . menace of' (*OED*, sense 3b)? My point is, of course, that the word sustains both meanings. The joys of (or at least promised by) the trumpet's voice are both exciting *and* intimidating to the boyish imagination.

Oblivious to these semantic niceties, Calidore is pleased at being called by the trumpet – as he should be, since on the face of it the poem is *about* a boy being summoned to manhood.[16] Impatient to mature – as Keats can appear to be impatient, particularly in the letters – the apprentice knight leaves the first island 'most eagerly' (l. 59), directing his little shallop towards a 'jutting point of land'. This second island is home to another edifice, a 'castle gloomy' (l. 65), full of 'halls and corridors' (l. 72), such as those Porphyro will negotiate in *The Eve of St Agnes*. Like Porphyro, Calidore (another archetypal 'aspiring boy', l. 128),[17] slips into a stronghold of conventional manliness. This castle, precursing the 'mansion foul' in *The Eve of St Agnes*, is about to become the scene where a pressing Keatsian anxiety will be played out.

Entering the courtyard, Calidore sets eyes on two ladies and their unmistakably bona fide knights as they gallop through the portcullis. The episode is described in terms that repay close scrutiny:

> . . . into the court he sprang,
> Just as two noble steeds, and palfreys twain,
> Were slanting out their necks with loosened rein;
> While from beneath the threat'ning portcullis

> They brought their happy burthens. What a kiss,
> What gentle squeeze he gave each lady's hand!
> (*Calidore*, ll. 76–81)

Keats's deep-seated fears about developing adult phonation are, I will be arguing, 'converted' into the image of the 'threat'ning portcullis'. To remain now, though, with the narrative of the scene, Calidore rushes over enthusiastically to help the ladies dismount – to all appearances, eager to play the man's part.[18] However, strategies of deferral similar to those we have observed in previous chapters soon become evident:

> . . . whisperings of affection
> Made him delay to let their tender feet
> Come to the earth.
> (*Calidore*, ll. 84–6)

This 'delay' exasperates the stalwart Sir Gondibert and his equally rugged companion, Sir Clerimond, model 'man of elegance, and stature tall' (l. 112). The latter moves to counter Calidore's boyish impulses:

> A dimpled hand,
> Fair as some wonder out of fairy land,
> Hung from his shoulder like the drooping flowers
> Of whitest cassia, fresh from summer showers:
> And this he fondled with his happy cheek
> As if for joy he would no further seek;
> When the kind voice of good Sir Clerimond
> Came to his ear, like something from beyond
> His present being: so he gently drew
> His warm arms, thrilling now with pulses new,
> From their sweet thrall, and forward gently bending,
> Thank'd heaven that his joy was never ending.
> (*Calidore*, ll. 93–104)

With 'kind voice' (l. 99), Sir Clerimond prompts Calidore to release the ladies. But despite his well-meaning nudge, the young hero lingers, pressing the ladies' dimpled hands to his forehead, thanking heaven that his 'joy' was 'never ending' (l. 104).

Why should Calidore insist his joy is 'never ending' in the very instant Clerimond effectively ends it? We can move towards resolving this conundrum by viewing the above lines, particularly 76–80 – 'two noble steeds, and palfreys twain, / Were slanting out their necks . . . / While from beneath the threat'ning portcullis / They brought their happy burthens' – as a deep-level rumination on the breaking voice: more specifically, on the wish to postpone this public manifestation of physical maturation for as long as possible. Lines

76–80 are doubly preoccupied with vocal ripeness. It's not only the horses' slanting necks that alert us to Keats's anxiety about throats and mature phonation. At some subterranean level of Calidore's – or rather, and let us not beat about the bush, Keats's – imagination, the 'threat'ning portcullis', with its wooden bars and opening/closing ropes and pulleys, constitutes a poetic instantiation of the out-sized larynx, of the ligaments and muscles of the matured vocal cords.[19] The portcullis reminds Calidore of what it is he has come to do, and with what consequences. I am ready to concede that this identification, dependent as it is on a surgical degree of familiarity with laryngeal anatomy, might seem far-fetched, or even frivolous. That is to say, I'm anticipating 'standing water' objections. But the identification starts to resonate and illustrate and illuminate when we remember that Keats was surgically trained. His medical career began with a five-year apprenticeship to Thomas Hammond, apothecary-surgeon (the early nineteenth-century equivalent to a general practitioner). This entailed learning basic medical procedures, assisting in childbirths, dressing wounds and performing postmortems.[20] Six months or so before composing *Calidore*, he moved on from Hammond's practice to study at Guy's Hospital with the innovative surgeon and political radical, Sir Astley Cooper.[21] The year-long post, which included courses in anatomy and physiology,[22] as well as morbid anatomy and dissection,[23] began in October 1815. Although friends from the period recall Keats dreamily composing Spenserian fragments during lectures,[24] if the poet's surviving anatomical and physiological notebook is anything to go by he was, for the most part, an attentive and diligent student.[25] It was just as well since the anatomy demonstrator, Joseph Henry Green, demanded that his pupils' knowledge be 'articulate and even minute'.[26]

At any rate, he would have owned a copy of the manual used by all anatomy students at Guy's, *The London Dissector*.[27] This closely describes the complexities of the laryngeal opening and closing mechanism. Under 'Dissection of the Throat' (subsections including 'Muscles of the Larynx'), we find a meticulous discussion of the 'Rima Glottidis' (glottis), detailing muscles around the larynx such as the 'Crico-Arythaenoideus Lateralis', whose function is 'To open the rima glottidis, by pulling the ligaments from each other'. Also described is the 'Arythaenoideus Transversus', whose function is 'To shut the rima glottidis, by bringing the arytenoid cartilages together'.[28] With advanced student manuals like *The London Dissector* forming part of Keats's prescribed reading, it would be perverse indeed to assume that the detailed physiology of the laryngeal apparatus could have remained mysterious to the poet. It is not at all unthinkable that a *rite de passage* poem on the progress of a young boy hoping to become a knight (a *rite de passage*, too, for *Calidore*'s literary apprentice hoping to become 'a poet'), could turn a portcullis into a symbolic projection of the matured, and thus in Keats's fragile psychology 'threat'ning', larynx. When Keats orchestrates events at line 76 so that his boyish adventurer comes face to face with the grown-up knights and ladies *just as* they ride in beneath the 'threat'ning portcullis' (on horses with conspicuously outstretched necks), he is registering profound disquiet at the prospect of imminent vocal mutation. I believe that *Calidore* not only inscribes its protagonist's deep unease about becoming a man, but also Keats's own alarm about facing up to adult responsibility. In addition, the episode logs Keats's ambivalence – which I shall discuss later – towards the idea of 'finding' a mature poetic voice.

Calidore springs into the courtyard, then, 'just as' the grown-ups gallop under the portcullis. Keats is very precise about the timing of this arrival, which, given the poem's larger concern with maturational anxiety, should not simply be ascribed to coincidence. The riders' mounts are 'slanting out their necks with loosened rein' (l. 78). These elongated necks are eye-catching within the context of ripening phonation. As Andrews and Summers note in their medical study of adolescent voices – and this is something Keats the anatomical expert would also have known – during puberty 'the neck lengthens and the larynx increases in length'.[29] An anonymous reviewer for Gold's *London Magazine* recognized the appositeness of outstretched necks to describe the literary pubescent, Keats himself – a writer who 'says nothing like other men, and appears always on the stretch for words to show his thoughts are of a different texture from all other writers'.[30] 'Always on the stretch for words', a striking image this. It anticipates the terms, and to some extent the sentiments, of Byron's contemptuous dismissal of Keats's 'outstretched poesy': poetry that tries too hard. But while the *London Magazine* deftly apprehends Keats's apparent eagerness to mature as a poet and a man, its reviewer also puts his finger on a central Keatsian dilemma. As a result of his efforts to find a unique voice (saying things that have not been said by men before), Keats finds that he 'says *nothing like other men*' (my emphasis). Keats's outstretched, but persistently childish, poetic timbre cuts him off from the male community that both calls and unnerves him.

One part of Keats's personality was self-consciously 'on the stretch' to mature – determined, like the fledgling knight, to join the manly heroes ('be among the English Poets') in the castle of high culture, resolved to demonstrate his prowess with 'sweet-lipp'd ladies' (l. 135). Nevertheless, an equally powerful desire inscribed in *Calidore* is for Keats's psychological surrogate to be granted a reprieve from the threatened onset of vocal development. The encounter at the castle gate dramatizes a defining moment of maturational crisis where the boyish imagination once again proves wholly incapable of contemplating ripeness without a shudder of repugnance and aversion.[31] If one thing becomes clear in lines 76–80, it is that the aspiring boy's eagerness to find his manly, broken voice and enter the grown-up sphere is compensated by an equally fervent wish to put off the arrival of mature phonation. The tension generated by these opposing partial drives visibly marks the portentous phrase 'threat'ning portcullis': the epithet itself is broken by an apostrophe (an element of grammar, but also a rhetorical device in speech).

'Threat'ning' is a curious term to affix to 'portcullis'– an odd conjunction all round, in fact, since portcullises are defensive rather than offensive structures.

They may be foreboding; they are certainly designed to dismay anyone contemplating forced ingress; but it is hard to imagine how one could feel *threatened* by a portcullis. Unless, of course, at some hidden stratum of consciousness, Keats is profoundly disturbed by the thought of his poetic voice maturing.[32] It can be no accident, at least not in terms of Calidore's boyish psychology, that the encounter with the virulently masculine Sir Clerimond and Sir Gondibert takes place in the shadow of the portcullis, the figurative projection of the oversized, manly voice-box.[33] In Chapter 1, we observed Keats's unease in the presence of excessively manly men. It is no different here, where vexed issues connected with 'legitimate' modes of masculinity are troped onto, and explored through, the voice. It can also hardly be coincidental that Calidore first becomes aware of Sir Clerimond when the grown-up knight's 'kind' – and interpellating – 'voice . . . came to his ear'; a voice, moreover, that is described as 'like something from beyond / His present being' (ll. 99–101). Tall in stature, unimpeachably manly, Clerimond, like his vocal cords, is truly 'beyond' Calidore's 'present being'. One part of Keats's awestruck/horrified young hero is perfectly content for things to stay this way.[34]

Similar ambivalence can be discerned in another '*p—ss a bed*' work: one that was composed immediately before *Calidore*, *Specimen of an Induction to a Poem*. After giving an excitable account of a tournament where 'stout' knights are 'grasping' tall lances in 'tremendous' hands, Keats abruptly breaks off, declaring: 'No, no! this is far off' (l. 31). On the surface, this histrionic piece of aposiopesis communicates despair at the passing of the age of jousting. But it is also possible to hear Keats reassuring himself that the point at which he will have matured sufficiently to enter what he cannot help but regard as a disconcerting world of hypermasculinity, is still 'far off'.

Having followed an early interloper into the 'halls and corridors' of the castle of masculine prowess, I want to conclude the first part of this chapter by returning to a later, better-known version of Keats's immature Romance hero: Porphyro. Let me begin by pointing out that the narrative of *The Eve of St Agnes* depends for its continuation (and its protagonist's survival) on silence. Moreover, on a specific *kind* of silence: the absence of voice. Lines 82–4: 'let no buzz'd whisper tell . . . / or a hundred swords / Will storm his heart'. Voice here is doubly de-amplified – reduced to a whisper, then erased altogether ('let *no* . . . whisper tell'; my emphasis). Framed thus, it is just as well (though in another sense, not surprising) that, by his own admission, Porphyro possesses a 'weak voice' (l. 147). Significantly, when utterance *is* raised to the level of audibility, it is its boyish timbre to which Madeline responds most passionately:

'Ah, Porphyro!' said she, 'but even now
Thy voice was at sweet tremble in mine ear,
Made tuneable with every sweetest vow;

. . . .
Give me that voice again, my Porphyro'
(*The Eve of St Agnes*, ll. 307–12)

'Sweet tremble' could simply be taken as a reference to Porphyro's singing voice: Porphyro has just sung an 'ancient ditty' into the sleeping Madeline's ear: 'La belle dame sans merci'. A little later in 1819, Keats *would* give this ditty again; what is more, in the same immature voice. But bearing in mind Keats's wider attention to adolescent phonation, it is tempting to see, or rather hear, in 'sweet tremble' – which contains a 'sweet treble' – a case of persistent puberphonia. It was no doubt salutary for Keats to imagine his most congenial, least threatening icon of sexualized femininity, Madeline, desiring, and even demanding, the unbroken voice of Porphyro, instead of the decisively broken voices of the ultra-masculine 'tiptoe, amorous cavaliers', whose advances are so pointedly spurned in stanza 7. Madeline's injunction, 'Give me that voice *again*' (my emphasis), is at any rate consonant with – and resonant within the context of – Keats's wish continually to re-present his boyish tones to the public.

What I have been attempting to establish are the ways in which Keats's work frequently dramatizes an unconscious impetus to defer vocal maturation, even while, at a manifest level, Keats's young heroes appear to long assiduously for physical manhood. There is also, however – and here we begin to appreciate the complexity of Keats's attitude(s) towards vocal development – a concurrent (and largely independent) readiness *deliberately* to address reading audiences in boyish or adolescent tones. It is this phenomenon to which I now attend.

'A space of life between'

Dead at seventeen, Thomas Chatterton was the archetypal 'young poet' for Romantic readers. His name, along with Kirke White's, conjured up an image of youthful poetic spirit blighted by the cruelty and neglect of the (adult) literary establishment. But whereas for Wordsworth and others Chatterton was the 'marvellous *boy*' (my emphasis), Keats addressed his memory in subtly but tellingly different terms. In an 1815 sonnet, 'Oh Chatterton! how very sad thy fate', Keats applies to the usual boyish clichés to describe his subject. We find, for instance, predictable apostrophes to the 'dear child of sorrow!' and 'son of misery!' (l. 2):

>Oh Chatterton! how very sad thy fate!
> Dear child of sorrow! son of misery!
> How soon the film of death obscur'd that eye,
>Whence Genius mildly flash'd, and high debate!
>How soon that voice, majestic and elate,

>   Melted in dying numbers! O how nigh
>   Was night to thy fair morning. Thou didst die
>   A half-blown flower which cold blasts amate.
>   But this is past. Thou art among the stars
>   Of highest heaven; to the rolling spheres   10
>   Thou sweetly singest – naught thy hymning mars.
>   Above the ingrate world and human fears.
>   On earth the good man base detraction bars
>   From thy fair name, and waters it with tears!

But by far the most interesting, because least formulaic, lines in this otherwise punishingly conventional early sonnet – Vendler goes too far, perhaps, in dismissing it as 'spastic [in the sense of 'involuntary'] exclamatory utterance'[35] – are those stressing Chatterton's *adolescent*, rather than simply boyish, tones. Chatterton's idiom is figured as prototypical of the always-just-breaking poetic voice, continually fluctuating between high and low registers: 'How soon that voice, majestic and elate, / Melted in dying murmurs' ('Oh Chatterton! how very sad thy fate!', ll. 5–6). One instant his voice is deeply intoned ('majestic'); the next it is raised in pitch ('elate').[36] Chatterton, indeed, could be said to speak to Keats with a quintessentially adolescent voice: breaking, but not yet broken. As suggested by the deferring participle in 'dying' (l. 6), his youthful tones are unended. From an adult perspective, Chatterton's phonic oscillation represented a vocal 'disorder'; but for Keats, as I will show, the wavering, continually murmuring voice, by turns 'majestic' and 'elate', has a thoroughly political quality.

Shortly after composing his elegy on the death of Chatterton, Keats produced a second sonnet, identical in rhyme scheme, entitled 'Written on the Day That Mr Leigh Hunt Left Prison' (1815). This, as Nicholas Roe points out, belongs to a group of early poems that clearly announce the 'oppositional values of dissenting culture'.[37]

>   What though, for showing truth to flatter'd state,
>   Kind Hunt was shut in prison, yet has he,
>   In his immortal spirit, been as free
>   As the sky-searching lark, and as elate.
>   Minion of grandeur! think you he did wait?
>   Think you he nought but prison walls did see,
>   Till, so unwilling, thou unturn'dst the key?
>   Ah, no! far happier, nobler was his fate!
>   In Spenser's halls he strayed, and bowers fair,
>   Culling enchanted flowers; and he flew   10
>   With daring Milton through the fields of air:
>   To regions of his own his genius true
>   Took happy flights. Who shall his fame impair
>   When thou art dead, and all thy wretched crew?

There is a particularly close phonal relationship between the sonnets on Hunt and Chatterton. The *-ate* rhyme, which Keats had picked up from reading Chatterton, sounds across parallel lines in both pieces: 'fate'/'state', 'debate'/ 'elate', 'elate'/'wait', 'amate'/'fate'. The phonic relationship between rhyming end vowels in the sonnets – 'eye'/'free', 'nigh'/'see', 'die'/'key' – is also interesting, built around open and closed vowels: or, rather, open and *shut* vowels. For it seems to me that where Chatterton's freedom from the 'ingrate world' is echoed in the open-mouthed vowels of 'eye', 'nigh', and 'die', Hunt's incarceration ('shut in prison', l. 2), is echoed in the 'shut' vowels of 'see', 'key', and, most ironically of all, 'free'. That Keats was attentive to phonation is attested by Benjamin Bailey, who reminisced about his friend's theory of 'open & close vowels' to Richard Monckton Milnes in 1849:

> One of his favourite topics of discourse was the principle of melody in Verse, upon which he had his own notions, particularly in the management of open & close vowels ... Keats's theory was, that the vowels should be so managed as not to clash one with the other so as to mar the melody, – & yet that they should be interchanged, like differing notes of music to prevent monotony.[38]

Returning to 'elate', we hear the word's contestational overtones more clearly in the sonnet on Hunt:

> What though, for showing truth to flatter'd state,
>   Kind Hunt was shut in prison, yet has he,
>   In his immortal spirit, been as free
> As the sky-searching lark, and as elate.
>   ('Written on the Day That Mr. Leigh Hunt
>   Left Prison', ll. 1–4)

Given the near contemporaneity of the lines on Chatterton's 'release' from the ingrate world (through death) with those on Hunt's release from prison, it is likely that Keats is making a political point – or at least registering a political association – when he uses 'elate' to describe the boyish quality apprehended in Chatterton's poetic voice.

While Keats doesn't allude to voice directly in 'Written on the Day That Mr Leigh Hunt Left Prison', vocality is at the heart of the poem. Look again at line 2: 'Kind Hunt was shut in prison'. Due to metrical constraints there is no room for an extra syllable; but usage actually demands not just 'shut', but 'shut up' (*OED*, 'to confine a person in prison'). There is, of course, a more colloquial meaning of 'shut up': *OED*, 'to cause (a person) to stop talking'. This connotation was certainly current in 1815 – it is found, for instance, in *Mansfield Park* (1814).[39] Hunt incurred his punishment specifically for speaking out (presumptuously) against the Prince Regent. In his case, incarceration was not only a punitive measure; it was also meant to prevent the radical editor from speaking out further. As things turned out, the government failed to 'shut up' the shut-up activist's voice, since Hunt stubbornly and flamboyantly continued editing his political journal, *The Examiner*, from his cell. (Keats is disingenuous when he suggests that Hunt spent his time gathering 'enchanted flowers' and straying in 'Spenser's halls'.)⁴⁰ He also held notorious prison soirées, attended by leading political reformers and friends, including Byron. Keats does not offer Hunt as a representative of youth (although Hunt was known for fostering youthful talent like Shelley's, and would shortly foster Keats's own), but the sonnet does underline his close association of political resistance and voice – especially the adolescent voice, which, Keats knew only too well, was especially vulnerable to adult attempts to shut it up.

If the two 1815 sonnets gesture in similar ways towards the political dimensions of adolescent intonation, boyish voices also possessed a distinctive radical charge for Keats. I shall develop this point by looking at two more early poems, *Sleep and Poetry* and *I Stood Tip-toe*, both composed at the end of 1816. In *Keats's Life of Allegory* – a study that still surprises – Marjorie Levinson frames various resonances of 'tip-toe' for Keats:

> The curiosity of the word 'tip-toe', and the metrical awkwardness of the line ['I stood tip-toe upon a little hill'] invite us to consider the simplest social meanings of the phrase. Why does one assume this stance? Or rather, who typically – what class of individuals – stands tip-toe? Children, short grown-ups, and people struggling to penetrate a defended view or to seize a remote one. Keats, from a political standpoint, was . . . all of those things.
>
> (p. 239)

We might add that the 'boyishness' of standing tip-toe would have been self-evident to Keats. Standing 'tip-toe' is, after all, the (im)postural analogue to 'speaking out loud and bold', a presumptuous act of utterance in the literary world, especially performed by someone like Keats who had a rudimentary command of Latin, and no Greek.

Sleep and Poetry, a companion piece to *I Stood Tip-toe*, is keenly aware of the politics of speaking:

> Will not some say that I presumptuously
> Have spoken? that from hastening disgrace
> 'Twere better far to hide my foolish face?
> That whining boyhood should with reverence bow
> Ere the dread thunderbolt could reach? How!
> If I do hide myself, it sure shall be
> In the very fane, the light of Poesy:
> If I do fall, at least I will be laid
> Beneath the silence of a poplar shade;
> And over me the grass shall be smooth shaven;

And there shall be a kind memorial graven.   280
But off, Despondence! miserable bane!
They should not know thee, who, athirst to gain
A noble end, are thirsty every hour.
What though I am not wealthy in the dower
Of spanning wisdom; though I do not know
The shiftings of the mighty winds that blow
Hither and thither all the changing thoughts
Of man: though no great minist'ring reason sorts
Out the dark mysteries of human souls
To clear conceiving: yet there ever rolls   290
A vast idea before me, and I glean
Therefrom my liberty; thence too I've seen
The end and aim of Poesy. 'Tis clear
As any thing most true; as that the year
Is made of the four seasons – manifest
As a large cross, some old cathedral's crest,
Lifted to the white clouds. Therefore should I
Be but the essence of deformity,
A coward, did my very eye-lids wink
At speaking out what I have dared to think.   300
          (*Sleep and Poetry*, ll. 270–300)

This long passage, doubly presumptuous, what with its Wordsworthian cadences at lines 288–93, anticipates and 'answers' detractors whom Keats suspected would – who *did* – denounce his entire poetic project as an act of impudence delivered in the preposterous voice of 'whining boyhood'.[41] Such lofty opposition notwithstanding, Keats bravely insists on the right to raise his voice. He would be a 'coward' should his 'eye-lids wink / At speaking out' what he has 'dared to think' (ll. 299–300). Personal 'liberty' for Keats derives from contemplating – what is more *articulating* or 'speaking out', that key phrase from the Chapman's Homer sonnet – the 'vast idea' that ever rolls before him (ll. 290–2). The very 'end and aim' of his poetry – and he is especially ardent on this point – is to enunciate that vision. From an early stage in Keats's work, then, the whine of boyish phonation and political autonomy are closely imbricated. Failure to speak out, indeed, is condemned as cowardice, a dangerous word in dangerous days when radical journals and pamphlets were demanding political activism, or even revolt, from Britain's populace. In Keats's view, though, as the sonnet on Hunt's release from prison makes uncompromisingly clear, brutal repression from Lord Liverpool's regime had left people with a stark choice: 'shutting up' or 'speaking out'.

While early poems like *Sleep and Poetry* and *I Stood Tip-toe* plainly possess an unreflectingly childish dimension, they also perform 'whining boyhood' in a knowing manner. To pursue this distinction, let us turn to a passage in the middle of *I Stood Tip-toe*, where Keats imagines parting from one of the many undifferentiated 'maidens' floating around his early work:

> O let me lead her gently o'er the brook,
> Watch her half-smiling lips, and downward look;
> O let me for one moment touch her wrist;
> Let me one moment to her breathing list;
> And as she leaves me may she often turn
> Her fair eyes looking through her locks auburne.
> (*I Stood Tip-toe*, ll. 101–6)

Keats, I suspect, is also looking through his locks here. We need to decide whether the patent boyishness enshrined in the awkward rhyme in the last couplet is consciously or unconsciously bad. Harold Bloom might argue that all bad poetry is sincere; but this passage, it seems to me, is anything but ingenuous. While there is nothing inherently awkward or boyish about rhyming on 'auburne', there is, I would suggest, everything awkward and boyish about rhyming on 'auburne'. Keats deliberately shifts the conventional stress onto the second syllable, a relocation accomplished with the aid of a diacritical mark. We might say that Keats, wilfully disposed not to heed the likely objections of critics, revels in the badness of the forced rhyme, going so far as to point out his transgression with a diacritical finger.

I Stood Tip-toe's rapport with puerility, then, organizes itself into a complex system of exchange. At least three discrete categories of boyishness can be distinguished. To begin with, the aspiring neophyte poet, conscious of his shortcomings, yearns to possess the 'mighty voice' of Apollo (l. 56). Keats is thus aspiring in the sense of being 'always on the stretch', but also in the sense of wanting to translate his childish, lisping sibilants into full-throated, mighty-voiced, masculine aspirants. For Keats, that is – literally – to say, aspiration is closely bound up with the developing voice. There is also a boyish dimension to the poem which Keats hardly seems aware of (this is its 'pronounced badness' – Marjorie Levinson's expression, borrowed from John Bayley – which has repelled generations of readers).[42] Finally, as we have just observed with 'auburne', Keats is closely and self-consciously attuned to boyish phonation as a tactical measure in his attack on established legislatures, where the 'vocality' of the poem – the whole 'grain of the throat', to use Barthes' phrase – identifies itself as a site of political contestation.[43]

As we have seen in *Calidore*, ambivalence towards manly voices is often registered latently. I do not think Keats *intended* the poem to explore his fear of developing adult intonation; or was even aware, necessarily, that it seems to do so. But there are other occasions where the wish to prolong, for political reasons, a state of vocal in-between (the always-just-breaking adolescent voice) is deliberately allowed to penetrate the surface of the text. When *Endymion* appeared in 1818, it was prefaced by what purported to be a prose apologia. In it, Keats declared he was only publishing a poem which he himself acknowledged bad because while it was 'dwindling' he might be 'plotting, and fitting [him]self for verses fit to live' (*Poems*, p. 102). He was, he added, acutely aware that merely to articulate this hope 'may be speaking too presumptuously'. His anxiety about speaking presumptuously, first heard in *Sleep and Poetry*, may or may not be genuine. Whatever the case, that curious formulation – 'plotting, and fitting myself for verses fit to live' – invites closer scrutiny. In view of the troubled times, 'plotting' is not only conspicuous, but *conspicuously* conspicuous. All importantly, Keats is not 'plotting and fitting' himself for 'verses fit to live'; he is 'plotting, and fitting' – the comma is decisive – which is something different altogether. The idiosyncratic punctuation invites us to read the first two verbs as separate actions, with separate consequences. We would, in any case, be ill-advised to gloss over 'plotting' from a writer whose poetic response to Peterloo, 'To Autumn' – an ode which on first and several subsequent readings seems to aspire to canonicity – hid allusions to dissent in innocent-looking, seasonal images of fruitful conspiracy and clammy cells. 'Plotting' does more than just signal Keats's readiness to invent new narrative schemes; it is also deployed as a means of alerting receptive readers to the Preface's subversive politics. Importantly for my argument, the Preface's revolutionary charge – the word does not seem overblown now – and that of *Endymion*, derives from Keats's faith in the capacity of presumptuous, youthful phonation to disrupt adult paradigms of authority and control.

Endymion, Keats declared in the Preface with rhetorical flourish, should never have appeared. It was, he confessed, a work of 'great inexperience, immaturity, and . . . error', denoting 'a feverish attempt, rather than a deed accomplished'. On the other hand, the age was full of feverish attempts that failed to become deeds accomplished: Leigh Hunt's endeavour to humiliate the Prince Regent (the joke backfired), the efforts of protesters at Peterloo, the plotting of the Cato Street conspirators. Reviewers may have been right to highlight the fact that *Endymion* was a poem with a weak plot; but of chief importance was the fact that it had been plotted by someone like Keats in the first place. To make matters worse, Keats had publicly announced that his boyish epic would be used to hatch other plots, which, next time around, *would* produce 'verses fit to live': plots, that is to say, which would not remain feverish attempts, but end in deeds accomplished.

In the final sections of the published Preface, Keats attributes *Endymion*'s weaknesses to the fact that the poem had been composed in the adolescent 'space of life' between the 'imagination of a boy' and the 'mature imagination of a man'.[44] In this suspended interval between immature and mature existence, he explains, the soul is in a 'ferment'; everything is 'uncertain' and 'undecided':

> The imagination of a boy is healthy, and the mature imagination of a man is healthy; but there is a space of life between, in which the soul is in a ferment, the character undecided, the way of life uncertain.
>
> (*Poems*, pp. 102–3)

For Keats, undecidedness captured the perpetual waver of the adolescent voice: the pulling of the vocal cords in two directions, towards boyhood *and* manhood, without either being able to establish primacy. On the one hand, Keats seems to regard this undecided, intermediate 'space of life' as a version of the 'second Chamber'. But it is also a political space. Those distinctive words in the Preface – 'ferment', 'uncertain', 'undecided' – are attractively ambiguous, polyvalent terms for Keats. Alongside 'plotting', at any rate, 'ferment' begins to suggest a chaotic, uncertain space resistant to attempts at governance; where things – 'way[s] of life', no less – remain undecided, and might indeed be decided differently.

The unpublished Preface to *Endymion* had also accentuated Keats's sense of the immaturity of his project: its status as a childish 'endeavour' rather than a 'thing accomplish'd' (*Poems*, p. 739). But in addition to moments of childish truculence – 'I have written to please myself' – the original prefatory remarks had also included passages that were closely attuned to political issues, especially to the need to engage in 'conversation' (another form of 'speaking out'):

> I would fain escape the bickerings that all Works, not exactly in chime, bring upon their begetters: – but this is not fair to expect, there must be conversation of some sort and to object shows a Man's consequence.
>
> (*Poems*, p. 739)

Recognizing that his long poem was not 'in chime', Keats boldly insists on the need for a rigorous exchange of contrary views; on the need for 'bickerings', to use his colloquial, knockabout expression. 'There must be conversation of some sort', he insists, resolving to speak out, however presumptuous his voice might sound (even to his own ears). For Keats, making *Endymion*'s defiantly out-of-chime/dissonant adolescent voice audible becomes an integral part of what it means 'to object' in troubled days.[45]

Dedicated to the memory of Thomas Chatterton – the voice of adolescence – *Endymion* is the poem of breaking voices par excellence. It is where Keats's poetic voice oscillates most markedly between 'trembling' and 'stedfastness' (*Endymion*, IV, 715).[46] This unpredictable rise and fall in poetic pitch was seized upon by reviewers, who produced verbal portraits of Keats as a 'boy of pretty abilities' and a 'very young man'.[47] Appraising *Lamia* in the *Eclectic Review*, the commentator, in all probability Josiah Conder, found some 'indication of *growth*' (Conder's emphasis), but complained that this was undermined by the poet's frequent lapses into 'school boy taste'.[48] Such critiques were levelled at Keats from the beginning.[49] A generally supportive reviewer for the *Edinburgh {Scots} Magazine* detected much worthy of approbation in *Poems* (1817), singling out the sonnet, 'Addressed to Haydon', for possessing 'so *deep a tone* of moral energy' (my italics). He qualified his applause, however, adding that this deeper tone was repeatedly marred by the '*high raised* passion' (my italics) of 'namby-pamby' phrases such as 'leafy luxury', 'jaunty streams', 'lawny slope', 'moon-beamy air', and 'sun-beamy tale' – Cockneyisms that represented the acme of jejune bad taste.[50]

I should like to examine one more example of the breaking voice deployed as a political weapon. On 21 December 1817, Keats reviewed Edmund Kean's performance of *Richard III* in the *Champion*. His critique, it seems to me, occupies an important place within the boyish project we have been investigating. The political reflex of the review is made immediately and starkly apparent in an ironic reference to Habeas Corpus (suspended 4 March 1817, and not restored until 28 January 1818):

> 'In our unimaginative days' – *Habeas Corpus'd* as we are, out of all wonder, uncertainty[51] and fear; – in these fireside, delicate, gilded days, – these days of sickly safety and comfort, we feel very grateful to Mr Kean for giving us some excitement by his passion in one of the old plays.[52]

What strikes Keats most forcibly about the actor is not his formidable physical presence, but rather the 'indescribable gusto in his voice'. This convinces Keats that Kean is 'thinking of the past and the future, while speaking of the instant' (*Complete Poems*, p. 528). A simultaneous pull towards past and future is, we might say, audible in the adolescent's breaking voice, where speaking *in* the instant involves both boyish and manly states of laryngeal physiology. Keats is alive to the inherent historicity of vocal fluctuation (as was Kean, in Keats's estimation – a man whom he evidently thought inhabited the same 'space of life'). For Keats, the present is always historical in Kean's verbal performances, and thus always politicized. The celebrated actor spoke for and to the '*Habeas Corpus'd*' times, for and to liberals and reformers who had suffered a period of major setbacks and reversals (not least of which was the suspension of habeas corpus for the second time in living memory). Playing a tyrannous king in *Richard III*, Kean found himself on the 'wrong side of the question'. But the important thing was that Keats's favourite actor articulated a guiding spirit of hope and resilience: 'Although so many times he has lost the battle of Bosworth Field, we can easily conceive him really expectant of victory, and a different termination of the piece.' This was precisely the spirit needed to sustain harried and demoralized reformers, many of whom, in Horsemonger Lane Gaol, the Tower of London, and countless other clammy cells, had been literally 'Habeas Corpus'd' out of all wonder – and out of existence.

If a careful use of voice could produce this extraordinarily transformative degree of uncertainty, overturning old certainties, old orthodoxies, and showing that things were indeed still 'undecided', then it is little wonder that Keats was so eager to explore the possibilities of boyish intonation. Given the political attractions of Kean's voice, it is also understandable why Keats was so impatient to secure the great actor's services for *Otho the Great*.[53]

'Beyond the reach of my voice'

In the summer of 1818, Keats's recently married brother George emigrated to America with his wife, Georgiana. Keats composed a number of long journal letters to the pair. Of particular interest in the context of my argument is correspondence added to over the course of two weeks at the end of September 1819. In the first two sections, dated Friday 17th and Saturday 18th, Keats is preoccupied with the 'bad times and misfortunes' which he felt had engulfed him. His 'bad reputation', he complained, hindered any attempts to make money from poetry. On top of that, Edmund Kean, whom he hoped would play the part of Ludolph in *Otho the Great*, had left England to tour America – 'the worst news I could have had', Keats exclaimed (*Letters*, II, 186). George and Georgiana were facing financial hardships of their own following the calamitous failure of a business venture: George had lost his entire inheritance (and arguably some of Keats's) after investing it in a Mississippi river-boat, which promptly sank. Not in the least censorious, Keats assures his correspondents that if he ever made money from writing, they would benefit, too: 'Your wants will be a fresh spur to me. I assure you you shall more than share what I can get, whilst I am still young – the time may come when age will make me more selfish' (*Letters*, II, 185). It is possible to see in this passage an economy of youthful largesse, pointedly at contrast with the self-interested logic of maturity.

Despite frequent allusions to adversity, Keats's letter contains a plenitude of lighter moments, including a transcription of the doggerel lines, 'Pensive they sit, and roll their languid eyes':

> Pensive they sit, and roll their languid eyes
> Nibble their to[a]sts, and cool their tea with sighs,
> Or else forget the purpose of the night
> Forget their tea – forget their appetite.
> See with cross'd arms they sit – ah hapless crew
> The fire is going out, and no one rings
> For coals, and therefore no coals betty brings.
> A Fly is in the milk pot – must he die
> Circled by a humane society?[54]
> ('Pensive they sit, and roll their
> languid eyes', ll. 1–8)

Lest we forget *our* purpose, the transcription is followed by a distinctly Keatsian aside: 'You see I cannot get on without writing as boys do at school a few nonsense verses' (*Letters*, II, 188). Schoolboy humour is recurrent in Keats's letters; but often, as here, it punctuates or disguises more pressing concerns. The couplet at the end of the quotation, which depicts a fly in a milk pot, is deliberately bathetic and turns on a preposterous slant rhyme. All the same, the fly's predicament conjures up an affecting image of neglect and isolation, poignantly paralleling the situation of Keats and his beleaguered brother and sister-in-law.

Saturday's entry registers yet another instance where maturational crisis is troped through images of laryngeal development. Keats takes up his pen determined to lift George's mood. Gloomy about past literary endeavours, he manages to talk in positive terms about his current project, *Lamia*: 'I am certain there is that sort of fire in it which must take hold of people in some way – give them either pleasant or unpleasant sensation' (*Letters*, II, 189). This well-known statement appears to show Keats in a confident frame of mind – as Motion says, 'Keats seems to have felt 'briefly confident that he had at last written something which honoured his poetic principles and would also prove popular'.[55] The less familiar passage which immediately follows, however, suggests that Keats was still plagued by what we can now recognize as habitual insecurities regarding manliness and adulthood:

> I wish I could pitch the key of your spirits as high as mine is – but your organ loft is beyond the reach of my voice.
>
> (*Letters*, II, 189)

This may look straightforward, bringing a buoyant Keats into favourable apposition with the downcast George. Keats wishes he could cheer his brother up, but acknowledges that, having emigrated to America, George is out of reach of his voice. A closer look, however, shows the sentence to be perilously overdetermined; so much so, that it struggles to maintain internal coherency. The first thing to note is the decoupling of sequential logic marked by the separating (rather than conjoining) dash. I am not suggesting that the sentence does not collocate at all; but it does not do so quite in the way Keats supposes. There are several things to unpick here if we are to expose the psychological impetuses that, time and again, propel Keats towards crisis. For instance, how can Keats's *voice* – and, equally perplexingly, its *reach* – raise the *key* of George's *spirits*? And why should the operation take place in an organ loft? For that matter, what exactly does Keats mean by his brother's 'organ loft'? At least two lines of thought – as well as the figures used to express them – have become entangled. The dead metaphor, 'to raise one's spirits', has been fused with, or invaded by, a metaphor of vocal pitch ('key'). The sentence *does* concatenate, but only within the terms of Keats's vexed psychic economy. Keats, that is, does not just think of his spirits as high-pitched, but, in figurative terms, also his voice. Let me add that by 'organ loft', Keats is alluding to the metaphorical pitch of George's voice. Quite aside from its *actual* tenor, this would have been deep for Keats in so far as George – the younger brother – was already married and engaged (if precariously) in the adult world of business. Organ lofts are situated high up in churches, not deep down, of course; but what is first and foremost at stake here is not George's deep organ 'loft', but his deep organ *tone*. Compare Moneta's 'deep organ tune' in *The Fall of Hyperion* (I, 350).[56] In other words, even though Keats starts the sentence – in one sense, positively – by comparing his brother's depressed emotional state to his own indefatigable light-heartedness, he ends it in a state of anxiety, nervously comparing the manly pitch of George's voice to his own persistently boyish accents.

While the letter, then, is ostensibly concerned with comparative levels of cheer, it simultaneously registers a more urgent fixation with high-pitched, boyish voices versus deep-toned, manly ones, just as we saw in *Calidore*. In fact a compelling verbal similitude links the portion of the letter under discussion to Keats's early poem. Just as Sir Clerimond's 'kind voice' comes to the young knight 'like something from beyond / His present being' (ll. 100–1), George's 'organ' tones are 'beyond the reach' of Keats's voice (*Letters*, II, 189). They are also, Keats seems to concede, beyond the reach of his present being. Pursuing the connection between poem and letter a step further, in the same way that Clerimond knows how to act in the company of 'sweet-lipp'd ladies', George has successfully wooed, married – and impregnated – Georgiana. Keats, on the other hand, had yet to develop a 'right feeling towards Women', and arguably never did.

The likelihood that Keats was thinking specifically – if unconsciously – in terms of comparative stages of maturation when he discussed the relative pitch of his and George's spirits, is strengthened a few paragraphs later. The topic has moved on to Charles Dilke, a friend who Keats complained was overly absorbed in fatherhood. 'Pitch' is deployed once more, this time within an overtly boyish context:

> Dilke is entirely swallowed up in his boy: 't is really lamentable to what a pitch he carries a sort of parental mania – I had a Letter from him at Shanklin – He went on a word or two about the isle of Wight which is a bit of hobby horse of his; but he soon deviated to his boy. 'I am sitting' says he "at the window expecting my Boy from School." I suppose I told you some where that he lives at Westminster, and his boy goes to the School there. where he gets beaten, and every bruise he has and I dare say deserves is very bitter to Dilke.
>
> (*Letters*, II, 190)

Note the position(ing) of 'pitch' mid-way between 'boy' and 'parental mania'. Exactly here, suspended in the space of life between boyhood and manhood, between boyish play and adult responsibility, is where Keats pitches his own voice. At times, this pitching is deliberate and political. When it is not, we discover Keats in the grip of maturation anxieties.

'Parental mania' – and by this Keats simply seems to mean 'parenthood', given the patently *un*manic nature of Dilke's 'deviation' – is obviously a powerful source of unease. (George's own status as married man and father would have contributed to this heightened level of apprehension.) In the entry from

17 September 1819, Keats claims to be able to 'bear any thing, any misery, even imp[r]isonment – so long as I have neither wife nor child' (*Letters*, II, 186). The passage not only expresses Keats's relief at the absence of financial dependants; it records *pleasure* at not having – makes pleasure virtually contingent on not having – the key proofs of a mature existence, a wife and children.

This particular economy of pleasure can also be discerned in *Lamia* – a poem, we have seen, which was very much on Keats's mind on 17–18 September. *Lamia* is precisely 'about' getting (or, more accurately, *not* getting) married, and having (or rather ensuring one does not have) children, the ultimate 'adult responsibility'.[57] Indeed, the semantic derailings and dissonances that complicate the letter to George and Georgiana are equally apparent in *Lamia*. In several respects, the entries for the 17th and 18th actually provide a gloss on the psychological interiors of the poem. At the manifest level of what Baudrillard calls – especially appropriate here – the text's 'laboured appearance',[58] *Lamia* is about a demon-enchantress waylaying a naïve young man. Lycius, however – wanting, it seems, nothing more than to mature along 'normal' lines – is 'preserved' by his teacher, Apollonius, who is determined that his protégé's normative maturational trajectory (setting up home, founding a family with a suitable wife) should not be subverted by a serpent woman. Disastrous consequences ensue. But despite the 'self-evidence' of this manifest reading, the letter to George and Georgiana, with its vocally focused anxieties and paranoia regarding 'parental mania', alerts us to more complex psychological swirls and eddies. The journal entries legitimize a reading of the poem in which Apollonius emerges as an aspect of Lycius's anxious Self, opposed to any set of circumstances that would result in the 'young Corinthian' growing up to marry not just Lamia, but *anyone*. Apollonius' goal, we are told, is to preserve Lycius from 'every / Ill of life' (ll. 296–7). And, as Keats's letters generally make clear, it is the *adult* world which is associated with the ills of life: 'adult' ills such as pain and heartache, bailiffs and debt, the 'weariness, the fever, and the fret' – *and marriage and children*. Apollonius' project, then, is to keep Lycius in a state of arrested development, staving off the arrival of grown-up responsibilities indefinitely. Lamia – whom Keats's boyish imagination conceives as the archetypal embodiment of the girl who wants to grow up as quickly as possible, marry and have children – is interpreted not so much as a threat to manly men, as to *boyish* men – to those with no desire to grow up, no urge to enter the world of marriage, offspring, and adult obligations. At every level, Lamia imperils Lycius' boyish wish to preserve an intermediate 'space of life' where everything can remain gloriously 'undecided' (to invoke once again that very decisive word from the published Preface to *Endymion*).

Lamia's will to mature, her wish to participate in the mad rush of mature desire ('the ruddy strife / Of hearts and lips'), is memorably stated at the beginning of Part 2, where she bewails the fact that her body is inappropriate to her physical appetites:

> 'When from this wreathed tomb shall I awake!
> When move in a sweet body fit for life,
> And love, and pleasure, and the ruddy strife
> Of hearts and lips! Ah, miserable me!'
> (*Lamia*, I, 38–41)

Lamia's fantasy of possessing an adult 'body fit for life' is resonant, read alongside Keats's own maturational crises. Think again of Keats in the Preface to *Endymion*, 'plotting, and fitting' himself for verses 'fit to live'. Lamia shares similar aspirations with that aspect of the poet which is 'always on the stretch' to develop and evolve – Keats wants to reify his juvenile scribblings into a corpus of mature verse (a 'body fit for life', *Lamia*, I, 39), just as Lamia longs to become a 'deed accomplished' (Preface to *Endymion*).

'Parental mania', then, is not only addressed in the letter to George and Georgiana, but is also pointedly at issue in the poem haunting (and haunted by) that letter. That is to say, the letter's preoccupation with *voice* – with 'organ' tones; with lengthening, but not yet lengthened, larynxes – is present, too, in sublimated form, in *Lamia*. At I, 146–67, for example, Lamia's feverish transformation into a 'lady bright' concludes with the arrival of a 'new voice', confirming the importance for Keats of vocal maturation as the final verification of physical ripeness.[59] It is worth emphasizing the vocality of *Lamia* as a whole, since the text is quite literally filled with voices. Typically these are subdued 'mutterings', 'murmurings', and 'undersongs' – white noise discerned at the edge of consciousness. We think of the constant 'muttering' in the streets of Corinth (I, 353), the 'murmurous vestibule' at the wedding (II, 163), and the guests' 'vowel'd undersong' (II, 200). Though muted, the significance of these 'voices off' is by no means marginal. On the contrary, at the beginning of Part 2, a seminal episode is precipitated by Lycius' growing awareness of this quiet, but steadily encroaching, cacophony of voices. The incident I am referring to offers an unique glimpse into the workings of Lycius' boyish imagination, and deserves to be read attentively.

The lovers have secreted themselves in Lamia's 'purple-lined palace of sweet sin' (II, 31), where Lamia has been enjoying Lycius' single-minded devotion – until, that is, the 'noisy world' (II, 33) outside – in particular 'a thrill / Of trumpets' (II, 27–8) – compare *Calidore* – causes his attention to wander beyond the walls of the palace. Lamia responds by playing a mixture of piqued lover and teacher who upbraids naughty schoolchildren for gazing out of the window. Swiftly fabricating an excuse, Lycius claims to have been imagining the joys of parading his 'prize' (Lamia) before Corinth's jealous males:

> My thoughts! shall I unveil them? Listen then!
> What mortal has a prize, that other men
> May be confounded and abash'd withal,
> But lets it sometimes pace abroad majestical,

And triumph, as in thee I should rejoice
Amid the hoarse alarm of Corinth's voice.

(*Lamia*, II, 56–61)

In this mealy-mouthed, grammatically opaque address, Lycius tells Lamia what he thinks she wants – what she *does* want – to hear. These are lies, of course: idealized lies, but lies none the less – and will prove his undoing. What Lycius imagines is a harmless fiction that will enable him to regain Lamia's favour soon gathers its own terrible momentum. Before long, it is impossible to conclude his oratory with anything less than a marriage proposal, delivered via an allusion to bridal cars. This is Lycius going too far:

Let my foes choke, and my friends shout afar,
While through the thronged streets your bridal car
Wheels round its dazzling spokes.

(*Lamia*, II, 62–4)

Lionel Trilling is wrong, I think, to ascribe the energies of these lines to Lycius' wish to excite a 'particularly ugly kind' of envy (although Trilling is quite right to want to 'involve Keats' in the psychology that prompts Lycius' speech).[60] Lycius has no *genuine* investment in exciting envy among potential rivals; the point is that he is playing a role (a manly role, at that). As with the equally decisive (and psychologically contiguous) scene played out in *Calidore* before the 'threat'ning portcullis', the primary, if submerged, concern is with voices and throats. Choking throats of enemies, shouting voices of friends (an earlier, cancelled version of line 62 – 'Life to my friends, and to my foes a curse' – had not contained this vocal reflex).[61] At the risk of going too far myself, the bridal car's 'dazzling *spokes*' (my emphasis) could also be seen as registering – in what Lycius hopes is a dazzling *speech* – an oblique preoccupation with (maturing) voices. Lycius's own voice proves to be his downfall. Only a few moments before his rash, improvised speech, marriage could not have been further from (although in another sense, *closer to*) his boyish mind. Hardly believing her luck at her lover's peroration, Lamia goes through the motions of decorous, accismustic protest, 'beseeching him . . . / To change his purpose' (II, 68–9), before finally acceding to his 'wishes'.

At some level, Lycius is aware that he is shaping a set of circumstances deeply inimical to his boyish desire (which is to prolong boyish desire). Let us look again, and more intently, at line 61, at Lycius' description of 'the hoarse alarm of Corinth's voice'. Ostensibly, Lamia's lover refers to the sounds of Corinth's busy streets. In any event, this seems to have been Keats's intention, since cancelled versions of the phrase in the draft manuscript included 'buzzs of the Citiy's', 'great buzz', and 'buzzd alam' (*sic*, see *Poems*, p. 465). The version Keats settled on, 'hoarse alarm', is an intriguing formulation, containing two parapractical slips, pregnant with all kinds of truths. Taking 'alarm' first, this is a strange word to choose to describe the noise of chattering citizens. If, however, Lycius unconsciously perceives the 'alarm' of the 'populous streets' as a 'warning sound [giving] notice of danger' (*OED*), as well he might, then the term is apt to the context (slips of the tongue usually are). As modern readers, we are accustomed to gloss over ostensible ripples in coherency in historically distanced works, particularly when they stem from linguistically inventive writers like Keats. We tend to accommodate words that disrupt sense – such as 'alarm' in line 61 – by approximating them to others more readily comprehensible.[62] Quite literally in other words, we ascribe now difficult terms alternative meanings, apparently more appropriate but often only more expedient. We assume, then, that by the 'hoarse alarm of Corinth's voice', Keats was simply casting about for a suitably poetic way to say 'background chatter'. It should hardly need pointing out that this strategy of convenience results in missed opportunities. It is, in any case, quite bizarre to want to read poems – by nature powerfully figurative entities – in a purely uninflected manner. All the more so since 'alarm', it seems to me, is placed carefully by Keats (although this is not to say that it is placed consciously). 'Alarm' rings out proleptically, alarming us to the fact that Lycius is about to propose marriage and thus endanger his boyish existence; at the same time, it reveals that Lycius is himself, in some sense, alert to the fact that he is on the verge of setting a truly calamitous series of events in motion.

I referred to two parapractical slips: the second is 'hoarse'. It is not that the idea of voices made hoarse by excessive chatter fails to make perfect sense. But I would propose that *other* considerations, other factors, suggest this particular word to Keats at this particular point in this particular narrative. For the 'hoarse alarm of Corinth's voice' is none other than the breaking, but not yet broken, voice of adolescence. It is the alarming voice of youth alarmed at its own hoarseness – a tonal characteristic instantly recognizable as the indubitable sign of maturity's onset, the prelude to the commencement of adult responsibilities. In one regard it is appropriate that, at the precise moment Lycius begins to utter his marriage proposal and thereby cross the threshold into the world of adult accountability, the poem's narrative voice itself cracks, exhibiting classic symptoms of vocal maturation (hoarseness).

Immediately after proposing, Lycius conforms to, or at least mimics, what Keats's boyish imagination envisages as a normative mode of aggressive masculine desire: his first act as a fiancé is to perform tyranny, which famously Lamia 'lov'd' (II, 81). His *essai* in domination is noted approvingly by the woman determined to make a man of him. None the less, Keats undermines the authenticity of Lycius' staged rage, unable to refrain from pointing up the comical side of his feverish attempt to 'play the man's part'. Look carefully at Keats's deflating depiction of Lycius' ingenuous, but far from genuine, act of tyranny as 'mitigated fury' (II, 78). What should be a defining maturational juncture, marked by the 'punctual incandescences' described by Lyotard in his

'Give me that voice again': Keats and puberphonia 71

whimsical but instructive book, *Libidinal Economy*;[63] what should be a crucial phase in the protagonist's journey towards manhood, degenerates into yet another amusing boyish interlude:

> His passion, cruel grown, took on a hue
> Fierce and sanguineous as 'twas possible
> In one whose brow had no dark veins to swell.
>
> (*Lamia*, II, 75–7)

The cruel joke is, of course, that Lycius' face cannot become 'sanguineous' (engorged with blood), because his immature brow has not yet any 'dark veins to swell'.[64] It is only in line 77 that the elided comparative 'as' which actually sits at the beginning of line 76, becomes 'visible' – what we first read as the manly attribute 'Fierce and sanguineous as 'twas possible', that is, revises itself into the distinctly unmanly '(As) fierce and sanguineous as 'twas possible / In one whose brow had no dark veins to swell'. At this undeniably funny, but nevertheless uncomfortable, moment of detumescence – detumescence notwithstanding – or perhaps hence – Lycius' (comically un-metonymic) red face, *Lamia* records Keats's deeply rooted fear about growing up and assuming adult obligations.[65] Although Lycius *seems* to embrace the prospect of an accelerated *rite de passage* by 'offering' to marry Lamia, things – as is so often the case in Keats – are not *only* what they appear to be.

It is not difficult to appreciate why Lycius has, for so long, come across to readers as someone who is eager to mature. Keats strains/stretches throughout *Lamia* to display the accoutrements of conventional manliness; hence Lycius' apparent impatience to make the transition from boyhood into adulthood and marriage. Like Keats, however, Lycius fails to convince. Our swooning hero (I, 289) is as unsure of his relationship with virile masculinity as Porphyro, Lorenzo, and the desolate woman-hater, the knight-at-arms. At the close of Part 1, for example, Lycius is portrayed 'charioting foremost in the envious race' (I, 217). Yet, even when he is winning, he displays a 'calm uneager face'. In short, he lacks the killer instinct, which is partly what makes his exhibition of youthful tyranny at lines 75–7 so amusing. While, on the one hand, *Lamia* is at pains to (be seen to) recount an archetypal tale of young love imperilled – either by the jealousies of age or by a demonic version of womanhood – it is probably best understood as a psychological exploration of the predominantly male apprehensions associated with growing up,[66] getting married, and having children.[67] It is, no doubt, not insignificant that, at the close of the tale, when Lycius' marriage ceremony ends in crisis and disaster, the 'young Corinthian' utters a protracted shriek (II, 269) – one of the best examples of high-pitched, male puberphonic utterance in Keats, rivalling even Apollo's squeaky aposiopesis at the end of *Hyperion*. Just as *Hyperion* depicts Apollo, another of Keats's reluctant adolescents, balking at the thought of assuming adult responsibilities – in Apollo's case, taking over as sun-god, no less –

Lamia shows Lycius recoiling at the prospect of marrying and having 'wife and child', to recall the letter to George and Georgiana.

With the aid of adjacent texts such as the correspondence of September 1819 and *Calidore*, we are able to appreciate that *Lamia* does not, primarily, dramatize the tragically thwarted efforts of a young man to marry and become a full adult. The terminally 'uneager' Lycius is not seeking a 'right feeling towards Women'. He is emphatically *not* Cinderella's Prince Charming, struggling to break out of the stasis of the fetish, finally to emerge as a grown-up lover. On the contrary, *Lamia*, at least as far as Lycius is concerned, is precisely about *not* wanting to grow up, about doing everything in one's conscious and unconscious power to avoid maturing.

4 Japing the sublime
Naughty boys and immature aesthetics

On 22 June 1818, Keats and Charles Brown left London to embark on a sightseeing tour of the north. Their ambitious itinerary included walks in the Highlands, Ireland, and the Lake District (where they planned to visit Wordsworth). For Keats, the trip was in part a chance to obtain a salutary dose of non-metropolitan 'experience', and thereby 'rub off his 'obstinate Prejudice' concerning women (*Letters*, I, 342). But it was also envisaged as an opportunity to 'gorge wonders' in textbook locations of the sublime (*Letters*, I, 268). The spectacle of natural wonders, Keats enthused to friends, was certain to 'enlarge' his vision and 'strengthen' his poetic 'reach' (*Letters*, I, 268, 342). Marginalized and alienated, worried about public perceptions of his youth, troubled by the poor reception of *Endymion*, Keats looked forward to mining raw material for a mature style that would persuade the custodians of literary orthodoxy to accept him. If he could master the grand style, of which sublime rhetoric was a key component, his claim to the status of grown-up author might be settled once and for all. In more ways than one, the walks in the north were contrived as crucial steps towards maturity.

'Gorge', from 'gorge wonders', turned out to be plurally resonant, defining important aspects of the northern excursions in ways Keats could hardly have foreseen as he set out. Gorges are chasms, narrow openings between hills: there is no shortage of these in the Lake District. 'Gorge' is also, the *OED* reminds us, an old word for 'throat'. It was a 'bad sore throat' caught on the Isle of Mull which forced Keats to leave his travelling companion prematurely and return to Hampstead (*Letters*, I, 364). 'Gorge' carries, too, not just the connotation of feeding, but of *over*feeding. Keats was no stranger to this phenomenon, confessing his fondness for eating a 'Monstrous Breakfast' every morning during the walks (*Letters*, I, 302).

He also overfed on the sublime. At the beginning of the tour, rushing from one sublime spot to the next, we find him eagerly mouthing the rhetoric of what Brown called 'fashionable guide-books' (*Letters*, I, 363),[1] performing Burkean awe, terror, and astonishment with characteristic élan: 'The Lake and Mountains of Winander – I cannot describe them – they surpass my expectation – beautiful water – shores and islands green to the marge – mountains all round up to the clouds' (*Letters*, I, 298). Yet just a few days after penning this conventionally breathless, wide-eyed passage, Keats was complaining about having to 'fag up hill, rather too near dinner time' (*Letters*, I, 306). Still fixated on gorging, as the reference to 'dinner time' suggests, he no longer wished to feed on sublime landscapes.

Keats began to express his growing antipathy towards scenery by puerilizing the descriptive conventions of travel narrative. 'Fagging' uphill is gloriously inappropriate where one expects to hear of mountains being scaled or conquered through manly exertion.[2] In similarly irreverent vein, instead of composing mature verse about craggy rocks or fathomless lochs, Keats dashed off smutty and pointedly juvenile doggerel inspired by irksome gadflies and lascivious mountains. He also produced a self-portrait, 'A Song about Myself'. This radically, and comically, subverted sublime subjectivity by infantilizing the viewing subject itself – the mediator of grand experience to readers awaiting vicarious immersion in 'wonders':

> There was a naughty Boy
>   A naughty boy was he
> He would not stop at home
>   He could not quiet be[3]

In refusing to take the sublime seriously, Keats plays the 'naughty boy'. Naughtiness, though – and this is the point I wish to elaborate – is enacted not simply for bathetic effect, but as a specific form of resistance. There is a further meaning of 'gorge' recorded by the *OED*: 'extreme disgust . . . resentment'.[4] My aim in this chapter is to investigate how Keats's mischievous bearing towards 'grand scenery' is inflected by disgust at the 'mature' aesthetics which made it visible as such. Keats started to realize – to have proved on his pulses – that ways of seeing landscape drew equally on an élite theory of the picturesque and a profoundly undemocratic model of political governance. Traditional travel literature shaped the world in a harmonious manner by removing disturbing human elements such as impoverished labourers and ragged children from scenes of natural wonder. Keats's own record of travel, by contrast, which reaches towards an ethical critique of the sublime, endeavoured to make newly visible the distresses of working people – the 'rags, the dirt and misery' (*Letters*, I, 321). In the journal of his tour, Keats repeatedly unsettles grand discourses by recording inappropriately juvenile japes in one splendid location after another. Immaturity is a frequently disregarded and misunderstood feature of Keats's challenge to authority. Yet boyish pranks and infantile responses, which I argue function as a system of interruption, prove a powerfully strategic means of disturbing the 'adult' focus of eighteenth-century aestheticians such as Edmund Burke, Thomas West, and William Gilpin. There is a deeply subversive purpose in Keats's politically freighted portrayal of himself as a 'naughty boy' who 'could not quiet be'.

It was, of course, a familiar phenomenon for young men on the Grand Tour to play pranks on their tutors, drink to excess, and be generally loud and promiscuous, instead of taking proper account of grand scenery, refined society, and the splendours of continental culture – the things that were supposed to improve or 'finish' them. Keats, touring the north of England and Scotland on a shoestring budget, was to a certain extent separated from such hedonistic subversions of classical education and aesthetics by class and limited financial resources; but it might be supposed that his naughtiness was simply a way of indulging some of the traditionally profligate responses of the sons of noblemen. It is my belief, however, that Keats's contestation of grown-up power begins to look distinctly less opportunistic and rather more programmatic – constituting, indeed, a careful schema of 'boyish' opposition to rigid aesthetic and political dogmas.

Maturing sons

As a partial consequence of the current endeavour to recuperate a politically sophisticated Keats, we find in critical orthodoxy a willingness to play up signs of the poet's maturity, and underplay or explain away episodes of his (all too evident) penchant for infantilism. It is easy to understand why this is so. In an influential piece of *ur*-Keats-criticism, Mrs Oliphant portrayed her subject as a 'fervid boy', disparaging his early letters for their 'weak boyish jokes and banter', which she did not consider 'worth preserving or reading'.[5] The terminus of Oliphant's puerilizing caricature was the assertion that 'Keats, though he was so little apart from his great contemporary [Shelley] in age, was no child of Revolution': 'He wanted nothing but to roam about the unimaginable tangles of the dewy woods and meet his goddess' (I, 140). 'Fervid boys', in other words, cannot be political beings (although Oliphant's own phrase to describe Shelley, 'child of the Revolution', somewhat militates against her distinction). Silently acceding to the judgement of Oliphant, modern attempts to establish Keats's political credentials frequently gloss over what can still appear as 'weak boyish jokes and banter'; or else measures are taken to represent boyishness – and this most misleadingly of all – as a form of incipient manliness, manliness *in potentia*, as it were.

Andrew Motion and John Woolford, two recent commentators on the political nuances of the 1818 walks, are equally at pains to project the now conventional, post-McGannian image of Keats as mature, or in any event rapidly maturing – someone who was (eagerly) developing a grown-up lyrical and political consciousness. So, for example, while they observe Keats's preoccupation with 'images of poverty'[6] and 'human relationships' in the Lake District[7] over scenery, and while they draw attention to his disinclination to perform the 'correct' responses to landscape, they neglect to point out that prominent displays of childishness are typically, indeed invariably, involved at these seminal junctures. Motion's and Woolford's aim is to trace how Keats's ripe demeanour (which according to orthodox criticism is explored more fully in *Hyperion*, and culminates in the 'quiet power' of 'To Autumn') received a vital boost during the northern tour. Both scholars work assiduously and resourcefully, that is, to fit Keats's writing on the walks into a larger schema in which the poet's short life can be depicted as a precociously brisk evolution towards poetical and, all importantly, political maturity.[8] To keep faith with this meta-narrative of accelerated, uni-directional development, we are obliged to ignore, or otherwise negotiate out of existence, all signs of recalcitrant juvenility that intrude on the walks. Such strategies dispense, however, with the need to ask the decisive question *why* Keats deploys immature imagery so persistently during his excursion. But by not asking it we miss – paradoxically enough, from the viewpoint of political criticism – an important dimension to Keats's challenge to established power.

The following passage from Motion's biography illustrates how its 'mature' subject is constructed:

> [Keats] knew that in a sense his early return [from the tour] was a failure. In other, more important ways, he had triumphed. His increased self-knowledge had prepared him to take a decisive step towards the next chamber of his existence.[9]

With interpretive sleight-of-hand, Keats's 'failure' to grow as a poet in the Lake District is reabsorbed within a narrative of progress, failure itself being cast as a critical component of personal and artistic development. Motion's study, steeped in new historicist assumptions, reads the walks unwaveringly in terms of their contribution to Keats's (political) 'self-knowledge'. The poet who steps into the Lake District to be 'vexed' (p. 265) by endemic poverty is still – or even more conveniently *is once again* – a political apprentice, although fast maturing. We discover a similar emphasis on process over achievement in John Glendening's elegantly written essay on Keats and hero worship: 'As tourist and literary pilgrim, Keats was largely unsuccessful . . . As a seeker after a capable self, however, he made headway.'[10] In the end, Glendening concludes, the trip north enabled Keats to 'resolve those ambiguities in his situation that were resolvable, leave those be that were not, and ultimately allow him to master a verse rich with the contrariety of life itself' (p. 99). This reproduces a familiar teleological narrative of trial and growth, failure and eventual triumph, where every hardship suffered bears mature fruit in the major poems. Marlon B. Ross is justly wary of reading the life of Keats too rigidly as an 'evolutionary parable'.[11] None the less, he, too, suggests that Keats's 'development' can be seen as a 'self-conscious movement from literary apprenticeship to master craftsman, from uncertain ventriloquism of other's voices to masterful articulation of his own unique voice, from modish pictorialism of "thoughtless youth" to visionary gleams of profound prophecy' (p. 157).

Of course, the element of Keats's personality that genuinely longed to 'evolve' encourages us to perceive the poet as a maturing son, and supplies a number of eye-catching models of youthful development (the best known being the concept of 'Chambers' of intellectual progress, which Keats outlined in a letter to Reynolds in May 1818). We observed in Chapter 1 that Keats was morbidly afraid that people would dismiss him as unripe: he complained bitterly that he was only a 'weaver boy' in the eyes of the reading public. 'Weaver boy' is an interesting phrase, doubly diminishing, conflating two of Keats's most deeply seated anxieties: weavers were 'beneath' physicians (turned poets) in professional terms, and boys were 'less' than men from a social standpoint. Yet for all this yearning to conform, and be seen to have conformed, to customary models of manliness, it is boyishness and regression, *not* maturation, that emerge as governing personal tropes in the tour journal, something neither Woolford nor Motion, doughty champions of a grow(i)n(g)-up Keats, acknowledge. For that matter almost all scholars of Keats, post-McGann, exhibit a near pathological reluctance to concede *any* evidence of infantilism in the poet. It is usual practice to skim over doggerel composed during the walks (unless it contains an obvious political reference); or simply to despair at infantile skits like 'Upon my life, Sir Nevis, I am piqued', summarily dismissed by Robert Gittings as a poem about a 'fat lady climbing [a] mountain'.[12] Alternatively, attempts are made to redeem tour works such as 'A Song about Myself' and 'Ah! ken ye what I met the day' from charges of boyishness by making them appear to fulfil the requisites of mature, politically aware composition. Motion urges us to see these pieces 'tip[ping] towards seriousness in the closing lines', arguing that they encode Keats's 'sense of alienation', 'solitude', and 'foreignness'. By the same token, any perceptible 'lack of interest in descriptive writing' in the walking-tour poems is ascribed to 'depression', usually understood as a grown-up affliction.[13] Such indubitable signs of ripeness (alienation, solitude, depression) are obviously essential ingredients for a political Keats. Yet by ignoring the poet's boyishness we are in danger of overlooking some of his sharpest contestations of established values.

The critical disinclination to dwell on performances of childishness in the Lake District and Highlands ultimately derives from a failure to appreciate their frequently self-conscious, ironized character. As a corrective, I will be scrutinizing episodes of juvenility in the journal letters to demonstrate how these often carefully staged events constitute integral components of Keats's larger political assault on the cultural institutions of mature power (thus returning to Oliphant's 'fervid boy' the fugitive radicality familiar to new historicist criticism). These are my contentions: first, that Keats's subversion of the Burkean sublime, and more urgently the 'natural sublime' (*Letters*, I, 224) represented by Wordsworth's grand style, is staged through images, verse forms, semantic registers and conversational/poetic topics that are deliberately and incongruously boyish; second, that Keats's repudiation of sublime rhetoric, his boyish counter-aesthetic, is not merely the precondition for an evolved political awareness, but is *already* the calculated manifestation of such an awareness;[14] and, third, that by insisting on viewing the poet's boyish japes as antithetical to political diligence, we risk constructing a Keats who is curiously detached from the aspect of his work that is arguably most

'Keatsian'. We should not, therefore, follow Motion and Woolford in striving to redeem Keats's northern doggerel, those hastily penned skits and dashed-off rhymes, by insisting on their serious moments; neither should we strain to recognize in them the germ of future mature poems. Their political capacity to disrupt lies precisely in their *boyishness*, rather than in signs of incipient maturity. These often Bakhtinesque interludes deserve to be acknowledged as part of a carefully considered political response to literary values that an appalled Keats began to reject as the belletristic expression of repressive social power.

Two naughty boys

Setting out on the walking tour, troubled by *Endymion*'s poor reception, Keats believed, or at least *wanted* to believe, that experience was the key to strengthening poetic 'reach'. A culturally marginal poet, denigrated by reviewers for his puerility and indifferent education,[15] for being over-aspiring and poetically insignificant, the lackey and tasteless imitator of poets like Leigh Hunt, who were themselves insignificant and tasteless, Keats needed to demonstrate that he had attained sufficient control over his idiom to be considered as a mature writer. One way of doing this was to master that type of over-heated landscape rhetoric which Thomas Weiskel has called the 'Romantic sublime'. In this compositional mode, the viewing subject typically conveys a sense of being overpowered, rising to terror and fear of personal annihilation.[16] Discourse itself breaks down at these epiphanic moments into breathy exclamations of 'grandeur', 'terror', and 'awe'. Coleridge is illuminating here:

> Gothic art is Sublime. On entering a cathedral, I am filled with devotion and with awe; I am lost to the actualities that surround me, and my whole being expands into the infinite; earth and air, nature and art, all swell up into eternity, and the only sensible expression left is, 'that I am nothing!'[17]

Keats was particularly fascinated by the Wordsworthian sublime, counting *The Excursion* (1814) as one of 'three things to rejoice at in this Age' (*Letters*, I, 203). The following passage is from Book IV of Wordsworth's poem:

> Has not the Soul, the Being of your Life
> Received a shock of awful consciousness,
> In some calm season, when these lofty Rocks
> At night's approach bring down the unclouded Sky,
> To rest upon their circumambient walls;   1160
> A Temple framing of dimensions vast,
> And yet not too enormous for the sound
> Of human anthems, – choral song, or burst
> Sublime of instrumental harmony,
> To glorify the Eternal![18]
>
> (*The Excursion*, 1814, IV, 1156–65)

'Lofty rocks' – 'A Temple framing of dimensions vast' – 'glorify the Eternal!' For Keats, Wordsworth's style, his 'grandeur', epitomized the highest form of the sublime. More of a byword for mature style even than *The Excursion*,[19] the 1805 *Prelude* is the paradigmatic Romantic poem 'on' maturation. Perhaps the best-known example of the sublime pitch occurs in Book 1, where Wordsworth describes how as a (naughty) schoolboy he stole a boat tethered on the shores of Patterdale:

> . . . lustily
> I dipp'd my oars into the silent Lake,
> And, as I rose upon the stroke, my Boat
> Went heaving through the water, like a Swan;
> When, from behind that craggy Steep, till then
> The bound of the horizon, a huge Cliff,
> As if with voluntary power instinct,
> Uprear'd its head: I struck, and struck again,
> And, growing still in stature, the huge Cliff   410
> Rose up between me and the stars, and still,
> With measur'd motion, like a living thing,
> Strode after me. With trembling hands I turn'd,
> And through the silent water stole my way
> Back to the Cavern of the Willow tree.
> There, in her mooring-place, I left my Bark
> And, through the meadows homeward went with grave
> And serious thoughts: and after I had seen
> That spectacle, for many days, my brain
> Work'd with a dim and undetermin'd sense   420
> Of unknown modes of being:
> . . . .
>   . . . huge and mighty Forms that do not live
> Like living men mov'd slowly through my mind
> By day and were the trouble of my dreams.
>   (*The Prelude*, 1805, I, 402–28)[20]

This is justly celebrated, spectacularly conceived. As the boat pulls away from the 'craggy Steep', the 'huge Cliff', previously hidden, appears to rear up in pursuit. Naturally, this only works if one reads the landscape from the same viewpoint as the boy on the lake, since the boat-stealing scene is wholly dependent on linear perspective theory for its sublime effect. This theory was a crucial component of eighteenth-century aesthetics, stressing as Peter de Bolla reminds us that 'one, and only one, place constitutes the "correct" place for viewing'.[21] Wordsworth's extraordinary trick of perspective, then, although a tour de force of the Romantic imagination, remains within the conventional bounds of what de Bolla, in a different context, calls a 'legislative theoretical discourse' of representational and spatial relations.

The scene's essential conventionality is not confined to perspective. The 'huge Cliff' itself could be seen as supremely legislative. Unmistakably tumescent in nature, 'uprear[ing] its head', 'growing still in stature' (I, 408–9), it functions as a potent sign of patriarchal power. The law (of the father) inspires sublime terror in naughty boys like the young Wordsworth, who returns the boat (which entered the text as a potential symbol of liberation) with 'trembling hands', and afterwards dreams guiltily of his act of theft. In other words, a formative experience of the phallic sublime becomes a grim rite of passage in which 'grave / And serious thoughts' are substituted for boyish play (I, 416–17). This crucial scene also demonstrates how the sublime is not simply produced by grown-up politics, but also propagates that politics, planting the seeds of mature ideology in young boys, who will one day grow up to own boats themselves.

Tim Fulford notes that 'in Burke's account, the sublime is an encounter with a patriarchal power to which we submit as to a father figure'.[22] Wordsworth's response to the pursuing mountain certainly appears to resolve itself into the paradigmatic Burkean engagement described by Fulford. But while Wordsworth is soundly reprimanded for his naughtiness on the shores of Patterdale, Keats is altogether more successful in disturbing the efforts of the sublime to impose the symbolic order. One of his major challenges to mature perspectives is directed at perspective itself, especially at the sublime perspective responsible for terrifying the young Wordsworth. Keats is unimpressed by terrifying vantages from mountain summits or by views over dizzy ravines. Scaling Skiddaw – the 'distant Skiddaw' of Wordsworth's boyhood (*Prelude*, I, 299) – for its renowned prospect, he was obliged to abandon his ascent due to inclement weather:

> It promised all along to be fair, & we had fagged & tugged nearly to the top, when at halfpast six there came a mist upon us & shut out the view; we did not however lose anything by it, we were high enough without mist, to see the coast of Scotland; the Irish sea; the hills beyond Lancaster; & nearly all the large ones of Cumberland & Westmoreland, particularly Helvellyn & Scawfell.
>
> (*Letters*, I, 306–7)

This vaguely admonitory passage ('it promised all along to be fair') registers disappointment; but Keats's endearing reaction to his failure to reach the mountain's peak – 'we were high enough' – is delightfully pragmatic at the same time as it disarms. While, as Marlon Ross asserts, climbing mountains 'perfectly embodies the poet's charge of self quest' and is 'another metaphor of masculine poetry', and while Byron in Canto 3 of *Childe Harold's Pilgrimage*, 'driven by desire that is intensified the more it is quenched', has 'no choice but to climb the Alps', Keats refuses to conform to prevailing notions of masculine prowess.[23] He is not climbing Skiddaw to strike Romantic attitudes; his 'fagging' and 'tugging' fail to produce a sublime climax – but Keats is not overly concerned. At any rate, nothing is said about returning to the mountain in fairer weather. The idea of a correct (manly/heroic) viewpoint leaves Keats unmoved. Three-quarters of the way up Skiddaw is 'high enough'.

'Safe in its own privacy' (and another naughty boy)

On the one hand, Keats could display remarkable equanimity at losing out on an astonishing view. However, the Wordsworthian sublime continued to preoccupy him periodically. Four weeks into the walking tour, he used the opportunity of writing to Benjamin Bailey to remind himself why he had undertaken his northern peregrinations:

> I should not have consented to myself these four Months tramping in the highlands but that I thought it would . . . identify finer scenes load me with grander Mountains, and strengthen more my reach in Poetry, than would stopping at home among Books even though I should reach Homer.
>
> (*Letters*, I, 342)

Despite early misgivings over the politics of the sublime, Keats was acutely aware that the grand style in poetry epitomized the mode of literary production readers were accustomed to accept as 'grown-up'. His original plan on setting out from Hampstead had been to acquire the cultural authority he felt (and knew) he lacked in the eyes of the public by acquainting himself with the principles of sublime rhetoric. It is, then, all the more striking that he used every occasion to jape grand discourses with childish exhibitions, 'trivial' comments, and inappropriate responses to impressive scenery. These improprieties are not conducted in an arbitrary fashion but amount to a calculated critique of high aesthetics. To probe this line of investigation, I want to examine an earlier – and possibly related – contestation of orthodox aesthetics: Mary Wollstonecraft's *Letters Written during a Short Residence in Sweden, Norway and Denmark* (1796).

Elizabeth Bohl's illuminating work on *A Short Residence* explores Wollstonecraft's firm rejection of the 'established political valence of taste'. In traditional eighteenth-century representations of nature, Bohls explains, undesirable human presences such as hungry children and impoverished labourers are removed through a process of 'verbal framing' which distances viewer from scene.[24] In stark contrast, Wollstonecraft focuses on the relationship between people and their environments, deliberately interjecting exploited peasants into otherwise formulaic descriptions of awe-inspiring scenes. The first extract I should like to look at from *A Short Residence*, taken from Letter 16, records Wollstonecraft's departure from Kvistram and begins as a routine invocation of the picturesque:

> The purple hue which the heath now assumed, gave it a degree of richness, that almost exceeded the lustre of the young green of spring – and harmonized exquisitely with the rays of the ripening corn.
>
> (*A Short Residence*, Letter XVI, p. 158)

Conventional enough, perhaps. 'Lustre', 'richness', 'young green of spring', 'harmonized exquisitely': this is the sublime's beautiful counterpart, as described paradigmatically by Burke in his treatise, *A Philosophical Enquiry into the Origin of our Ideas of the Sublime and Beautiful* (1757). Wollstonecraft, though, suddenly pulls into focus a group of labourers 'busy in the fields cutting down the corn, or binding up the sheaves'. The serenity of the conventional pastoral idyll is pressured by the intrusion of labour, activity, and feudal economy. The figurative 'richness' (Wollstonecraft's term) of the heath is ironized by the all too real poverty of the peasants who are gathering in the harvest, a contrast that was also to strike Keats forcefully in the summer of 1818. In Bohls's words, Wollstonecraft 'revises the canons of scenic description to make a seamless transition from aesthetic to practical . . . plac[ing] rural dwellers and their subsistence at the centre of the landscape'.[25] There is a brief return to formula in the notice of some 'unusually rugged rocks', but any hopes that a passage of Burkean sublimity is about to ensue are dashed when Wollstonecraft remarks that the Scandinavian winters are 'so long, that the poor cannot afford to lay in a sufficient stock of hay'. Wollstonecraft, we might say, makes political hay, affording rural communities and their precarious, exploitative economy precedence over the travelogue's customary inventory of natural wonders and carefully scripted exclamations of amazement.

The second passage, from Letter 17, details the author's visit to the Trollhättan 'cataracts'. Wollstonecraft's accounts of these natural splendours merit attention because, for a brief period, her prose seems less confident of its subversive mission, more than half in love with the sublime. We could say that Wollstonecraft allows herself to be constructed by the sublime, her prose temporarily losing its historical awareness. Retreating into formula, she claims to have been 'scarcely conscious *where* [she] was' (my italics), or *when*, gazing 'I know not how long' at the waterfalls. Spatial and temporal disorientation constitutes a standard effect of the sublime, of course. Surveying the spectacle of the falls in conventional eighteenth-century mode, Wollstonecraft also employs punishingly orthodox rhetoric: the water 'rushing from different falls', 'struggling with the huge masses of rock', and 'rebounding from . . . profound cavities' ('profound cavities', in particular, has the tell-tale sound of landscape jargon, loud without force). But all this is merely to set up Wollstonecraft's next astounding move. An abrupt and crucial shift in focus occurs as the author's eye is distracted from the 'grand object' of cascading water by the astonishing presence of an unlikely interloper:

> I gazed I know not how long, stunned with the noise; and growing giddy with only looking at the never-ceasing tumultuous motion, I listened,

scarcely conscious where I was, when I observed a boy, half obscured by the sparkling foam, fishing under the impending rock on the other side. How he had descended I could not perceive; nothing like human footsteps appeared; and the horrific crags seemed to bid defiance even to the goat's activity.
(*A Short Residence*, Letter XVII, pp. 159–60)

Jane Moore is surely mistaken to argue that when Wollstonecraft notices the boy 'sublimity is henceforth forgotten'.[26] The sublime has not been forgotten in this critical scene; it has never been more at issue. The focus of sublimity, though, has moved from the waterfall to the marvellous figure of the boy, who leaves no 'human footsteps' and scales 'horrific crags' too steep even for goats: a boy – and this should *not* be forgotten – who is impossibly and disturbingly present in the midst of a scene where, according to Burkean aesthetics, he does not belong and is certainly not welcome. No abstract spirit of nature to be idealized or deified by the Romantic sublime, he is performing a specific act of labour: fishing. Given the hardship of Scandinavian life catalogued elsewhere in *A Short Residence*, the boy is unlikely to be engaged in sport or pleasure.

This perilous act of necessity surprises and embarrasses the polite reader in much the same way that Wordsworth, the polite poet, is embarrassed in the fourth section of *Poems on the Naming of Places*, which documents a more famous fishing encounter.[27] Wordsworth and his entourage have set off into the picturesque, travelling within a vicinity of the Lake District which is sheltered from public view, 'framed' by the craggy lakeside topography:

A narrow girdle of rough stones and crags,
A rude and natural causeway, interposed
Between the water and a winding slope
Of copse and thicket, leaves the eastern shore
Of Grasmere safe in its own privacy.
(*Poems on the Naming of Places*, IV, 1–5)

The group notice a man 'angling beside the margin of a lake' (IV, 52). Assuming the angler is enjoying himself while his more industrious fellows labour at the harvest, Wordsworth bristles with indignation. Closer inspection, however, reveals a gaunt, emaciated figure, too 'worn down / By sickness' to work (IV, 64–5), a man who is eking out an existence from the 'dead unfeeling lake' (IV, 71). Once the parameters of misapprehension have become clear, the group's collective gaze turns uncomfortably inward, the travellers falling to 'serious musing and to self-reproach' (IV, 76). What starts out as an appreciation of the 'sweet morn / With all its lovely images' (IV, 74–5) ends in chastened introspection. Traversing a seemingly unproblematic stretch of the picturesque – 'safe in its own privacy' – Wordsworth is confronted with an embodiment of hardship which he is not meant to see (at least, not at close proximity). Eighteenth-century aesthetics, with its safe, 'framed' views, enabled polite audiences to continue in their 'unthinking fancies', as Wordsworth puts it soberly, concerning the lives of labourers (IV, 46): fancies in which 'Reapers, Men and Women, Boys and Girls' at work could be imagined as engaged in 'busy mirth' (IV, 42), rather than trapped in a structure of inequitable exchange. It is exactly to dispel this kind of deceiving fancy that Keats performs and records intransigent acts of boyishness on his walking tour.

Returning to *A Short Residence*, similar to Wordsworth's angler the Trollhättan fisher-boy is a secret which Wollstonecraft's text is not keen to divulge. We could go so far as to say that every effort is made to keep him from view. To start with, he is 'half obscured by the sparkling foam'; and just as the 'crags' in section IV of *Poems on the Naming of Places* form a screening causeway (ll, 1–2), 'horrific crags' at the Trollhättan waterfalls create an excluding frame which discourages intrusion into a site of polite cultural consumption. None the less, the fisher-boy (and the desperate economy of need that has summoned him) insists on visibility, breaking into the author's sublime revery, usurping the waterfalls to become a sublime object himself.

I will be elaborating how, just like Wollstonecraft's 'naughty' boy, Keats – self-proclaimed 'naughty Boy' ('A Song about Myself'), literary pretender, and preposterous Cockney tourist – is troublesomely 'out of place' as he tramps irreverently through the Lake District and other 'high' cultural locales.

'No such thing as time and space'

One of the most popular travel primers of the period was Thomas West's *Guide to the Lakes*, which identified for 'persons of genius, taste, and observation' a series of 'select stations' from which to enjoy the most picturesque scenes in the Lake District.[28] Stipulating where to go to secure the finest views – to the extent of detailing hidden gates and 'secret' paths – West's *Guide* aimed to obviate the polite traveller from the 'burthen of those tedious enquiries on the road, or at the inns, which generally embarrass, and often mislead' (p. 1). Used properly the *Guide* offered a means – and took for granted the desirability – of keeping local people at a distance. Even the task of providing directions, an important opportunity for employment in the incipient Lake tourist industry, is thus withdrawn from local inhabitants. Social and economic disengagement rather than engagement is the premise of West's primer. Bohls comments astutely that the *Guide* constructs the picturesque viewer into a 'pure organizing eye, with no physical connection to the landscape':

> Instead of being in nature, the viewer is positioned as in a picture gallery, opposite a framed, contained scene. As the viewer is cut off from the scene, visual aesthetic satisfaction is correspondingly cut off from other dimensions of experience. The consequences are finally political.[29]

It was precisely these prohibited 'other dimensions of experience' that began to preoccupy Keats, just as they had Wollstonecraft.

Another popular guide, William Gilpin's *Observations, Relative Chiefly to Picturesque Beauty . . . Particularly the Mountains and Lakes of Cumberland, and Westmorland*, performed a similar act of aesthetic distancing, even as it claimed to be doing exactly the opposite. The purpose of the *Observations* was to explain 'the *rules of picturesque beauty*' by which landscape was to be examined.[30] For the polite traveller, Gilpin explained, this meant learning how to experience nature through an artist's eyes. The implications were far-reaching, going beyond aesthetics as we can gauge from Gilpin's discussion of pictorial veracity in the illustrations of landscapes interleaved throughout his volume:

> Trees [the artist] may generally plant, or remove, at pleasure. If a withered stump suit the form of his landscape better than the spreading oak, which he finds in nature, he may make the exchange – or he may make it, if he wish for a spreading oak, where he finds a withered trunk. He has no right, we allow, to add a magnificent castle – an impending rock – or a river, to adorn his foreground. These are *new features*. But he may certainly break an ill-formed hillock; and shovel the earth about him, as he pleases, without offence. He may pull up a piece of awkward paling – he may throw down a cottage – he may even turn the course of a road, or a river, a few yards on this side, or that. These trivial alterations may greatly add to the beauty of his composition; and yet they interfere not with the truth of *portrait*.
>
> (*Observations*, pp. xxxi–xxxii)

Keats was not prepared to 'throw down a cottage' in his walking journal, for all that Gilpin considered this to be a 'trivial alteration' in representational terms. Similarly, he refused to erase traces of human struggle, joy, or despair from his descriptions of sublime scenes. For Keats, the depiction of what was actually, rather than ideally, present came to embody the real 'truth of portrait'.

On 24 June, Keats and Brown arrived in the industrial town of Lancaster. They were greeted by the sound of looms and shuttles, which Keats judged the 'most disgusting of all noises' (*Letters*, I, 321). Lancaster was exceptionally lively since parliamentary elections were due to take place the next day. Not only was there the noise of last-minute canvassing to contend with – Whig lawyer Henry Brougham was challenging the Tory incumbent Lord Lowther,[31] whose family had held the seat for generations – disgruntled factory workers had also taken to the streets en masse to demand labour reform.[32] The latter was a disenfranchised body of dissent: without property, workers were not recognized as fully matured subjects, and thus could not vote. The vehemence of their protestations had alarmed Lowther into summoning government troops to keep order, creating a spectacle of violent repression that appalled the two travellers. As well as being 'framed out' of landscapes, labourers – as Keats witnessed at first hand – were also removed from the political process. It began to dawn on Keats that both kinds of exclusions were ideologically contingent on each other. As if the sight of soldiers clashing with factory workers was not sufficiently disconcerting, dining at Bowness later that day Keats was informed by a waiter that Wordsworth had dropped in a short while ago to drum up support for Lowther. 'Sad – sad – sad' was Keats's dismayed reaction to the news (*Letters*, I, 299). Landscape may have provided initial distraction from unpleasant actualities of this kind; but the thought of the greatest living purveyor of the sublime pressing Lowther's claim to authority would have confirmed to Keats the close relationship between high aesthetics and élite politics.

In spite of all he had seen in Lancaster, Keats tried to cling to his original plan to 'gorge wonders' in the Lake District. He was not disappointed by a long view of Lake Windermere, exclaiming jubilantly to Brown: 'How can I believe in that?'[33] This response falls wholesquarely into the category of astonishment identified by Burke as the 'passion caused by the great and sublime in *nature*':

> Astonishment is that state of the soul, in which all its motions are suspended, with some degree of horror. In this case the mind is so entirely filled with its object, that it cannot entertain any other, nor by consequence reason on that object which employs it. Hence arises the great power of the sublime, that far from being produced by them, it anticipates our reasonings, and hurries us on by an irresistible force. Astonishment . . . is the effect of the sublime in its highest degree.[34]

Overwhelmed by the lake, Keats declared that there was 'no such thing as time and space' (*Letters*, I, 298). Here, for once, we miss the fiercely autonomous bent of his imagination. The report has a well-rehearsed feel to it, constituting a virtual set-piece within the rhetorical mode Keats is invoking. Compare Wollstonecraft's comments at Trollhättan: 'I gazed I know not how long' (time), 'I listened, scarcely conscious where I was' (space). The force of sublime astonishment works assiduously to empty the scene of history, voiding it of any disagreeable specificity. But it would not be long before the historical re-interposed itself in the Lake District, just as it had in Trollhättan with the intrusion of the fisher-boy's labouring body into a vicinity of polite aesthetic consumption. Increasingly, Keats will be drawn to the time-and-space plight of silenced, displaced labourers.

A 'noble assemblage of words'

> On our return from Bellfast we met a Sadan – the Duchess of Dunghill – It is no laughing matter tho – Imagine the worst dog kennel you ever saw placed upon two poles from a mouldy fencing – in such a wretched thing sat a squalid old Woman squat like an ape half starved from a scarcity of Buiscuit in its passage from Madagascar to the cape, – with a pipe in her

mouth and looking out with a round-eyed skinny lidded, inanity – with a sort of horizontal idiotic movement of her head – squab and lean she sat and puff'd out the smoke while two ragged tattered Girls carried her along – What a thing would be a history of her Life and sensations.

(*Letters*, I, 321–2)

The best thing about this remarkable passage is its attention to detail, its vividness. The 'Duchess' is not just 'round-eyed', but 'skinny lidded' as well. She is not simply 'squat like an ape', but squat like an ape that has been 'half starved from a scarcity of Buiscuit'. This is inspired, mischievous detail that animates and exhilarates. Its emphasis laid firmly on poverty, the portrait registers disgust (gorge) at the callousness of a political system that tolerated such abjectness. But Keats's meticulous, thickly idiosyncratic narrative challenges the mature sublime in other crucial respects.

The concluding section of *A Philosophical Enquiry* constitutes a linguistic disputation in which Burke vigorously denies that individual words produce 'any representation . . . in the mind of the things for which they stand'. Single terms, he contends – especially in poetry – do not convey 'precise notions' at all, since before any 'real idea emerges to light' speakers would have to move from 'one set of general words to another . . . in a much longer series than may be at first imagined' (p. 315). This process, Burke objects, could only result in the effect of the composition being 'utterly lost'. His theory of language is summarized in the following passage:

> Words are in reality mere sounds . . . used on particular occasions, wherein we receive some good, or suffer some evil, or see others affected with good or evil; or which we hear applied to other interesting things or events; and being applied in such a variety of cases, that we know readily by habit to what things they belong, they produce in the mind, whenever they are afterwards mentioned, effects similar to those of their occasions.
>
> (*A Philosophical Enquiry*, p. 316)

The above advances a concept of semantic conditioning in which aural thumbprints of words communicate meaning through association and habitual context. Listeners are not obliged to cogitate on single expressions, Burke stresses. Individual words, indeed, 'utterly lose their connection with the particular occasions that gave rise to them' – but language continues to 'work' because sounds conjure impressions or create second-hand 'effects', owing to the familiarity of the constellations in which they habitually occur.

Philological polemic, although left to the final section of *A Philosophical Enquiry*, is an important component within Burkean aesthetics. Since Burke does not believe that the principal effect of words is generated 'from their forming pictures of the several things they . . . would represent in the imagination' (p. 320), he sees little to be gained by retailing precise, mimetic descriptions of landscape. Such attempts are, in fact, rejected as counter-productive:

Suppose we were to read a passage to this effect. 'The river Danube rises in a moist and mountainous soil in the heart of Germany, where winding to and fro it waters several principalities, until, turning into Austria and leaving the walls of Vienna it passes into Hungary; there with a vast flood augmented by the Saave and the Drave it quits Christendom, and rolling through the barbarous countries which border on Tartary, it enters by many mouths into the Black Sea.'

(*A Philosophical Enquiry*, p. 321)

No one wading through this detail, Burke insists, could form 'any pictures of a river, mountain, watery soil, Germany, &c.' (p. 322), let alone *sublime* pictures. If poetry sought for its effects in a similar manner, endeavouring to raise 'sensible images' with words, it would 'lose a very considerable part of its energy' (p. 328). In Burke's eyes, poetry, too, should eschew idiosyncratic detail, aiming instead to present a 'noble assemblage of words, corresponding to many noble ideas, which are connected by circumstances of time or place, or related to each other as cause and effect' (p. 320). Pope's portrayal of Helen of Troy is enlisted to underscore Burke's theory of detached language:

> They cry'd, no wonder such celestial charms
> For nine long years have set the world in arms;
> What winning graces! what majestic mien!
> She moves like a goddess, and she looks like a queen.

These lines are praised because 'not one word' is said of the 'particulars of [Helen's] beauty', 'nothing which can in the least help us to any precise idea of her person'. Pope affects Burke more deeply than 'long and laboured descriptions of Helen . . . handed down by tradition . . . which are to be met with in some authors' – authors such as George Chapman, whose 'uncouth' 1614 translation of Homer had been replaced by Pope's polished volumes.

Keats, on the other hand, rejected Pope's habitual Homer in favour of Chapman's earthier English textures – the preference he recorded in 'On First Looking Into Chapman's Homer'.[35] In Charles Cowden Clarke's well-known account of the sonnet's composition, the two men read from the epic translation late into the night.[36] Keats was utterly delighted to find that where Pope's circumlocutious idiom loftily and distantly depicted the 'briny torrent' running from Ulysses' 'mouth and nose', Chapman had referred with kinetic immediacy to the hero's 'cheeks and nosthrils flowing' with 'froth'. It is exactly this kind of physical detail which informs Keats's description in *Endymion* of Venus' lips and eyes 'closed in sullen moisture', her sighs coming 'vexed and pettish through her nostrils small' (II, 468–70). The portrait of the 'Duchess of Dunghill' owes just as much to Keats's election of Clarke's Chapman over Burke's Pope.

In Burke's estimation, the sublime force of poetry, like prose, depended on the use of familiar, *sanctioned* signifiers such as 'majestic', 'depthless', and 'terrible'. Idiosyncratic detail, by contrast, is regarded with suspicion. Readers are supposed to be 'lost to the actualities' (as Coleridge explained) which surround them. Keats was *not* content, however – not when 'actualities' signalled the indignities suffered by impoverished people encountered in muddy fields, in smoky cottages, or carried aloft on two poles from a piece of mouldy fencing. Resisting the prescriptive, dehumanizing drift of eighteenth-century aesthetics, Keats started to record the 'particulars' and 'actualities' of northern life, resulting in such memorable verbal renderings as the 'squalid old Woman' from Belfast, 'squat like an ape' on a sedan chair. 'No laughing matter', as Keats says. In another sense, though, it was very much a laughing matter. For it is in vivid, inappropriately humorous interludes (and the description of the old woman 'squat like an ape' *is* humorous, even as it appals) that Keats penetrates through the élite postures of sublime discourse into the lived experiences of ordinary people. Disregarding what eighteenth-century aesthetics told him was, and was not, in front of his eyes, Keats began to see, and more to the point *sing*,[37] in a series of neglected 'minor' poems, 'by his own eyes inspired'.[38]

Learning poetry

The waterfall at Ambleside was the location for Keats's second encounter with the sublime. His reaction repays citing at length:

> The waterfall itself, which I came suddenly upon, gave me a pleasant twinge. First we stood a little below the head about half way down the first fall, buried deep in trees, and saw it streaming down two more descents to the depth of near fifty feet – then we went on a jut of rock nearly level with the second fall-head, where the first fall was above us, and the third below our feet still – at the same time we saw that the water was divided by a sort of cataract island on whose other side burst out a glorious stream – then the thunder and the freshness. At the same time the different falls have as different characters; the first darting down the slate-rock like an arrow; the second spreading out like a fan – the third dashed into a mist – and the one on the other side of the rock a sort of mixture of all these. We afterwards moved away a space, and saw nearly the whole more mild, streaming silverly through the trees. What astonishes me more than any thing is the tone, the coloring, the slate, the stone, the moss, the rock-weed; or, if I may so say, the intellect, the countenance of such places. The space, the magnitude of mountains and waterfalls are well imagined before one sees them; but this countenance or intellectual tone must surpass every imagination and defy any remembrance. I shall learn poetry here and shall henceforth write more than ever, for the abstract endeavour of being able to add a mite to that mass of beauty which is harvested from these grand materials.
>
> (*Letters*, I, 300–1)

Ostensibly, Keats adheres to customary travel rhetoric in this account, with its audible gasps of astonishment and general sense of breathy wonder. Indeed, the sublime appears to be invoked in a conventional manner. Robert Gittings goes so far as to call the passage a 'prose *Prelude*'.[39] And yet on closer inspection things are seriously amiss. What affects Keats most deeply, what 'surpass[es] every imagination and def[ies] any remembrance', are the small details of the scene – the humble, trivial, *un*sublime 'moss' and 'rock-weed' – things seen from a child's perspective – rather than the 'magnitude' of mountains and waterfalls. The aspect most glaringly askew, most at odds with Burkean precept, however, occurs at the beginning: 'The waterfall itself, which I came suddenly upon, gave me a pleasant twinge'. Coming 'suddenly upon' something is rhetorically commensurate with sublime discourse (things are either come upon unexpectedly, or they leap up at one). But a 'pleasant twinge' is hardly an appropriate reaction where convention demands that the viewing subject profess his or her certitude of annihilation.

Intriguing filaments of connection link Keats's account of the Ambleside waterfalls and Wollstonecraft's description of the cataracts at Trollhättan, cited earlier. Indeed, Wollstonecraft throws revealing light on Keats's boyish challenge to authority at Ambleside. The following is a fuller report from *A Short Residence*:

> Arrived at Trollhättan, I must own that the first view of the cascade disappointed me: and the sight of the works [on a new canal], as they advanced, though a grand proof of human industry, was not calculated to warm the fancy. I, however, wandered about; and at last coming to the conflux of the various cataracts, rushing from different falls, struggling with the huge masses of rock, and rebounding from the profound cavities, I immediately retracted, acknowledging that it was indeed a grand object. A little island stood in the midst, covered with firs, which, by dividing the torrent, rendered it more picturesque; one half appearing to issue from a dark cavern . . .
>
> I gazed I know not how long, stunned with the noise; and growing giddy with only looking at the never-ceasing tumultuous motion, I listened, scarcely conscious where I was . . . There were so many appearances to excite the idea of chaos, that, instead of admiring the canal and the works, great as they are termed, and little as they appear, I could not help regretting that such a noble scene had not been left in all its solitary sublimity. Amidst the awful roaring of the impetuous torrents, the noise of human instruments, and the bustle of workmen, even the blowing up of rocks, when grand masses trembled in the darkened air – only resembled the insignificant sport of children.
>
> One fall of water, partly made by art, when they were attempting to construct sluices, had an uncommonly grand effect; the water precipitated itself with immense velocity down a perpendicular, at least fifty or sixty yards, into a gulph, so concealed by the foam as to give full play to

the fancy: there was a continual uproar: I stood on a rock to observe it, a kind of bridge formed by nature, nearly on a level with the commencement of the fall. After musing by it a long time, I turned towards the other side, and saw a gentle stream stray calmly out . . . I retired from these wild scenes.

Wollstonecraft's waterfall is 'covered with firs', Keats's is 'buried deep in trees'. Wollstonecraft views hers by standing 'on a rock . . . nearly on a level with the commencement of the fall'; Keats stands 'on a jut of rock nearly level with the second fall-head'. Where Wollstonecraft describes a 'little island . . . dividing the torrent', Keats recounts how 'the water was divided by a sort of cataract island'. Wollstonecraft tells how, at the 'other side' of this island, she saw 'a gentle stream stray calmly out'. On the 'other side' of Keats's island 'burst out a glorious stream'.

We would certainly expect to find *some* rhetorical convergence in Keats's and Wollstonecraft's letters, given that both writers are describing the same phenomenon: a many-headed waterfall. I would be the first to concede that the presence of verbal similitudes such as 'cataract' can be ascribed to the ubiquity of such 'elevated' terms in texts of this kind (in the same way that sublime rhetoric invariably transforms humble cliffs into brain-giddying 'precipices'). By the same token, we need not read too much into the duplication of mundane phrases like 'different falls'. But even when these qualifications are taken into account, the two passages have enough idiosyncratic features in common to oblige one to consider seriously the possibility that Keats is remembering Wollstonecraft's depiction of a waterfall when he comes to describe his own. What are the implications of such textual affiliations? It is, I think, significant that at an early stage in the walking tour, a point at which Keats was still equivocal about adopting or rejecting the grand style, he turns to Mary Wollstonecraft – least trustworthy, least conventional, least ideologically inert of travel writers – to be his 'guide' in the sublime. Keats's stagy declaration on seeing the falls, 'I shall learn poetry here', receives an added twist of irony when read in the context of Wollstonecraft's less than committed approach to mature aesthetic discourse. At any rate, there is something fascinating, not to mention unsettling, about a fledgling poetics of the sublime (Keats's), based on a theory of the sublime (Wollstonecraft's) that is primed to deconstruct its grand material, poised to expose inner contradictions, divisions, and conflicting interests. Keats's 'pleasant twinge', viewed in the light of Wollstonecraft's own mischief-making, begins to appear not simply as a surprising intervention, but as a thoroughly calculated one.

'Squashy holes' and 'tittle bats'

In a second descriptive account of the waterfalls at Ambleside, written a few days later for George and Georgiana, the cascade has dwindled to a mere 'teapot spout' which Keats does not consider worth describing at length. He promises to deliver reports of far more spectacular specimens; but these wonder narratives fail to materialize. By the end of the first week of walking, the sublime climax itself was imperilled. We have already seen how, instead of heroically gaining the summit of Skiddaw, Keats and Brown 'fagged & tugged nearly to the top' only to have their view 'shut out' by mist (*Letters*, I, 306). Now, as the pair were about to conquer the 'Fall of Low-dore', another unfortunate (and distinctly 'boyish') incident occurred:

> I had an easy climb among the streams, about the fragments of Rocks & should have got I think to the summit, but unfortunately I was damped by slipping one leg into a squashy hole.
>
> (*Letters*, I, 306)

Not only is the mishap a childish one, but the language used to relate the event – a 'squashy hole' – is self-consciously infantile. Such comical anti-climaxes keep sublimity firmly at bay.

As Keats's interest in descriptions of inanimate splendour plainly began to flag, his attention turned instead to the inhabitants of towns and villages dotted between tourist spots. At Ireby, for example, Keats was fascinated by a country dancing school, where the dancers 'kickit & jumpit with mettle extraordinary, & whiskit, & fleckit, & toe'd it, & go'd it, & twirld it, & wheel'd it, & stampt it, & sweated it, tattooing the floor like mad' (*Letters*, I, 307). He was especially captivated by 'as fine a row of boys & girls as you ever saw', a vision of youth eulogized as an alternative to both mature politics ('making ... a country happier') and high aesthetics ('scenery'): 'I never felt so near ... the glory of making by any means a country happier. This is what I like better than scenery' (*Letters*, I, 307).

On 2 July, traversing the environs of Dumfries, Keats wrote to his sister, Fanny. He joked that he had been 'employed in going up Mountains, looking at Strange towns prying into old ruins and eating very hearty breakfasts' (*Letters*, I, 310). No attempt is made to conjure a sense of the sublime. On the contrary, Keats is more concerned with recording scenes of Scottish poverty, commenting sadly: 'Girls are walking about bare footed and in the worst cottages the Smoke finds its way out of the door.'[40]

The next day, Keats composed 'A Song about Myself'. A joyously slap-dash affair, the poem's narrative is plainly subordinate to rhyme:

> There was a naughty boy
>   And a naughty boy w[as] he
> He kept little fishes
>   In washing tubs three
>   In spite
>   Of the might
>   Of the Maid,
>   Nor affraid

Of his Granny-good –
He often would
Hurly burly
Get up early
And go
By hook or crook
To the brook
And bring home
Miller's thumb
Tittle bat
Not over fat,
Minnows small
As the stall
Of a glove
Not above
The size
Of a nice
Little Baby's
Little finger –
O he made
'T was his trade
Of Fish a pretty kettle,
A kettle – A kettle
Of fish a pretty kettle
A kettle!
   ('A Song about Myself',
      Letters, I, 314–15)

These lines make inventive use of nursery-rhyme idiom and employ infantile vocabulary such as 'tittle bat', a variant of *stickleback* which, as John Barnard points out, is a name 'usually used by children'.[41] However, without exactly tipping towards seriousness (as Motion urges us to see things), the last stanza does provide an insight into the ways in which the walking tour was changing in status from a field trip to gather materials for Keats's grand poetic style into a chronicle of human degradation:

  There was a naughty Boy
    And a naughty Boy was he
 He ran away to Scotland
    The people for to see

The new accentuation on people rather than scenery is equally apparent in Keats's next letter to Tom, written 3–9 July, which dispenses with the sublime in a single, devastatingly cool sentence: 'Yesterday Morning we set out from Glenluce going some distance round to see some Ruins – they were scarcely worth the while' (*Letters*, I, 319). In place of reveries on sublime wonders, we find Keats declaiming on the plight of Scottish girls under 'the horrible dominion of the Scotch kirk':

> A Scotch Girl stands in terrible awe of the Elders – poor little Susannas – They will scarcely laugh – they are greatly to be pitied and the kirk is greatly to be damn'd. . . These kirkmen have done Scotland harm – they have banished puns and laughing and kissing.
>
> (*Letters*, I, 319)

Keats had humourless Scottish Elders of his own to deal with, attached this time to the literary establishment. Both sorts, kirkmen and Edinburgh reviewers, were to be resisted, Keats resolved, by means of childish 'puns and laughing and kissing'.

The first letter Reynolds received from the Highlands was dated 11 July. Three weeks into his tour, Keats was unable to muster the energy – or interest – to bring his friend up to date on routes taken and sights seen. He merely quipped that his journey so far could be summarized by 'put[ing] down Mountains, Rivers Lakes, dells, glens, Rocks, and Clouds, With beautiful enchanting, gothic picturesque fine, delightful, enchancting, Grand, sublime', and adding 'a few Blisters &c' (*Letters*, I, 322). Although Keats trivializes sublime discourse here (a little later in the letter he talks about crushing 'scenery . . . between two Puns'), he was nevertheless moved by spectacular vistas glimpsed on the approach to Robert Burns's cottage. Especially impressive were the 'Mountains of Annan Isle, black and huge over the Sea' (*Letters*, I, 323).[42] This formulation, 'black and huge', deserves scrutiny since it strikingly anticipates a phrase Wordsworth added to the famous boat-theft scene in the 1850 edition of *The Prelude*:

> . . . from behind that craggy Steep till then
> The horizon's bound, a huge peak, black and huge,
> As if with voluntary power instinct,
> Upreared its head.[43]
>
> (*The Prelude*, 1850, I, 377–80)

In 1805, the passage had stood:

> . . . from behind that craggy Steep, till then
> The bound of the horizon, a huge Cliff,
> As if with voluntary power instinct,
> Uprear'd its head.
>
> (*The Prelude*, 1805, I, 406–9)

Keats's mountain is 'Black and huge over the Sea'; Wordsworth's, 'black and huge' over a lake. Though by now almost completely disenamoured of scenery,

Keats is capable of attuning himself so subtly to the Wordsworthian sublime that he instinctively hits on a phrase that will later appeal to Wordsworth in an identical sense when he came to revise his great poem.[44] This complicates Keats's lament, heard at various points in the correspondence, that he was technically and emotionally unable to master the grand style; it also supports the idea that Keats drew back from the aesthetics and ethics of the sublime primarily as a result of 'gorge' (in the sense of 'disgust . . . resentment'), rather than due to feelings of poetic inadequacy. Politically, the distinction is vital.

'Press a Piece'

The walking tour, Keats explained to Bailey, was intended to 'strengthen [his] reach in poetry'. This is an odd metaphor, not least because it does not quite work. It is entirely possible to *lengthen* one's reach in poetry (which may have been what Keats intended to write, or thought he was writing), but not to *strengthen* it. With its suggestion of mental *and* physical development, however, the metaphor's double reflex hints at how Keats conflated physical, manly strength with poetical proficiency.[45] Indeed, the orthographical slip acts as a marker of Keats's conviction that poetic prowess and physical maturity were mutually contingent.

Famed for his stature as a writer, but also for his ability to walk great distances, Wordsworth was the archetype for this sort of muscular poetics. One of Keats's recent meetings with the sinuous bard had been at Benjamin Robert Haydon's 'immortal dinner' in December 1817. Wordsworth had been forty-seven then. In addition to being the oldest of the assembled guests, he was, as Penelope Hughes-Hallett points out, 'also the fittest, having climbed Skiddaw twice the previous summer without noticing any diminution of the vigour and strength of his youth'.[46] In a very real sense, Wordsworth's poetic achievement was enabled by his physical resilience, by his superhuman acts of perambulation in the Lake District. But if Wordsworth presented Keats with a model for the manly poet writing manly poetry, he was also a focus of resentment and anxiety. Keats's entire journey through the Lake District, a locale firmly associated with the older poet, could be seen as a version of patrifilial struggle, Wordsworth embodying the father whom Keats initially wants to equal or surpass, but ends up rejecting once he confronts the impossibility of doing either. Keats was certainly no match for Wordsworth in terms of physical endurance. He found himself 'fagging' and 'tugging' up mountains with no great enthusiasm, where Wordsworth had 'panted up / With eager pace' (*The Prelude*, 1805, XIII, 31–2). Equally dismaying, poetically speaking, was the circumstance that great peaks inspired Keats to mere doggerel whereas Wordsworth was moved to compose anthems to glorify the eternal. In short, Keats felt powerless alongside, and disempowered by, the Lake poet. Travelling north to look for Wordsworth – literally and figuratively – he is simultaneously in flight from him. Marlon Ross perceives in Keats a 'need . . . to construct an Oedipal parable of filial adoration giving way to paternal separation and patricide, and then of separation giving way to rightful inheritance of the father's acclaimed domain'.[47] Ross may or may not be right about paternal separation and patricide; but in so far as Keats experienced Wordsworth as a poetic Father, he did not inherit the acclaimed paternal domain. What he did gain during the walks, though, was the insight into human suffering and injustice that allowed him to disavow and turn from his 'rightful inheritance', even as it was within his grasp.

Robert Burns, another northern father figure, precipitated a second crisis for Keats as he half-heartedly tried to adhere to his resolution to acquire the outward signs of conventional literary maturity. Having made a pilgrimage to the Scots poet's cottage in the second week of July, Keats composed, in situ, what he hoped would be an appropriately grand sonnet. The resulting lines ('This mortal body of a thousand days'), he confided to Reynolds despairingly, were 'so bad' that he refused to transcribe them (*Letters*, I, 324). His experience in the cottage had been uniformly depressing. The first thing was the cottage itself, that hallowed literary abode in which Keats had been looking forward to an epiphanic experience: it had been turned into a whisky house. The present owner, a man who had known Burns, talked incessantly and drunkenly about his acquaintanceship, proving 'a great Bore with his Anecdotes' and utterly destroying the reverent atmosphere Keats had hoped to find so inspiring. 'His gab', Keats complained, 'hindered my sublimity.' A heightened impression of the 'actuality' of Burns's life, then, proved to be profoundly disabling. Keats left the cottage convinced that '[Burns] talked with Bitches . . . drank with Blackguards' and 'was miserable'. What is more, he had lost his sense of wonder. 'I cannot write about scenery and visitings' (*Letters*, I, 325), he announced disconsolately, before quickly changing the subject.

Correspondence with Tom begun at this time subjects the sublime to further pressure, even as Keats appears to be courting conventional aesthetics most assiduously. The letter opens with an account of Keats's and Brown's journey through a 'delightful Country', a walk that culminated in the sight of Ailsa Rock:

> I shall endeavour that you may follow our steps in this walk – it would be uninteresting in a Book of Travels – it can not be interest-{ing} but by my having gone through it – When we left Cairn our Road lay half way up the sides of a green mountainous shore, full of Clefts of verdure and eternally varying – sometimes up sometimes down, and over little Bridges going across green chasms of moss rock and trees – winding about every where. After two or three Miles of this we turned suddenly into a magnificent glen finely wooded in Parts – seven Miles long – with a Mountain Stream winding down the Midst – full of cottages in the most happy Situations – the sides of the Hills coverd with sheep – the effect of cattle lowing I never had so finely – At the end we had a gradual ascent and got among the tops of the Mountains whence In a little time I descried in the Sea Ailsa Rock

940 feet hight – it was 15 Miles distant and seemed close upon us – the effect of ailsa with the peculiar perspective of the Sea in connection with the ground we stood on, and the misty rain then falling gave me a complete Idea of a deluge – Ailsa struck me very suddenly – really I was a little alarmed.

(*Letters*, I, 329)

This passage discloses a familiarity but also an uneasiness with Burkean precept. Ayumi Mizukoshi claims that 'Keats's awestruck response to Ailsa Crag, and his almost visionary grasp of the sublime landscape of unspoiled nature' were 'quite conventional'.[48] This is to miss entirely the aesthetic subversiveness of the way in which Keats describes his hike to the celebrated tourist spot. His prose might seem, on initial reading, to be consonant with eighteenth-century techniques of picturesque framing. There are no impoverished, dirty labourers to spoil the scene; there are no people at all. What is more, the cottages that are visible this time are placed in the 'most happy Situations', paradigms of the beautiful in complete contrast to the 'wretched Cottages' described earlier, where the smoke had 'no outlet but by the door' (*Letters*, I, 309). The sublime, too, seems to be handled adroitly. The misty rain gives Keats a 'complete Idea of a deluge', and Ailsa Rock strikes him 'very suddenly'. And yet, instead of professing climactic awe, terror, or astonishment, Keats manages only the diminutive and faintly paradoxical: 'really I was a little alarmed' – a sensation akin to his earlier 'pleasant twinge' at Ambleside. In any case, Keats undercuts the significance of the episode from the outset, insisting that it would be 'uninteresting in a Book of Travels', and could only engage Tom's attention in so far as it involved his brother.

The next letter to Tom (haphazardly dated 'Cairn-something July 17th__'), rather than presenting customary descriptions of picturesque land- or seascapes, begins with a smutty parody of conventional sight-seeing:

The Lady of the Lake went to Rock herself to sleep on Arthur's seat and the Lord of the Isles coming to Press a Piece and seeing her Assleap remembered their last meeting at Corry stone Water so touching her with one hand on the Vallis Lucis while [t]he other un-Derwent her Whitehaven, Ireby stifled her clack man on, that he might her Anglesea.

(*Letters*, I, 333)

Keats's own angle on the sublime is equally plain to see. By japing grand terms like 'precipice', rendered here as the bawdy 'Press a Piece', Keats uses schoolboy humour and linguistic inventiveness to subvert the habitual rhetoric of travel discourse.

Keats stops sniggering briefly, regaining his composure to describe the banks of the Clyde as 'extremely beautiful', Loch Lomond as 'grand in excess', and to mention with delight a 'rich Pink Cloud' at the head of Ben Lomond. However, he and Brown did not trouble themselves with climbing the famous mountain, and Keats's poetic extemporizing was confined to a hastily scribbled poem on gadflies, 'All gentle folks who owe a grudge'.[49] This gleefully picks up the smutty tone of the letter's opening paragraphs:

> Has any here a daughter fair
>   Too fond of reading novels
> Too apt to fall in love with care
>   And charming Mister Lovels[50]
>
> O put a gadfly to that thing
>   She keeps so white and pert
> I mean the finger for the ring
>   And it will breed a Wert

In the midst of this absurdity, Keats evokes the political circus witnessed a few weeks earlier in Lancaster:

> Is there a Man in Parliament,
>   Dum founder'd in his speech
> O let his neighbour make a rent
>   And put one in his breech
>
> O Lowther how much better thou
>   Hadst figur'd to'ther day
> When to the folks thou madst a bow
>   And hadst no more to say
>
> If lucky gad fly had but ta'en
>   His seat upon thine A—e
> An put thee to a little pain
>   To save thee from a worse

'Worse' pain alludes to Lowther having 'Dum founder'd in his speech' during the elections. But Keats's ingenuity is to transpose 'dumfounded' from sublime registers (travellers are supposed to be dumbfounded by spectacular sights), and deploy it ironically against a tongue-tied agent of the élite politics that conspired with and undergirded the high aesthetics Keats had begun to despise.

After the skit on gadflies, all traces of sublime deportment evaporate from Keats's letter. Following a brief interlude on the Duke of Argyle's castle, which Keats describes as 'very modern magnificent', and an approving mention of the 'solemn' approach to Loch Awe, attention switches to the raucous 'horrors of a solo on the Bag-pipe' and the absence of a 'watercloset', or 'anything like it', at the inn where Keats and Brown were staying. It is difficult to conceive of any object more at odds with the sublime than a flush-toilet.

Knocked up on a mountain

By the time he began his letter to Benjamin Bailey on 18 July, Keats had become more or less inured to the aesthetic and emotional effects of grand scenery:

> I have been among wilds and Mountains too much to break out much about the[i]r Grandeur. . . The first Mountains I saw, though not so large as some I have since seen, weighed very solemnly upon me. The effect is wearing away.
>
> (*Letters*, I, 342)

These sentiments were recapitulated in the next letter to Tom: 'I assure you I often long for a seat and a Cup o' tea at well Walk[51] – especially now that mountains, castles and Lakes are becoming common to me' (*Letters*, I, 351). The extent to which mountains really had become 'common' to Keats can be gauged from his antics on Ben Nevis, which he climbed with Brown on 3 August. The journal attests to Keats's initial admiration for the famous peak, and contains a suitably mesmerized report of chasms like 'great rents in the very heart of the mountain'. 'These Chasms', Keats waxes, 'are 1500 feet in depth and are the most tremendous places I have ever seen – they turn one giddy if you choose to give way to it' (*Letters*, I, 353). None the less, despite these touristy swoons, the account is punctuated with schoolboy irreverence. I do not think I am making up the programmatic character of Keats's assault on the practised poses and attitudes of sublime reportage. The climb up 'old Ben', for instance, is described as a 'fag and a tug', made bearable only by tipples of whisky that made Keats and Brown 'tipsy' (the climbers do not even achieve the 'adult' state of drunkenness). Higher up, Keats is exhilarated to find himself among clouds like 'large dome curtains which kept sailing about, opening and shutting at intervals'. At the summit, however, he japes the sublime with a unmistakably boyish prank, cheerfully recounting to Tom how he clambered onto a pile of stones 'and so got a little higher than old Ben himself'. This absurd act of one-upmanship – which amounts to standing tip-toe on a mountain – has added poignancy performed by one so acutely conscious of stature as Keats.

The penultimate journal letter to Tom includes a transcription of Keats's often overlooked lines, 'Upon my life, Sir Nevis, I am piqued',[52] a burlesque on the celebrated ascent of Ben Nevis by Mrs Cameron, 'the fattest woman in all inverness shire' (*Letters*, II, 354). Routinely dismissed as trivial, this 'throw-away' composition, properly considered, registers a significant shift in Keats's critique of the sublime. To this point, Keats has been chiefly concerned with the sublime's pernicious bearing on the impoverished. Now he suggests that sublimity can be just as perilous – albeit differently so – for the polite viewers qualified to enjoy it. Having 'panted tugg'd and reek'd' her way up Ben Nevis,[53] Mrs Cameron petitions the mountain to wake from its thousand-year slumber and pay her a compliment in return. Duly aroused – in more ways than one – Old Ben advances on the horrified mountaineer, declaring:

> I must – I shall – I meet not such tit bits
> I meet not such sweet creatures eve[r]y day
> By my old night cap night cap night and day
> I must have one sweet Buss – I must and shall!

Old Ben wants more than a 'Buss', it transpires. The remainder of the poem constitutes a smutty conceit on tumescence:

> Block-head,[54] d'ye hear – Blockhead I'll make her feel
> There lies beneath my east legs northern heel
> A cave of young earth dragons – well my boy
> Go thithers quick and so complete my joy
> Take you a bundle of the largest pines
> And where the sun on fiercest Phosphor shines
>   turn to the beginning
> Fire them and ram them in the Dragon's nest
> Then will the dragons fry and fizz their best
> Until ten thousand now no bigger than
> Poor Aligators poor things of one span
> Will each one swell to twice ten times the size
> Of northern whale.

Hearing the mountain's design to 'complete' his 'joy', Mrs Cameron promptly faints:

>   O Muses weep the rest –
> The Lady fainted and he thought her dead
> So pulled the clouds again about his head
> And went to sleep again

Safely back at home, she 'bless'd her fate / That fainting fit was not delayed too late'.

Casting about for a way to excuse the schoolboyish tenor of this composition (and also to explain the lack of more substantial writings, or anthems to glorify the eternal, on Ben Nevis), Robert Gittings suggests that a combination of ill-health and exhaustion left Keats 'too knocked up to do more than write some comic verse about a fat lady climbing the mountain'.[55] By dismissing the poem in this manner, Gittings overlooks an important point, possibly even *the* point. The poem is not trivial, but *trivializing*. The lines on Ben Nevis actually represent the culmination of an adolescent aesthetic systematically deployed by Keats over the previous two months against the politics of privilege intimately bound up with the sublime.

Japing the sublime: immature aesthetics 101

The political dimensions appear more tangibly, perhaps, when we realize that there is a degree of alter-egoity about Mrs Cameron. Like Keats, she 'tugs' up the mountain rather than scaling it heroically; also like the poet, she fails to conform to textbook descriptions of a walker – where Keats is under-dimensioned, she has dimensions in excess. The poem continues Keats's practice of lampooning polite sight-seeing trips, parodying and reversing habitual components of traditional voyages into the picturesque with images of puerility and boyish humour. Even Mrs Cameron's fainting fit can be interpreted as a comical version of the orthodox sublime response of awe, astonishment, loss of control, and terror: by passing out, the portly mountaineer could be said to transport Burkean aesthetics to their logical extreme. However, the lines have a second, more acutely dissident purpose. They craftily depict the power of sublimity to overwhelm the viewing subject as a form of rape. This, after all, is precisely what is at stake when Old Ben rounds on Mrs Cameron, demanding first a 'Buss' and then the completion of his joy. Although Jack Stillinger refers disparagingly to 'the silly dialogue between Mrs. Cameron and Ben Nevis', there is a good deal more at issue in their exchange.[56] At some level, Gittings seems to acknowledge the exact nature of the danger, choosing 'knocked up' (slang usage denoting pregnancy) to describe Keats's supposed state of mental and physical exhaustion when he composed the poem.

What Gittings refers to regretfully as 'some comic verse', then, effectively and artfully uses childish idiom to deconstruct the mature sublime, exposing its foundations in tyrannical power and a violent sexual economy. Routinely written off, the cunningly assembled 'Upon my life, Sir Nevis' actually constitutes a fitting conclusion to a series of 'minor' poems in which virtually every aspect of the sublime has been presented as pernicious in some way.

'*Werry* romantic'

The last entry in Keats's journal, addressed to Mrs Wylie, George Keats's mother-in-law, is a rollicking affair which repeatedly pokes fun at the cult of the sublime.[57] The highlight of the letter occurs in Keats's response to Mrs Wylie's concern that he was the 'Gentleman in a Fur cap' reported in a newspaper as having 'fall[en] over a precipice in Kirkudbrightshire' (*Letters*, I, 358; my square brackets). Keats initially denies the identity, but reconsiders once the comic possibilities dawn on him. He then fires off gleeful jibes at sublime culture, romantic novels, and their (female) readers:

> Stop! let me see! – being half-drowned by falling from a precipice is a very romantic affair – Why should I not take it to myself? Keep my secret & I will. How glorious to be introduced in a drawing room to a Lady who reads Novels, with – "Mr so & so – Miss so & so – Miss so & so. this is Mr so & so. who fell off a precipice, & was half drowned . . . No romance lady could resist me. . . being tumbled over a precipice into the sea – Oh it

would make my fortune – especially if you could continue to hint, from this bulletins authority, that I was not upset on my own account, but that I dashed into the waves after Jessy of Dunblane – & pulled her out by the hair.

(*Letters*, I, 359)

This expertly deflates grand posturings, even as it acknowledges Keats's still-present desire to take advantage of the apparently insatiable taste for sublimity ('Oh it would make my fortune'). His jesting masks other anxieties, though. Even as Keats sends up romance heroes, he is painfully aware of how far he was from being one himself. Humour remained his best defence against such psychically corrosive thoughts; although he promises to 'leave joking', he continues in a light-hearted manner:

> I have been *werry* romantic indeed, among these Mountains & Lakes. I have got wet through day after day, eaten oat cake, and drank whiskey, walked up to my knees in Bog, got a sore throat, gone to see Icolmkill & Staffa, met with wholesome food, just here & there as it happened; went up Ben Nevis, & N.B. came down again; Sometimes when I am rather tired, I lean rather languishingly on a Rock, & and long for some famous Beauty to get down from her Palfrey in passing; approach me with – her saddle bags – & give me – a dozen or two capital roast beef sandwiches – When I come into a large town, you know there is no putting ones Knapsack into ones fob . . . Tell Henry I have not Camped quite on the bear Earth yet; but nearly as bad, in walking through Mull – for the Shepherds huts you can scarcely breathe in, for the smoke which they seem to endeavour to preserve for smoking on a large scale.
>
> (*Letters*, I, 359–60)

This paragraph, the last in Keats's tour correspondence, gestures, in one form or another, towards all four meanings of 'gorge' outlined at the beginning of this chapter. A preoccupation with overfeeding is registered in the urge for a 'dozen or two capital roast beef sandwiches'. Valleys and crevices are implied in the reference to being among 'Mountains & Lakes'. Keats's throat is mentioned directly ('got a sore throat'). Finally, resentment and disgust are detectable in the allusion to impoverished shepherds' huts which 'you can scarcely breathe in'. The fact that Keats quickly turns the huts to comic advantage, joking that shepherds use them for 'smoking on a large scale', should not blind us to the politically radical nature of the journal. Levity, japing, schoolboy antics, Keats concludes, are the most appropriate because most unsettling responses to the oppressive relationship of mature politics and 'grown-up' aesthetic theory. It is entirely in keeping with the tone of the tour letters as a whole that Keats should end his tales of gorging wonders by affecting a childish lisp: 'I have been *werry* romantic indeed'.

Playing up, acting the kid – this is not to relinquish agency in a grown-up world. For a culturally marginalized writer like Keats, it is exactly to find a means of asserting it. The capacity of 'naughty boys' (and girls) to disrupt structures of authority should not be underestimated. Ask any school teacher. In Rome, listening to Joseph Severn play piano arrangements of Haydn symphonies, Keats exclaimed that the composer was like a child, 'for there is no knowing what he will do next'.[58] This observation neatly encapsulates the potential of immaturity to wrong-foot established power. I am not suggesting that Keats does not mature at all, in Motion's and Woolford's sense, during the walking tour. In an important respect though he is *already* politically mature. This is not always apparent, primarily because his maturity manifests itself precisely in an unwillingness to perform the conventional signs of adulthood, in a refusal to be interpellated into what Keats had good reason to consider the oppressive ideology of the adult world. Recent commentators tend to regard the tour letters as a depressing sea of puerility, broken up by little islands of mature thought (such as Keats's denouncement of Lord Lowther). But the journal in its entirety represents a highly subversive document, asserting a powerful and coherent counter-aesthetic founded on cultivated impropriety, on performances of naughtiness, on cutting capers, telling cock-and-bull stories, on the production of doggerel, smut, and the absurd – all sources of a particularly disconcerting political energy. Although Keats did not compose his journal letters with publication in mind, he uses them to record humorous incidents for members of his literary and political circle in a way that progressively undermines the authority of mature cultural edifices, notably sublime literature.

5 'Stifling up the vale'
Keats and 'c――ts'

The title of this chapter may appear deliberately provocative, but there is, let me assure readers, a reasonably serious – if, from Keats's perspective, rarely reasonable – point behind it. Besides, the title's partially obscured word, including (vitally, for my argument) the partial obscuration, is taken from Keats himself, from one of his letters. In the discussions that follow, I want to propose that the semantic and psychic contours of genitally focused episodes in Keats are further shaped by the poet's equivocal relationship with two ostensibly discrete, but in fact mutually complicating, epistemologies regarding women's 'reality' (*Letters*, I, 341). The first was circulated through male communities, disseminated in 'Card playing Clubs', and in colourful, sexually explicit drawing-room badinage.[1] While a whole continuum of inter-male relational dynamics – as explored by Eve Kosofsky Sedgwick in her book, *Between Men* (1985) – may be supposed to have existed in these homosocial settings,[2] I am interested in Keats 'among Men' (*Letters*, I, 341) primarily in so far as these 'knowing' communities presented him with legitimized modes of masculine desire for women. The second educational tradition was absorbed during medical tutelage, which entailed, among other things, obstetric training with apothecary-surgeon Thomas Hammond, and physical anatomy lectures at Guy's Hospital.[3] Both traditions of knowledge – what I am calling 'social' and 'medical' – actually unsettled Keats profoundly, and never more so than when they cut against each other in complex ways. Nevertheless, I want to demonstrate, Keats was compulsively drawn in his writings to confront the dual epistemic grounds of his physiological aversion.

I began this book with feet, by arguing that these appendages appear in Keats in ways that are nearly always, in crucial respects, psychically disclosing. I wish to end with the notorious (and notoriously difficult to write about) monosyllable which Keats never utters directly, but whose psychosexual orbit he returns to repeatedly, obsessively, in gauche allegories of amorous encounter, in anxious uses of medical imagery, in would-be bawdy letters, and in wide-eyed reports of 'after-dinner' banter. The following sections seek to deepen our understanding of what Jean Hagstrum, in his influential book, *The Romantic Body: Love and Sexuality in Keats, Wordsworth, and Blake* (1985), referred to as the 'driving, torturing, shaping sexuality' in Keats which 'many have failed to see'.[4] I will be arguing that allusions to sexual intercourse and sexual anatomy in Keats typically mark excruciating textual junctures where coherencies of Self, as well as poetic register and diction, break down and threaten to dissolve altogether.

My approach is structured around close reading; but again what is read is a kind of sub- (or parallel) text, a shadowy linguistic correlative of the author's unconscious. The aim is to tease out an implicitly eroticized subtext in what are beyond doubt psychologically charged passages of writing – passages which seem in a literal sense *fraught* with the partially unspoken, with that which Keats cannot, or cannot allow himself, to speak fully. The result, I hope, will be to illuminate complex aspects of the work itself, as well as the psychological complexity – and maladjustments – of the author. (I do not concur with John Bayley's judgement that the 'sexual psychology' of Keats is 'in every sense . . . commonplace'.)[5] Fittingly, the model for this kind of reading is provided by Keats himself:

My dear Reynolds

I have parcell[e]d out this day for Letter Writing – more resolved thereon because your Letter will come as a refreshment and will have (sic parvis &c) the same effect as a Kiss in certain situations where people become over-generous. I have read this first sentence over, and think it savours rather; however an inward innocence is like a nested dove; or as the old song says.

> O blush not so! O blush not so!
>   Or I shall think you knowing;
> And if you smile, the blushing while,
>   Then maidenheads are going.
>   (*Letters*, I, 219)

'Certain situations where people become over-generous' – occasions, that is, when the polite/social kiss can (inadvertently?) carry sexual connotations or intimations. On reading his sentence over, which is also a reading *under*, Keats suspects that it 'savours rather', that it possibly says something more than he intends regarding his letter to, and relation with, Reynolds. But he isn't *entirely* sure. He acknowledges, however, that like a kiss in 'certain situations' words are meant (we assume) to carry one meaning, but can 'inadvertently' ('over-generously') convey another. He leaves it up to the reader, as all writers must, to determine the exact parameters of reference, accepting that interpretation will depend on whether we, as readers, have preserved an 'inward innocence', or blush in a manner that identifies us as 'knowing'. Preserving such readerly innocence, of course, is an especially difficult feat if we are professional students or teachers of literature; indeed, a prelapsarian state of mind may be incompatible with the demands of our profession. The point, though, is this: Keats concedes that he may (or may not) be saying what he does not (or perhaps does) intend. What is more, he alerts us to the necessity of – while supplying the paradigm for – precisely the kind of hermeneutic deliberation that might resolve the matter.

In one sense, this chapter constitutes an instructive coda to those preceding it, since it demonstrates how, despite Keats's conscious efforts to deploy immaturity in a tactical fashion, the deeper workings of the boyish imagination always threaten to impinge on the coherency of his project.

'After the ladies had retired'

> I was at a Dance at Redhall's and passed a pleasant time enough – drank deep and won 10.6 at cutting for Half Guinies there was a younger Brother of the Squibs made him self very conspicuous after the Ladies had retired from the supper table by giving Mater Omnium – Mr Redhall said he did not understand any thing but plain english – where at Rice egged the young fool on to say the World plainly out. After which there was an enquirey about the derivation of the Word C––t when while [*sic*] two parsons and Grammarians were setting together and settling the matter Wm Squibs interrupting them said a very good thing – 'Gentleman says he I have always understood it to be a Root and not a Derivitive.'
> (Letter to Tom and George Keats, 5 January 1818; *Letters*, I, 200)

In his riveting, and riveted, account of the etymological 'enquirey' at Redhall's – which could be seen as an example of men competing over 'knowledge' of the female body (even down to questions of etymology) – Keats, as Hyder Rollins notes, 'observed the taboo' that since about 1700 made printing 'cunt' in full a legal offence. One of my purposes is to show that there were not only pressing legal reasons, but also *psychological* grounds for Keats's self-censorship where pudenda were concerned.

'Cunt' had not always been a transgressive word. For medieval surgeons, it was an available medical term.[6] An early surgical manual, Lanfranc's *Cirurgia* (published around 1400), observed: 'In wymmen þe necke of þe bladdre is schort, & is maad fast to the cunte'.[7] By 1815, when Keats arrived at Guy's, a new vocabulary had evolved with which to describe the lineations of female anatomy. Take a comparable passage from Chapter 3 of Keats's student textbook, *The London Dissector*, entitled 'Dissection of the Organs of Generation in the Female': 'The Urethra is short in females, and . . . is connected to the cartilaginous arch of the pubis by the ligamentum inferius vesicae'.[8]

The word had become taboo in literary culture, too, though this did not deter Robert Burns – one of Keats's favourite authors (whose cottage he visited while touring northern vistas with Charles Brown in 1818). Burns made liberal (and illegal) use of the term in his notorious collection of bawdy, *The Merry Muses of Caledonia* (1799), a volume banned in America until 1964, and in Britain until 1965.[9] The following lines from the last stanza of 'Cumnock

Psalms', one of the lyrics 'collected' by Burns, are entirely representative of his gleeful idiom:

> And he grippet her fast by the goosset o' the arse
> And he gae her cunt the common law.
>   With a hey &c.
> ('Cumnock Psalms', *The Merry
> Muses of Caledonia*, p. 74)

Keats, as Jack Stillinger's edition of the complete works shows, made various attempts of his own at composing bawdy verse, including a handful of poems that allude transparently, and – Keats hoped – knowingly and urbanely, to the female genitals. Line 4 of an early draft of the obscure 'Unfelt, unheard, unseen' (1817) contains a striking colloquial allusion to sexual intercourse and sexual anatomy: 'stifling up the Vale'. Robert Gittings points out that within early nineteenth-century slang, 'stifling' meant 'occupying sexually', while 'Vale' was an euphemistic way of evoking the female pudendum.[10] In a subsequent go at the poem, Keats stifled the bawdy reference itself, substituting the anodyne, 'Ah! through their nestling touch'. Even so, he did not permit the poem to see the light of day in print.[11] It was finally published in 1848, in Richard Monckton Milnes's *Life, Letters, and Literary Remains of John Keats*. Milnes's text of the fugitive piece was based on Charles Cowden Clarke's transcription of Keats's now lost fair manuscript. Partially sanitized, an innuendo-laden phrase still nestles in the penultimate line:

> Unfelt, unheard, unseen,
>   I've left my little queen,
> Her languid arms in silver slumber lying:
>   Ah! through their nestling touch,
>   Who – who could tell how much
> There is for madness – cruel, or complying?
>
>   Those faery lids how sleek!
>   Those lips how moist! – they speak,
> In ripest quiet, shadows of sweet sounds:
>   Into my fancy's ear
>   Melting a burden dear,
> How "Love doth know no fullness, and no bounds."
>
>   True! – tender monitors!
>   I bend unto your laws:
> This sweetest day for dalliance was born!
>   So, without more ado,
>   I'll feel my heaven anew,
> For all the blushing of the hasty morn.
>   (*Life, Letters, and Literary Remains*, II, 258)

But while Keats speaks bawdily of 'feeling his heaven', there is a world of difference between 'Unfelt, unheard, unseen' and 'Cumnock Psalms'. Burns's raw, unblinking accounts of sexual exploits robustly affirm ideals of manly prowess; lyrics such as 'Put Butter in my Donald's Brose' and 'Nine Inch Will Please a Lady', for example, are cheery paeans to the over-dimensioned, over-active phallus. Keats's coy brand of ribaldry, by contrast, seems reluctant to meet anyone's eyes.[12] Lacking, at any rate, the directness of Wm Squibs, the two parsons, and the grammarian at Redhall's, 'after the Ladies had retired', 'Unfelt, unheard, unseen' merely, although not uncomplicatedly, testifies to Keats's uncertainty and indecision when it came to replicating 'after-dinner' modes of masculine address. Keats may aim for knowing bluffness and social urbanity, but his narrative voice fails to escape the callow self-consciousness of the sniggering schoolboy. The creative imagination does not, in this instance, effect the liberation from embarrassment celebrated by Christopher Ricks.[13] Both versions of the lyric, indeed, stand in nervous misalignment to the debauchery joyfully and *manfully* retailed by Burns, who more than most could be said to have championed the 'goatish winnyish lustful love' denounced by Keats as a form of 'raw scrofula' in the phlegmatically envious notes inscribed in his copy of Burton's *Anatomy of Melancholy*.

Bursting with lascivious energy, Burns's songs in *The Merry Muses of Caledonia* move with instinctive assurance towards disclosure and completion; Keats's awkward *essai* at 'bawdy', on the other hand, is entirely predicated on concealment, 'cold retreat', and withdrawal. The mere contemplation of physical, as opposed to idealized, womanhood finds Keats 'in a hurry to be gone' (*Letters*, I, 341).[14]

A further insight into the fundamental discrepancy between the two authors' erotic idiom is offered by 'Dainty Davie' from Burns's illicit collection, narrated this time from a female perspective (the lyric's gender ventriloquism in no way undercuts the hyper-masculinity of Burns's project):

> My minnie laid him at my back,
>   I trow he lay na lang at that,
> But turn'd, and in a verra crack
>   Produc'd a dainty Davie.
>
> Then in the field amang the pease,
>   Behin' the house o' Cherrytrees,
> Again he wan atweesh my thies,
>   And, splash! Gaed out his gravy.
>   ('Dainty Davie', *The
> Merry Muses of Caledonia*, p. 97)

The speaker is unabashed, lyrically inventive ('splash!'), candidly engaged in the act described. Keats's narrative persona, by contrast – particularly in the 1848 text, and arguably in the earlier draft, too[15] – elides the sexual act itself, doing little more, in fact, than imply it has just taken place (the perennial adolescent boast). The lyric remains firmly and fixedly in the realm of the scopic, the lover *watching* his lady's 'languid arms', 'faery lids', and 'moist' lips, rather than enjoying them physically. If there has been any manly accomplishment, it has been followed by a familiar Keatsian 'cold retreat', his lyric persona having hurriedly 'left' his lover 'unfelt, unheard, unseen'.[16]

It is easy to see why Keats replaced the original fourth line. 'Stifling up the Vale' is out of character, out of place (alternatively, too much *in* place). It involves too much agency. Unlike Burns – and despite the thin bravado of the poem's Rochester-like final three lines – Keats could hardly have written, let alone retained, a 'manly' phrase like 'grippet her fast' ('Cumnock Psalms'). His caress is more tentative, less assured. Even the libertine's boastful swagger, 'I'll feel my heaven anew', is swiftly followed by 'blushing', not all of which – *we* can't help but feel – may be ascribed to the 'hasty morn'.

In one facet of self-perception, Keats imagined himself as a beau about town, a virile cavalier who gathered maidenheads at every turn, like the narrator of his 'bawdy' lyric, 'O blush not so!': 'O blush not so! O blush not so! / Or I shall think you knowing; / And if you smile, the blushing while, / Then maidenheads are going' (ll. 1–4).[17] This poem, John Barnard notes, 'attempts to catch the tone of seventeenth-century rondeaus'.[18] But there are problems. Despite its 'tone', it fails to convince. The logic of the opening stanza is topsy-turvy: do 'knowing' maids possess maidenheads to lose? And do *knowing* lovers blush? It is Keats, of course, who wishes to be thought of as 'knowing' (while knowing that, in the social arena, he was anything but). In any case, braggadocio performances such as 'O blush not so!' could not be sustained for very long, and the larger corpus of Keats's work reveals the poet palpably ill at ease with anything but the most soft-focused, transcendent images of physical love.

Agency is often the sticking point for Keats in sexual matters. Even one of his boldest attempts at bawdy, already discussed in Chapter 4, is recounted, crucially, at one remove:

My dear Tom,

Here's Brown going on so that I cannot bring to Mind how the last two days have vanished – for example he says 'The Lady of the Lake went to Rock herself to sleep on Arthur's seat and the Lord of the Isles coming to Press a Piece and seeing her Assleap remembered their last meeting at Corry stone Water so touching her with one hand on the Vallis Lucis while [t]he other un-Derwent her Whitehaven, Ireby stifled[19] her clack man on, that he might her Anglesea and give her a Buchanan . . .'

(*Letters*, I, 333–4)

These are Brown's words, not his own, Keats assures us, before relaying them at length to Tom (on a walking tour, it is worth remembering, supposedly undertaken in part to overcome an 'obstinate Prejudice' regarding women).[20] As in his account of the notorious 'enquirey' at Redhall's (also conveyed to Tom), Keats parrots what other men – manly, sexually gregarious men like Charles Brown – have said on the subject of sexual encounter. Keats is uneasy with his friend's lewdness, shrugging off the passage as only 'Brown going on'; none the less, accepting that his own ribald verses were disappointingly 'boyish', lacking the courage of their convictions, Keats exhibits prurient and admiring interest in the genuine mature bawdy composed at the drop of a hat by the lecherous Brown.

This is not to say that during his 1818 excursion Keats deferred completely to his older companion where risqué jokes – what he called 'rascalliest' puns – were involved. By way of concluding this section, I want to highlight a portion of the letter to Reynolds documenting Keats's pilgrimage to the cottage in which Burns was born. The passage interests me for two reasons. First, Keats hints at his own facility with 'after-dinner' discourse, while (characteristically) disowning and wishing it censored at the same time. Second, Keats's obstetric knowledge collides with his social knowledge in a spectacular and psychologically intriguing manner:

> O scenery that thou shouldst be crush'd between two Puns – As for them I venture the rascalliest in the Scotch Region – I hope Brown does not put them punctually in his journal – If he does I must sit on the cutty<school>-stool all next winter. We went to Kirk allow'y "a Prophet is no Prophet in his own Country" – We went to the Cottage and took some Whiskey – I wrote a sonnet for the mere sake of writing some lines under the roof – they are so bad I cannot transcribe them – The Man at the Cottage was a great Bore with his Anecdotes – I hate the rascal – his Life consists in fuz, fuzzy, fuzziest . . . he is a mahogany faced old Jackass who knew Burns – He ought to be kicked for having spoken to him. He calls himself "a curious old Bitch" – but he is a flat old Dog . . . O the flummery of <the> a birth place! Cant! Cant! Cant! It is enough to give a spirit the guts-ache.
>
> (*Letters*, I, 324)

To dispense with some possibly unfamiliar vocabulary: the *OED* defines a 'cutty-stool' as a 'particular seat in a church, where offenders against chastity . . . had to sit during the time of divine service and receive a public rebuke'. 'Flummery' is a name given to 'various sweet dishes made with milk, flour, eggs'.

The two puns between which Keats wishes to see scenery crushed are to be the 'rascalliest', the most sexually explicit, he can muster – puns, that is, that would deserve a winter's chastisement in the cutty-stool, the seat of repentance for those who give offence to 'chastity'. But not only does Keats *not* tell these rude jokes; he also hopes that, if he did, Brown would not be 'punctual' about recording them in his own journal of the walks. While Burns represents an inspirational figure to whose 'merry' excesses Keats aspires (later in the letter he confesses to having tried, and failed, to write a 'merry Sonnet' in the cottage), the young poet stops – on a conscious level, that is – short of his goal.

*Un*consciously, it is a rather different matter. Keats may have lacked the famous obduracy of Burns, the unabashed poet of 'cunts', though no 'Prophet in his own Country', Keats notes (finely attuned to the sort of schoolboy 'Puns' that merited a spell in the 'cutty*school*', his first go at writing 'cutty-stool'). He gave in to pressure to rewrite his bad-tempered Preface to *Endymion*; he also replaced stifled vales with nestling touches; and, as we shall see, changed back sexually frank changes to *The Eve of St Agnes* at his publisher's insistence. But even on those occasions where Keats seemed prepared to curb the transgressive energies of his boyish imagination, things are rarely as clear-cut as they might appear. In a return of the repressed which must be at least as comical as either of the 'two Puns' now lost to posterity, Keats's subdued, sexually charged imagination, together with the morbid anxieties that have prompted self-repression in the first place, finds a way to express itself in a line supremely pregnant with meaning: 'O the flummery of <the> a birth place! Cant! Cant! Cant! It is enough to give a spirit the guts-ache.'

After Keats's reference to 'the birth place' (anatomical as well as geographical) and 'guts-ache' (birth-pangs?), we could view the expletive 'Cant!' – whose task of 'filling in' is completed by knowing readers – as, in a very real sense, a piece of 'jargon used for the purpose of secrecy' (*OED, n*³ sense 4a), which Keats's unconscious has employed to satisfy (and negotiate) the requirements of legality. Once we are alerted to the exigencies of the letter, however, we see that the 'secrecy' of the triply conspicuous 'Cant!' only conceals an open secret, one Keats cannot, and given the triple repetition, capitalization, and exclamation marks, does not actually seem to *want* to hide.

All this may be going too far, of course: as Keats comments in the same epistle, 'a Witty humour will turn anything to Account' (*Letters*, I, 324). On the other hand, as Keats also says a paragraph later, 'Many a true word . . . is spoken in jest'.

I would not, however, want to make too extravagant a claim for Keats's unconscious capacity here to resist censorship, self- or externally imposed. Looking across at a similarly-preoccupied letter by Byron, we discover a far more plain-spoken connection forged between 'Cant' and its consonant but (for Keats) unnameable Other. Byron laments how he, a man 'of experience', had been 'frightened' by the popular outcry at *Don Juan*'s sexual candour into affecting poetic modesty when composing the third stanza of his bawdy epic:

> I have written about a hundred stanzas of a third Canto – but it is damned modest – the outcry has frightened me. – I had such projects for the Don – but the *Cant* is so much stronger than the *Cunt* – now a days, – that the benefit of experience in a man who had well weighed the worth of both monosyllables – must be lost to despairing posterity.[21]

By exposing to view the taboo word's internal anatomy – the illegal *u* and *n* – Byron purposefully breaches (once again) the mores which had temporarily inveigled him into tempering the insinuating energies of his signature idiom. Indeed, the morphological momentum of Canto–Cant–Cunt, which governs the passage, gloriously reasserts the excesses of Byron's unrepentantly erotic project, as well as mapping out the sexual trajectory of his poetic narrative. But where Byron's cantos move assuredly from 'cant' to 'cunt' – their author having 'weighed the worth of both monosyllables' – Keats's transgressive imagination is contained within his cant. The cutty-stool – all joking aside – is a powerful deterrent for the schoolboy: the contextually incongruous 'flummery', a word denoting childishly sweet dishes, merely underlines the boyish processes of mind that have given rise to this section of Keats's correspondence. By contrast, for Byron – no schoolboy – the cutty-stool merely acted as a spur. Not only did he complete the third immodest canto of his epic, but he composed fourteen more, to boot.

Pouring forth splendours

Notwithstanding his apparent eagerness to be accepted by a polite reading public, Keats regularly smuggled bawdy elements into his work. There are more sexual allusions in his writing than one might expect, even after reading Robert Gittings's colourful catalogue of previously suppressed instances of the poet's 'sexual slang'.[22] (Appendices to Gittings's 1968 biography generously elucidate phrases from Keats's letters such as 'her Anglesea' and 'Vallis Lucis', as well as glossing references to 'secrets', 'puddles', 'concerns', and tickling 'feathers', all of which either invoke, or are focused on, the female pudendum.)[23] Keats's often, we might say obsessively, exercised penchant for erotically charged expressions was emphatically noted by 'knowing' readers in his own day, however. Indeed, as we have seen, there was something of a vogue among Keats's contemporaries for depicting the marginalized writer as an adolescent masturbator. This is Byron: 'His is the *Onanism* of Poetry – something like the pleasure an Italian fiddler extracted out of being suspended daily by a Street Walker in Drury Lane.'[24] Even George Felton Mathew, onetime confidante, hinted perfidiously in the *European Magazine* at the onanistic nature of his friend's work. Keats – we sense Felton nudging and winking – was always 'pouring forth his splendours' in verse.[25]

Byron (who despised Keats because of his attack on Pope in *Sleep and Poetry*) and Mathew (who was vindictively envious of Keats's rapid rise within Leigh Hunt's literary circle) had personal reasons for disparaging Keats in this manner. But there was nevertheless more than a grain of truth in their charges. Keats's poetry often displays – often aspires to – an erotic febrility. Take stanza 9 of *Isabella*:

> 'Love! thou art leading me from wintry cold,
>   Lady! thou leadest me to summer clime,

>   And I must taste the blossoms that unfold
>   In its ripe warmth this gracious morning time.'
>   So said, his erewhile timid lips grew bold,
>   And poesied with hers in dewy rhyme:
>   Great bliss was with them, and great happiness
>   Grew, like a lusty flower in June's caress.
>   (*Isabella*, ll. 65–72)

Christopher Ricks notes the 'vital turgescence' of the passage.[26] But while he is eloquent on its general 'erotic fervour', he omits to mention its specifically *boyish* character: for the allusion at the end turns on the time-honoured schoolboy joke over the homophony of 'happiness' and 'a penis' (growing 'like a lusty flower in June's caress'). Keats worried that *Isabella* was 'too smokeable', by which he not only meant 'too naïve', but also 'too easily found out'. Stanza 9 doubtlessly figured in his thoughts.

A second, comparable instance of schoolboy innuendo occurs more famously at line 317 of *The Eve of St Agnes*:

>   Beyond a mortal man impassion'd far
>   At these voluptuous accents, he arose,
>   Ethereal, flush'd . . .
>   (*The Eve of St Agnes*, ll. 316–18)

The 'joke' – for such it almost certainly is – was all the better, although *Keatsian* (rather than Burnsian), for being, as Thomas McFarland points out, hidden behind the trope of sinking to one's knees and arising.[27] While, McFarland also remarks, 'generations of schoolboys [and schoolgirls] have missed the tumescent reference' (or at least their teachers have), Keats's contemporary readers, not to mention reviewers and acquaintances who advised him to ration his 'splendours', were morbidly alert to the explicit eroticism of the poem.[28] Richard Woodhouse, a close friend of Keats, and literary and legal adviser to his publisher, John Taylor, was horrified by changes made to stanzas 35–6, which spelled out the fact that Porphyro, in Woodhouse's words, 'acts all the acts of the bonâ fide husband' (*Letters*, II, 163). Most scandalously and reprehensibly of all, the altered lines depicted Madeline in 'serene repose' when the 'acts' took place. These are Keats's emendations:

>   See, while she speaks his arms encroaching slow,
>   Have zoned her, heart to heart, – loud, loud the dark winds blow!
>
>   For on the midnight came a tempest fell;
>   More sooth, for that his quick rejoinder flows
>   Into her burning ear: and still the spell

Unbroken guards her in serene repose.
With her wild dream he mingled, as a rose
Marrieth its odour to a violet.
Still, still she dreams, louder the frost wind blows . . .
   (*The Eve of St Agnes*, ll. 314–22 of the revised manuscript)[29]

'His arms encroaching slow, / Have zoned her, heart to heart' – it's still not 'grippet her fast', in Burns's virile, aggressive version of masculine desire. But it *is* getting close. Keats's alterations were conceived as a means of redeeming his poem from the charge of naïvety. The revisions to stanzas 35–6 were dropped when *The Eve of St Agnes* was being prepared for the press in late spring 1820; but it is worth emphasizing with Jack Stillinger that it was Woodhouse and Taylor, not Keats, who were 'almost certainly responsible for the return to the draft's more innocent description of the lovers' union'.[30] Woodhouse's objections to what the poet plainly thought were manly additions had, in fact, elicited a furious 'rhodomontade', duly reported to Taylor:

> He says he does not want ladies to read his poetry: that he writes for men – & that if in the former poem [the earlier version of *The Eve of St Agnes*] there was an opening for doubt what took place, it was his fault for not writing clearly & comprehensibly – that he sh^d despise a man who would be such an eunuch in sentiment as to leave a <Girl> maid, with that Character about her, in such a situation.
>
>   (*Letters*, II, 163)

This is an arresting passage, remembering that the words are mediated. It strongly suggests to me that, for a short period at least, Keats seriously contemplated abandoning his efforts to find a 'right feeling' towards women, seeking to ward off a female readership – and with it, he hoped, vexing thoughts – with barely concealed sexual references.[31] By claiming to be writing 'for men' instead of for women, Keats is now thinking about his standing to the knowing male 'after-dinner' culture epitomized by Redhall's, 'after the ladies had retired', rather than about resolving his problems with women, and women's bodies.

John Barnard correctly detects an 'ugly "manliness"' in the rhetoric of the passage.[32] However, the manly flourish at the end – that he 'sh^d despise a man who would be such an eunuch in sentiment as to leave a <Girl> maid, with that Character about her, in such a situation' – is pure bluster from one who had already revealed himself, in verse at any rate, prone to leaving the amorous field 'unheard, unseen'. It is Keats who worries about being unable to act all the acts of the bona fide husband;[33] of being, as Byron, speaking about Keats, puts it indelicately but penetratingly in a letter to Murray, 'emasculated'. The self-hindering logic that underpins Keats's professed indifference towards his female audience struck Taylor forcibly. He lamented to Woodhouse: '[Keats] does not bear the ill opinion of the World calmly, & yet he will not allow it to form a good Opinion of him & his Writings' (*Letters*, II, 182). Displaying considerable insight into what were for Keats the scarcely apprehended depths of his boyish psyche, Taylor added: 'So far as he is unconsciously silly in this Proceeding I am sorry for him.'

Hairs and heirs

> The Nymphae are two prominent doublings of the integuments, extending from the glans of the clitoris to the sides of the vagina.
>
> (*The London Dissector*, p. 58)

The nomenclature employed in Keats's student manual continued the seventeenth- and eighteenth-century medical tradition of referring to the labia minora as 'nymphae' – because, as Tobias Pencer's 1691 translation of Blancaert's *Reformirte Anatomie* pointed out, 'they are situated around the urethral orifice like two water goddesses'.[34] (The politics of this labelling have recently been explored in a splendid essay by Bettina Mathes.) In Joseph Henry Green's[35] *The Dissector's Manual*, originally circulated in 1815 as *Outlines of a Course of Dissections* (a printed edition of Green's lectures at Guy's), the *Nymphae* are described as 'two folds, which begin at the clitoris, and separating from each other, are lost upon the internal surfaces of the labia'.[36] Keats, an attentive reader of *Outlines* and *The London Dissector*, is unlikely to have written – unlikely to have been able to write – about 'nymphs' without some degree of association with genital anatomy, as can perhaps be gathered from this schoolboy nympholeptic fantasy:

> 'O Arethusa, peerless nymph! why fear
> Such tenderness as mine? Great Dian, why,
> Why didst thou hear her prayer? O that I
> Were rippling round her dainty fairness now,
> Circling about her waist, and striving how
> To entice her to a dive! then stealing in
> Between her luscious lips and eyelids thin.
> O that her shining hair was in the sun,
> And I distilling from it thence to run
> In amorous rillets down her shrinking form!
> To linger on her lily shoulders, warm
> Between her kissing breasts, and every charm
> Touch raptur'd!'
>
> (*Endymion*, II, 936–48)

For Keats, a nymph's lips would have been an attractively, if unsettlingly, plural site of erotic signification, the loci where neophyte social knowledge of women's reality ('Circling about her waist, and striving how / To entice her to a dive! Then stealing in / Between her luscious lips') once again intersected with medical expertise ('The Nymphae are two prominent doublings of the integuments . . .').

Let us remain with lips for the moment. At Guy's, Keats studied up-to-date textbooks in the hospital's famed medical library. He also purchased key manuals. In May 1818, two years after leaving Guy's, he informed Reynolds that he had not disposed of these when he gave up his studies: 'Every department of knowledge we see excellent and calculated towards a great whole. I am so convinced of this, that I am glad at not having given away my medical Books, which I shall again look over' (*Letters*, I, 277). These 'medical Books' were detailed – perhaps *too* detailed for Keats's delicate sensibility. Given Keats's claim to have had neither the heart nor hand for surgical training, it is notable that tracts on contemporary medical ethics, an expanding genre at the time, such as James Wallace's *Letters on the Study and Practice of Surgery*, were soon to recommend that 'children' under the age of sixteen should not be apprenticed (as Keats had been to Hammond), 'lest the responsibility' weigh too heavy upon their health and sanity.[37] While Wallace is thinking primarily in terms of the horrors surgical apprentices routinely witnessed in a preanaesthetic age, state-of-the-art medical manuals such as *The London Dissector* and *Outlines of a Course of Dissections* were also – in Keats's case demonstrably so – deeply disconcerting. In as much as the knowledge they contained was 'calculated towards a great (w)hole', this was certainly true. The following extract is from Chapter 3 of *The London Dissector* ('Dissection of the Organs of Generation in the Female'):

> The Labia Externa, called also the labia or alae pudendi: they are continued downwards and forwards in the direction of the symphysis pubis, and terminate in the perineum anterius: they consist of integuments, cellular substance, and fat, – are thicker above than below, – and are red and vascular on their inner side . . . The Clitoris, a red projecting body, situated below the arch of the pubis, and partly covered by its Prepuce: The prepuce is a fold of skin, continued from the inner surface of the labia, so as to cover the superior and lateral part of the clitoris.
>
> (*The London Dissector*, p. 57)

We can readily imagine the 'Schoolboy' aspect of Keats, for whom a 'fair Woman' was a 'pure Goddess' (*Letters*, I, 341) – that part of him which yearned for transcendent love, for the ethereal union of pure virgins – inwardly shuddering on encountering such minute and intimate taxonomies. He may well have regarded passages like the above as putting fly to all charms, conquering all mysteries by rule, and unweaving rainbows.

But while his student textbooks sought to provide an objective, dispassionate guide to the lineaments and ligaments of the human body, there are moments, especially when the dissecting gaze alights on the 'Organs of Generation', where a self-consciously scientific vocabulary yields to the pressure of rather more problematic terminology. The American edition of *The London Dissector*, published in 1818 and based on the fifth English edition of 1816, contains a misprint as fascinating as it is revealing. The typographical error is powerfully, comically parapractical; but while it would doubtlessly have amused Keats if he had seen it, at a deeper level it would surely also have profoundly dismayed him:

> The Mons Veneris is a rounded prominence, covered with heirs after puberty, situated at the lower part of the belly, and arising on each side gradually from the groins.
>
> (*The London Dissector*, American edition, 1818, p. 47)

The printer has inadvertently changed 'hairs' from the 1816 English edition into 'heirs'. We might, though, pause to contend that there is no such thing as an innocent slip where male writing on the female genitals is concerned. It is tempting, indeed, to read the passage as an example of medical bawdy ('heirs' being what virile men get from the female genitals 'after puberty'). In any event, it is plain that 'objective' medical discourse has a tendency to break down when applied to the genitalia. Here, a professional, detached vocabulary has degenerated into a 'manly', we might say *Burnsian*, rhetoric of knowing nudges and winks.

The London Dissector offers further glimpses into the ways in which 'precision' vocabularies flounder when applied to genital physiology:

> The Vagina is the canal leading from the vestibulum to the uterus. It lies betwixt the rectum and inferior surface of the urethra and bladder, and is connected to them by cellular membrane. It is composed of fibrous substance, partly ligamentous, and perhaps in part muscular; its inner surface is rugose, vascular, and occupied by mucous glands. On slitting it up, we see, at its posterior extremity, the Os Uteri, a rounded projection, with a transverse fissure.
>
> (*The London Dissector*, pp. 61–2)

'On slitting it up' is a shocking phrase. Scalpel incisions are generally referred to in a neutral fashion as 'making a cut' (p. 51), the process being one of 'separating' (p. 48) and 'carefully removing' (p. 52). 'Slitting it up' plainly belongs to a wholly different discourse. Given *The London Dissector*'s meticulous avoidance of such turns of phrase elsewhere, as well as its wider endeavour to present an impartial, scientific catalogue of the human body, the reference to 'slitting up' the vagina is jolting and disturbing. It illustrates how scientific discourse is conditioned by, even as it reinforces, certain 'social' attitudes towards the female body. An educational comparison may be drawn with a section from Chapter 2, on the *male* organs of generation, which adopts a register that is equally surprising, but this time for incongruous tenderness:

> The rectum having been cleansed, a little baked hair may be introduced into its extremity, which will keep the anus gently protruding during the dissection.
>
> (*The London Dissector*, p. 42)

Here there is no, because medically speaking there can be no, confusion over 'hairs' and 'heirs'.

It is scarcely conceivable that Keats, the curious schoolboy, could have possessed a copy of *The London Dissector* without reading Chapters 2 and 3 on the male and female genitals. Indeed, if he read *any* sections from his student manual, it is safe to assume that he read these. We know from scholarly studies by Donald Goellnicht and Hermione de Almeida that a wide range of clinical descriptions, including images of blood and putrefaction, found their way from Keats's medical studies into his poems. It is clear in my own mind that genital imagery from surgical manuals also entered Keats's poetry – in often startling ways.

For instance, *The London Dissector*'s description of the vaginal canal, cited earlier from pages 61–2, resonates intriguingly with the all-important scene in *Lamia* where Lycius' 'protector', Apollonius, arrives (like the medical images) uninvited at the wedding feast:

> He met within the murmurous vestibule
> His young disciple. "'Tis no common rule,
> Lycius," said he, "for uninvited guest
> To force himself upon you, and infest
> With an unbidden presence the bright throng
> Of younger friends; yet must I do this wrong,
> And you forgive me." Lycius blush'd, and led
> The old man through the inner doors broad-spread.
> (*Lamia*, II, 163–70)

Suggestive parallels may be drawn between 'murmurous vestibule'/'inner doors broad-spread' in *Lamia*, and pages 61–2 of *The London Dissector*, which depict the vagina as the 'canal leading from the vestibulum to the uterus', and describe the vascularity of its 'inner surface' (on page 57, the 'Labia Externa' are depicted as 'red and vascular on their inner side'). Could the semantic proximity of *Lamia*/labia really have escaped Keats's attention? I think his portrayal of Lamia as a 'virgin purest lipped' (I, 189) is, in all probability, a medical pun, an attempt at urbanity which uses medical knowledge to supply a lack of social accomplishment where female 'conquests' were concerned. For that matter, I suspect that Keats has cast Lamia's dwelling, her 'purple-lined palace of sweet sin' (II, 31), as an architectural embodiment of the female genitalia. This reading is doubly enticing, since Apollonius would then confront his protégé, fittingly enough, directly on the troubled, vascular ground of women's biological 'reality' (vascular for Lycius, too, whose excruciating adolescent blush curiously escapes Ricks's attention). We have already seen in Chapter 3 that one of the overriding anxieties explored in *Lamia* coheres around Lycius' desire to evade the adult responsibilities associated with having children. *The London Dissector* helps us to recognize that Apollonius' 'preservation' of the boyish Corinthian from paternal duties takes place – and if this is unwitting then it is further proof of Keats's instinctive genius, and deep-level crisis – in a poetic projection of the uterus, the primary site of pregnancy.

Part 2 of *Lamia* is replete with phrases like 'inner doors broad-spread', which seem to aim for knowing sophistication (even as they snigger, boyishly), and which are clearly directed at a male, after-dinner readership. Consider, for example, the advice given to Lycius by *Lamia*'s (smirking) narrator not to 'show to common eyes' the serpent woman's 'secret bowers' (II, 149). Note, too, a differently knowing passage; that is, a passage about different kinds of knowing:

> . . . each guest, with busy brain,
> Arriving at the portal, gaz'd amain,
> And enter'd marveling: for they knew the street,
> Remember'd it from childhood all complete
> Without a gap, yet ne'er before had seen
> That royal porch
>
> (*Lamia*, II, 150–5)

These lines represent a metaphorically rich assemblage of boyish (mis)understandings of – and initiations into – the reality of female anatomy. We've just seen that Lamia's 'purple-lined palace', with its striking 'portal'/'royal porch',[38] is about to be identified, via its vestibule, with the vaginal 'vestibulum'. The 'street', that is to say, emblematizes the female genitals, which the boy perceives to be – like the unyielding pudenda of Greek statues – 'without a gap'. Freud recognizes the 'helpless perplexity' of the boy for whom the reality of sexual union is problematized at a conceptual level by the fact that 'the existence of the cavity which receives the penis remains undiscovered by him'.[39]

The extract also documents the dramatic moment of revelation in which the 'marveling' subject, with 'busy brain', perceives the genital reality of women for the first time: 'they knew the street, / Remember'd it from childhood all complete / Without a gap, yet ne'er before had seen / That royal porch'. But while giving voice to a general truth about sexual maturation, Keats is arguably recording a specific (obstetric) memory: his *own* traumatic recollection of having, while assisting Hammond, first 'gaz'd amain' at – first looked *into* – the 'royal porch'.

'Some backward corner of the brain'

Keats may have given up his medical career for poetry, but years of training had left him with several unbanishable images. Not all medical imagery in

Keats's poetry is psychologically burdened, of course. Take, for instance, the depiction of blood in what Hillas Smith calls a 'medical way' in Book 4 of *Endymion*:

> ... My Indian bliss!
> My river-lily bud! one human kiss!
> One sigh of real breath – one gentle squeeze,
> Warm as a dove's nest among summer trees,
> And warm with dew at ooze from living blood!
>   (*Endymion*, IV, 663–7)

The image of plasma oozing from 'living blood' is mildly eccentric in the context of a love apostrophe; but there are no obvious traces of anxiety.

Other passages are more troubled. Look at the following lines from Canto 1 of *The Fall of Hyperion*:

> ... As I had found
> A grain of gold upon a mountain's side,
> And twing'd with avarice strain'd out my eyes
> To search its sullen entrails rich with ore,
> So at the view of sad Moneta's brow,
> I ached to see what things the hollow brain
> Behind enwombed: what high tragedy
> In the dark secret chambers of her skull
> Was acting
>   (*The Fall of Hyperion*, I, 271–9)

A discourse of surgical probing appears to have been subtroped to the mining simile. While there may be something absurdly comical about a surgeon's apprentice unable to make new acquaintances without speculating on their internal anatomy ('I ached to see what things . . .'), the fact that women prompt fantasies of dissection in Keats is disturbing, to say the least. We find ourselves returned to familiar terrain, since the sinister thoughts buried in the above lines recapitulate the poet's recurring problems with women's interior 'reality': close inspection of Keats's figurative register – references to searching Moneta's 'enwombed' brain and 'dark secret chambers' – suggests that we are confronted with yet another nervous medical rumination on the female body, specifically the genitals.

Donald Goellnicht's elegant study, *The Poet-Physician: Keats and Medical Science* (1984), shows that by adapting his medical education for use in poetry and letters, Keats was able to give 'a vividness and concreteness to many of his images'.[40] This vividness is supremely evident in *Isabella*, in the scene where the murderous brothers kill Lorenzo: 'these men of cruel clay / Cut Mercy with a sharp knife to the bone' (ll. 173–4).[41] Surgical training also lends edge to Keats's description of the decapitation of Lorenzo's corpse by Isabella and her nurse (or surgeon's dresser): 'With duller steel than the Perséan sword / They cut away no formless monster's head' (ll. 393–4). As Goellnicht says, this 'smack[s] of anatomical dissection' (p. 113).

Medical expertise is apparent, too – although in ways that have not yet been noticed – in Keats's portrayal in stanza 60 of the second exhumation of Lorenzo:

> . . . they contriv'd to steal the basil-pot,
>   And to examine it in secret place:
> The thing was vile with green and livid spot
>   (*Isabella*, ll. 473–5)

A possible medical 'source' for this line may prove surprising. In Chapter 3 of *The Dissector's Manual* (1820) compiled by Joseph Henry Green (Keats's anatomy demonstrator at Guy's), immediately following a full-page engraving of a dissected vagina, we discover the following:

> The vagina is lined by a *mucous membrane* of a greyish colour, often interspersed with livid spots.
>   (*The Dissector's Manual*, p. 189)

Keats, to clarify, used Green's 1815 *Outlines of a Course of Dissections*, rather than the expanded volume of 1820; the above citation does not appear in *Outlines*. That said, given that the *Dissector's Manual* simply constituted a fuller version of Green's anatomy lectures at Guy's, it is entirely possible – likely even – that Keats had heard, and mentally noted, Green's description of the vagina as it would appear in the 1820 treatise. I believe that line 475 of *Isabella* owes a great deal to Green's lectures – Keats even (mischievously?) acknowledges the debt, incorporating his demonstrator's name into the memorable passage: 'vile with *green* and livid spot' (my emphasis).

The severed head in *Isabella* is usually seen as an image of phallic castration. The possibility that the iconic presence derives from a medical description of a *vagina* – an examination *of* (rather than in) a 'secret place' – puts things in rather a different light. It certainly enables us to reconcile Keats's association of the adored 'thing' (l. 475) rotting and putrefying inside the basil pot with a 'monster' (l. 394), since the boyish imagination is both repulsed by and terrified at the idea of the female genitals. Additional significance is also extended to Andrew Bennett's insight into the 'pathology' of *Isabella*'s 'hidden centre': 'Inside both the pot of basil and "The Pot of Basil" [Keats's original name for his romance] is an uncontainable, scandalous, terrifying, and gruesome secret.'[42] The secret – we now see – is women's genital reality, shared even by a 'fair Woman'/'pure Goddess' like Isabella.

Keats is at pains, Diane Long Hoeveler reminds us, to warn us away from the poem by claiming *Isabella* is 'mawkish', 'weak-sided', with 'too much inexperience of li[f]e and simplicity of knowle[d]ge' (*Letters*, II, 162, 174).

From this attempt to direct our attention elsewhere, Hoeveler concludes cannily, 'we know that the text contains material that was threatening to the poet for highly personal reasons'.[43] Whether or not 'vile with green and livid spot' (l. 475) is, in both senses, a Guy's 'in-joke' (one, by the way, that relies on anything but 'simplicity of knowle[d]ge; although, like Keats's spelling of the word, this knowledge is troublesomely incomplete), the semantic environment of the textual extract – furtive examinations, secret places, and vileness – is richly suggestive in the context of Keats's deeper (but none the less evident) boyish aversion to pudenda.

Immediately after outlining the disfiguring, but artfully figured, 'inexperience' of *Isabella*, Keats assures Woodhouse that there would be 'very few' readers who 'would look to the reality' of the poem (*Letters*, II, 174).[44] When it came to looking to *women's* 'reality', however, Keats was, on the whole, loath to put his professional knowledge to conscious poetic use. Book 2 of *Endymion* even suggests that he actively sought to suppress the workings of his medical imagination:

> One kiss brings honey-dew from buried days.
> The woes of Troy, towers smothering o'er their blaze,
> Stiff-holden shields, far-piercing spears, keen blades,
> Struggling, and blood, and shrieks – all dimly fades
> Into some backward corner of the brain.
> (*Endymion*, II, 7–11)

This constitutes a remarkably vivid – and, reading through the figures, physiologically accurate – account of genital arousal. But despite displaying medical and social knowledge, these lines regress to a boyish understanding of sexual union as an act of coercion involving struggle, shrieks, and blood. Extraordinarily self-reflexive, the opening of Book 2 acknowledges Keats's attempt to repress 'into some backward corner of the brain' not only his 'anatomically correct' allegory, but also the epistemic sources that gave rise to it.

Jean Hagstrum may be right in maintaining that abstract images of sexual intercourse ('love-embraces') are more abundant in Romantic poetry than explicit depictions: even in the notorious stanza 36 of *The Eve of St Agnes*, the genital reality of Porphyro's and Madeline's union ('as the rose / Blendeth its odour with the violet, – / Solution sweet') is 'etherealized', to use Hagstrum's word.[45] But the graphic nature of the *Endymion* passage is unquestionably startling. The psychological 'truth' it communicates can be compared with the equally, and similarly, revealing lines that commence Tennyson's *Maud*:

> I hate the dreadful hollow behind the little wood;
> Its lips in the field above are dabbled with blood-red heath,
> The red-ribb'd ledges drip with a silent horror of blood,
> An Echo there, whatever is ask'd her, answers "Death".
> (*Maud*, ll. 1–4)

Here, as in *Endymion*, the female genitalia become a locale (literally in a geographical sense) of 'horror' and 'blood', where unspeakable acts take place – social acts that Keats the medical man could have described with professional candour, but which the boyish imagination preferred to push away and forget about.

'Stifle', that key verb from 'Unfelt, unheard, unseen' also turns up in stanza 23 of *The Eve of St Agnes*, a section of the poem intimately detained by the theme of suppression/(self-)censorship of speech. Preparing for bed, Madeline adheres to the strictures of the legend of St Agnes's Eve, taking care not to utter a single syllable before sleeping. Her heart, by contrast, is:

> ... voluble,
> Paining with eloquence her balmy side:
> As though a tongueless nightingale should swell
> Her throat in vain, and die, heart-stifled, in her dell.
> (*The Eve of St Agnes*, ll. 204–7)

But more is being suppressed than speech alone. 'Departments' of knowledge, to recall the letter to Reynolds, are also at stake. The 'tongueless nightingale' in line 206 is an obvious allusion to the myth of Philomel, whom Tereus raped then mutilated, cutting out her tongue in an effort to prevent her reporting his crime. In Ovid's version of the tale, the tongueless Philomel was transformed into a nightingale. The quiet but carefully placed reference strongly suggests that one aspect of Keats's psyche indeed regarded Porphyro's actions in stanza 36 (even in what Stillinger calls the 'more innocent' original version) as, essentially, an act of rape, perpetrated while Madeline lay helpless in 'serene repose'. The proleptic quality of the tongueless nightingale allusion gestures, in fact, towards the fraught nature of *all* sexual acts, boyishly conceived. Freud is helpful here:

> If, through some chance domestic occurrence [children] become witnesses of sexual intercourse between their parents . . . [t]heir perceptions of what is happening are bound, however, to be very incomplete. Whatever detail it may be that comes under their observation – whether it is the relative positions of the two people, or the noises they make, or some accessory circumstance – children arrive in every case at the same conclusion. They adopt what may be called a *sadistic view of coition*. They see it as something that the stronger participant is forcibly inflicting on the weaker . . . [T]hey have interpreted the act of love as an act of violence.[46]

The heart-stifled, tongueless nightingale in Keats's Romance marks a conflicted site in the boy's efforts to interpret physical sexuality correctly (which is, after all, what *The Eve of St Agnes*, one long ratiocination of sexual conduct, attempts to do). It suggests that part of the author persisted in envisaging sexual relations, not as comprised of Hagstrum's ethereal 'love-embraces', but as a disturbingly non-consensual act ('a *sadistic view of coition*'), more in line with the Philomel/Tereus paradigm. Keats's anxiousness in this regard is disclosed in his instinctual desire to cover up (stifle) and forget about (in 'some backward corner of the brain') any illicitly won knowledge – even that which is voyeuristically gleaned in stanza 36 – of the physical reality of sexual consumption.

At the end of 1817, Keats began attending a 'Card playing Club' which met on Saturday evenings at James Rice's (*Letters*, I, 190). Its 'members', most of whom were sons of businessmen, formed a lively group of mainly non-literary figures. Keats professed to enjoy homosociality, confiding to Bailey that while the presence of women was distressing to him, he felt 'comfortable' with men:

> When among Men I have no evil thoughts, no malice, no spleen – I feel free to speak or to be silent – I can listen and from every one I can learn – my hands are in my pockets I am free from all suspicion and comfortable.
> (*Letters*, I, 341)

Actually, as Keats's nervous contemplation of life's 'tiptoe cavaliers', titanically proportioned father figures, and lecherous, sexually accomplished friends attests, we would be within our rights to suspect that he was not being wholly ingenuous with Bailey (or with himself) so far as having, or not having, evil thoughts and suspicions 'among Men' was concerned. That said, Keats seems to have welcomed the chance to learn from his fellows.

The last months of 1817 were socially crowded for Keats. In the letter to George and Tom describing the Saturday Club, he also talks about his plans to dine with Wordsworth at Mortimer Street, 'sup' with Wells[47] in Featherstone Buildings, and gives the famous account of the 'immortal dinner' at the painter B. R. Haydon's house, where Keats 'astonished Kingston[48] at supper with a pertinacity in favour of drinking – keeping my two glasses at work in a knowing way' (*Letters*, I, 198). He also mentions dining with Haslam,[49] and reports back on the dance at Redhall's where the 'enquirey' into the etymological derivation of 'C––t', this chapter's point of departure, took place. In one sense, Keats is simply showing off a little to his brothers about how hectic his social diary had become. But he is recording, too – perhaps unwittingly – his endeavour to acquire an urbanity which would make him appear less 'smokeable', as we can evaluate from references to drinking 'in a knowing way' before the astonished Kingston, and being 'initiated' by Rice's gang into 'Cant' expressions such as 'knocking out an apple' (giving birth):

> I have had a great deal of pleasant time with Rice lately, and am getting initiated into a little Cant – they call dr[i]nking deep dying scarlet ... they call good Wine a pretty tipple, and call getting a Child knocking out an apple, stopping at a Tave[r]n they call hanging out – Where do you sup? is where do you hang out?
> (*Letters*, I, 197)

We should note this second example of suggestive proximity between 'Cant' and images of childbirth – think again of 'O the flummery of <the> a birth place! Cant! Cant! Cant! It is enough to give a spirit the guts-ache'. That Keats's attempt to mature socially was, at best, only partially successful, is palpable in the variously unsettled lines of articulation we have been exploring over the course of this chapter, particularly those that engage, consciously or otherwise, with female pudenda.

Keats's knowledge of the anatomy and biological function of the female body, acquired through years of obstetric and surgical training, greatly exceeded that of any of his 'knowing' friends and acquaintances. But, we have also seen, far from being able to harness medical knowledge to mitigate an often acute sense of social neophytism, Keats's professional expertise merely brought additional irresolvable anxieties to the fore, further obstructing his attempts to develop a 'right feeling' towards women. Keats's social and medical education proved to be a mutually vexing admixture. I have tried to make explicit the ways in which some of the most undermining, tormenting – and tormented – moments in the poet's on-going efforts to resolve his 'obstinate Prejudice' concerning the opposite sex occur in, or are commemorated by, episodes where social and medical knowledge intersect and invariably problematize each other.

Afterword

In 'Lines on Seeing a Lock of Milton's Hair', composed 21 January 1818, Keats seems to look forward to poetic development: in Walter Jackson Bate's words, 'evolution in thought'; in Andrew Motion's, 'personal progress':[1]

> When every childish fashion
>   Has vanish'd from my rhyme,
> Will I, grey-gone in passion,
>   Leave to an after time   25
>   Hymning and harmony
> Of thee, and of thy works, and of thy life;
> But vain is now the burning, and the strife,
> Pangs are in vain – until I grow high-rife
>   With old philosophy;   30
> And mad with glimpses of futurity!

Commentators have traditionally seen this poem as marking Keats's 'recommitment' to poetry after the lull following *Endymion*'s completion;[2] it has also been seen as articulating Keats's desire to mature as a writer. But it is possible to retrieve a rather different message. For far from eagerly anticipating the production of 'high-rife', mature verse with which to honour Milton, the ode actually, it seems to me, strives to keep at bay any thoughts of the day when such austere offerings (a 'burnt sacrifice of verse / And melody', ll. 9-10), can reasonably be expected. It would be 'in vain' to try to offer these things now, Keats assures others, and reassures himself: 'in vain – until I grow high-rife / With old philosophy / And mad with glimpses of futurity' (we almost hear the rhyme on 'maturity'). The reference to madness in old age is possibly a sly allusion to George III. The idea that Keats may have been thinking of the king is strengthened by the fact that on the following day, 22 January, he wrote his famous sonnet 'On Sitting Down to Read *King Lear* Once Again'. The point is, performances of Shakespeare's play had been banned in London because its portrayal of a deluded old monarch was felt to be too close for comfort. Together with Milton and Shakespeare, George III would have made up a triumvirate of aged father figures who, in Keats's imagination, collectively stood for repressive authority.[3]

Bate thinks that Keats saw *King Lear* as 'a symbol of what he hoped ultimately to reach' (p. 287). But unless Bate is referring to the fact that Lear grows immature with age, the relationship is distinctly more problematic than that. After all, Shakespeare's tragic, supremely *mature* masterpiece threatens to annihilate Keats's boyish infatuation with boyish 'Romance' (which a few months earlier had produced the boyish *Endymion*). Reluctantly instructing Romance to 'shut up thine olden pages, and be mute' (l. 4), Keats prepares to grapple 'humbly' with Shakespeare's familiar 'bitter-sweet' fruit. The literary lesson evokes for Keats all the pain of fiery consumption:

> O golden-tongued Romance, with serene lute!
>   Fair plumed syren, queen of far-away!
>   Leave melodizing on this wintry day,
> Shut up thine olden pages, and be mute.
> Adieu! for, once again, the fierce dispute
>   Betwixt damnation and impassion'd clay
>   Must I burn through; once more humbly assay
> The bitter-sweet of this Shakespearian fruit.
> Chief Poet! and ye clouds of Albion,
>   Begetters of our deep eternal theme!   10
> When through the old oak forest I am gone,
>   Let me not wander in a barren dream:
> But, when I am consumed in the fire,
> Give me new phoenix wings to fly at my desire.

At the sonnet's conclusion, Keats yearns for rebirth. The obstetric image actually occurs twice in different forms. It is first articulated in line 12: 'Let me not wander in a *barren* dream' (my italics); then restated in Keats's wish to be reborn like a phoenix after being consumed in the white heat of Shakespeare's majesty (ll. 13–14). In other words, liberation from authority – the essential freedom to 'fly at my desire', to write in a manner unprescribed by Albion's 'Chief Poet' – constitutes Keats's last thought in the poem.

The irregular ode on the lock of Milton's hair is similarly – if equally fugitively – non-conformist. Reluctantly accepting the challenge set by Leigh Hunt (another ambiguous father figure, and the new owner of Milton's hair) to write on the literary patriarch, Keats comes up with a poem that is really and intricately about *refusing* to write on Milton. It would be a 'mad endeavour', Keats announces in line 6. Indeed, the ode's conceit of age versus youth is worked out in such a way that Keats is exonerated from having to pay homage ('offer a burnt sacrifice') to Milton until an unspecified 'after time' when 'every childish fashion' has vanished from his work – something Keats has no intention of allowing to happen. The feudal relations supposed to pertain between Keats and Milton, 'Chief of organic numbers' (organ-like tones), are certainly suggested in Keats's 'hot and flush'd' reaction to the mere 'vassal' of 'Milton's power' (an authenticated lock of his hair). However, elsewhere the poem strenuously contests the terms of the relationship. In seeming to honour Milton, Keats artfully pushes him away. Moreover, he banishes his great predecessor into distant 'futurity', rather than returning him again to the disturbingly ever-present past, where 'Thy spirit never slumbers, / But rolls about our ears / For ever, and for ever' (lines 3–5 begin to sound like a complaint). All of which is to say that Keats's 'young Delian oath' to pay homage to Milton in line 18 cannot be taken at face value, since the hour when the monstrous debt is to be paid is projected into an impossible future (the mere glimpse of which is enough to send the young poet 'mad').

These performances of seemly deference, then, are in fact sniping acts of insolence which allow Keats to assert the self-governance of the boyish imagination. They are entirely consistent with the contestative exploits we have been exploring throughout this book. Whether protesting expectations that he conform to available models of masculine behaviour, mould the myriad energies of his sexual longings to circumscribed patterns of mature articulation, internalize standard textbook theorems of aesthetic pleasure, or prune his literary idiom of 'namby-pamby' phrases, Keats stubbornly retains his childish capacity – his 'childish fashion' – to frustrate and elude the manifestations of adult power. Boyishness could be a double-edged concept, of course. Just as we have seen Keats deploying the logic of puerility in a calculating, strategic manner to unpick and deconstruct matrices of authority, a 'genuine' and psychically vexing infantilism can also be discerned unsettling the young poet in his political project. At various points in Keats, these two distinct kinds of boyishness operate simultaneously, further underscoring the complexity of the issue.

But what we are left with after the fever-fret of a book-length study . . . is still Keats: elusive, tricksy, unquantifiable – an unknown quantity for enemies and detractors who were unable or incapable of deciding whether he stood mischievously tip-toe on a little hill, or reverently silent on a peak in Darien. If this book has shown anything, though, it is that Keats and his work are always doing both: pulling in two directions at once, maddening expectations, growing older by becoming younger, offering a fine example for us all.

Appendix

Calidore: A Fragment

Young Calidore is paddling o'er the lake;
His healthful spirit eager and awake
To feel the beauty of a silent eve,
Which seem'd full loath this happy world to leave;
The light dwelt o'er the scene so lingeringly.
He bares his forehead to the cool blue sky,
And smiles at the far clearness all around,
Until his heart is well nigh over wound,
And turns for calmness to the pleasant green
Of easy slopes, and shadowy trees that lean   10
So elegantly o'er the waters' brim
And show their blossoms trim.
Scarce can his clear and nimble eye-sight follow
The freaks, and dartings of the black-wing'd swallow,
Delighting much, to see it half at rest,
Dip so refreshingly its wings, and breast
'Gainst the smooth surface, and to mark anon,
The widening circles into nothing gone.

And now the sharp keel of his little boat
Comes up with ripple, and with easy float,   20
And glides into a bed of water lillies:
Broad leav'd are they and their white canopies
Are upward turn'd to catch the heavens' dew.
Near to a little island's point they grew;
Whence Calidore might have the goodliest view
Of this sweet spot of earth. The bowery shore
Went off in gentle windings to the hoar
And light blue mountains: but no breathing man
With a warm heart, and eye prepared to scan
Nature's clear beauty, could pass lightly by   30
Objects that look'd out so invitingly

On either side. These, gentle Calidore
Greeted, as he had known them long before.

The sidelong view of swelling leafiness,
Which the glad setting sun in gold doth dress;
Whence ever and anon the jay outsprings,
And scales upon the beauty of its wings.

The lonely turret, shatter'd, and outworn,
Stands venerably proud; too proud to mourn
Its long lost grandeur: fir trees grow around,   40
Aye dropping their hard fruit upon the ground.

The little chapel with the cross above
Upholding wreaths of ivy; the white dove,
That on the windows spreads his feathers light,
And seems from purple clouds to wing its flight.

Green tufted islands casting their soft shades
Across the lake; sequester'd leafy glades,
That through the dimness of their twilight show
Large dock leaves, spiral foxgloves, or the glow
Of the wild cat's eyes, or the silvery stems   50
Of delicate birch trees, or long grass which hems
A little brook. The youth had long been viewing
These pleasant things, and heaven was bedewing
The mountain flowers, when his glad senses caught
A trumpet's silver voice. Ah! it was fraught
With many joys for him: the warder's ken
Had found white coursers prancing in the glen:
Friends very dear to him he soon will see;
So pushes off his boat most eagerly,
And soon upon the lake he skims along,   60
Deaf to the nightingale's first under-song;
Nor minds he the white swans that dream so sweetly:
His spirit flies before him so completely.

And now he turns a jutting point of land,
Whence may be seen the castle gloomy, and grand:
Nor will a bee buzz round two swelling peaches,
Before the point of his light shallop reaches
Those marble steps that through the water dip:
Now over them he goes with hasty trip,
And scarcely stays to ope the folding doors: 70
Anon he leaps along the oaken floors
Of halls and corridors.

Delicious sounds! those little bright-eyed things
That float about the air on azure wings,
Had been less heartfelt by him than the clang
Of clattering hoofs; into the court he sprang,
Just as two noble steeds, and palfreys twain,
Were slanting out their necks with loosened rein;
While from beneath the threat'ning portcullis
They brought their happy burthens. What a kiss,   80
What gentle squeeze he gave each lady's hand!
How tremblingly their delicate ancles spann'd!
Into how sweet a trance his soul was gone,
While whisperings of affection
Made him delay to let their tender feet
Come to the earth; with an incline so sweet
From their low palfreys o'er his neck they bent:
And whether there were tears of languishment,
Or that the evening dew had pearl'd their tresses,
He feels a moisture on his cheek, and blesses   90
With lips that tremble, and with glistening eye,
All the soft luxury
That nestled in his arms. A dimpled hand,
Fair as some wonder out of fairy land,
Hung from his shoulder like the drooping flowers
Of whitest cassia, fresh from summer showers:
And this he fondled with his happy cheek
As if for joy he would no further seek;
When the kind voice of good Sir Clerimond
Came to his ear, like something from beyond   100
His present being: so he gently drew
His warm arms, thrilling now with pulses new,
From their sweet thrall, and forward gently bending,
Thank'd heaven that his joy was never ending;
While 'gainst his forehead he devoutly press'd
A hand heaven made to succour the distress'd;
A hand that from the world's bleak promontory
Had lifted Calidore for deeds of glory.

Amid the pages, and the torches' glare,
There stood a knight, patting the flowing hair   110
Of his proud horse's mane: he was withal
A man of elegance, and stature tall:
So that the waving of his plumes would be
High as the berries of a wild ash tree,
Or as the winged cap of Mercury.

His armour was so dexterously wrought
In shape, that sure no living man had thought
It hard, and heavy steel: but that indeed
It was some glorious form, some splendid weed,
In which a spirit new come from the skies   120
Might live, and show itself to human eyes.
'Tis the far-fam'd, the brave Sir Gondibert,
Said the good man to Calidore alert;
While the young warrior with a step of grace
Came up, – a courtly smile upon his face,
And mailed hand held out, ready to greet
The large-eyed wonder, and ambitious heat
Of the aspiring boy; who as he led
Those smiling ladies, often turned his head
To admire the visor arched so gracefully   130
Over a knightly brow; while they went by
The lamps that from the high-roof'd hall were pendent,
And gave the steel a shining quite transcendent.

Soon in a pleasant chamber they are seated;
The sweet-lipp'd ladies have already greeted
All the green leaves that round the window clamber,
To show their purple stars, and bells of amber.
Sir Gondibert has doff'd his shining steel,
Gladdening in the free, and airy feel
Of a light mantle; and while Clerimond   140
Is looking round about him with a fond,
And placid eye, young Calidore is burning
To hear of knightly deeds, and gallant spurning
Of all unworthiness; and how the strong of arm
Kept off dismay, and terror, and alarm
From lovely woman: while brimful of this,
He gave each damsel's hand so warm a kiss,
And had such manly ardour in his eye,
That each at other look'd half staringly;
And then their features started into smiles   150
Sweet as blue heavens o'er enchanted isles.

Softly the breezes from the forest came,
Softly they blew aside the taper's flame;
Clear was the song from Philomel's far bower;
Grateful the incense from the lime-tree flower;
Mysterious, wild, the far heard trumpet's tone;
Lovely the moon in ether, all alone:
Sweet too the converse of these happy mortals,
As that of busy spirits when the portals

Are closing in the west; or that soft humming 160
We hear around when Hesperus is coming.
Sweet be their sleep. * * * * * * * * *

To Autumn

1

Season of mists and mellow fruitfulness,
   Close bosom-friend of the maturing sun;
Conspiring with him how to load and bless
   With fruit the vines that round the thatch-eves run;
To bend with apples the moss'd cottage-trees,
   And fill all fruit with ripeness to the core;
     To swell the gourd, and plump the hazel shells
With a sweet kernel; to set budding more,
And still more, later flowers for the bees,
Until they think warm days will never cease, 10
     For summer has o'er-brimm'd their clammy cells.

2

Who hath not seen thee oft amid thy store?
   Sometimes whoever seeks abroad may find
Thee sitting careless on a granary floor,
   Thy hair soft-lifted by the winnowing wind;
Or on a half-reap'd furrow sound asleep,
   Drows'd with the fume of poppies, while thy hook
     Spares the next swath and all its twined flowers:
And sometimes like a gleaner thou dost keep
   Steady thy laden head across a brook; 20
   Or by a cyder-press, with patient look,
     Thou watchest the last oozings hours by hours.

3

Where are the songs of spring? Ay, where are they?
   Think not of them, thou hast thy music too, –
While barred clouds bloom the soft-dying day,
   And touch the stubble-plains with rosy hue;
Then in a wailful choir the small gnats mourn
   Among the river sallows, borne aloft
     Or sinking as the light wind lives or dies;
And full-grown lambs loud bleat from hilly bourn; 30
   Hedge-crickets sing; and now with treble soft
   The red-breast whistles from a garden-croft;
     And gathering swallows twitter in the skies.

Notes

Introduction

1. Jeffrey C. Robinson, 'Leigh Hunt and the Poetics and Politics of the Fancy', in *Leigh Hunt: Life, Poetics, Politics*, ed. Nicholas Roe (London: Routledge, 2003), p. 171.
2. This drew on Charles Brown's unpublished manuscript, 'Life of John Keats', and on the personal reminiscences of many of Keats's surviving friends.
3. Richard Monckton Milnes (ed.), *Life, Letters, and Literary Remains of John Keats*, 2 vols (London: Moxon, 1848), II, 53.
4. M. R. Ridley, *Keats's Craftsmanship* (Oxford: Clarendon Press, 1933), p. 16. Further page references are given parenthetically in the main body of text.
5. Stephen Coote, *John Keats: A Life* (London: Hodder and Stoughton, 1995), p. 242.
6. Andrew Motion, *Keats* (London: Faber and Faber, 1997), pp. xxv–xxvi.
7. Jack Stillinger, 'The "Story" of Keats', in *The Cambridge Companion to Keats*, ed. Susan Wolfson (Cambridge: Cambridge University Press, 2001), p. 247.
8. Christopher Ricks, *Keats and Embarrassment* (Oxford: Oxford University Press, 1974), p. 12.
9. Roger Sharrock, 'Keats and the Young Lovers', *A Review of English Literature*, 2 (1961), 76–86, at p. 77.
10. Helen Vendler, *Coming of Age as a Poet: Milton, Keats, Eliot, Plath* (Cambridge, MA: Harvard University Press, 2003), p. 1. Vendler's determination to present an end-stopped narrative of achievement is clear throughout her criticism. While conceding that Keats's early poetic trajectory is 'one of ups and downs', Helen Vendler resolves, when discussing his sonnets, to 'begin at the worst and rise toward the best' (*Coming of Age as a Poet*, p. 46).
11. Motion, *Keats*, pp. 95, 134.
12. Ibid., p. 382.
13. Ibid., p. 484.
14. Walter Jackson Bate, *John Keats* (London: Hogarth, 1992), p. 623.
15. In his manuscript, 'Life of John Keats', Charles Brown referred to *The Cap and Bells* as Keats's 'comic faery poem'; see *The Keats Circle: Letters and Papers 1816–1878*, ed. Hyder Edward Rollins, 2 vols (Cambridge, MA: Harvard University Press, 1948), II, 72.
16. Joanna Richardson, *The Everlasting Spell: A Study of Keats and his Friends* (London: Jonathan Cape, 1963), p. 27.

1 'Strange longings': Keats and feet

1. See also *Lamia*, I, 15.
2. Similar uses occur in 'Hush, hush! tread softly! hush, hush, my dear!' (l. 5), and

'Specimen of an Induction to a Poem' (l. 41).
3 'Women! When I behold thee flippant, vain' (ll. 17–18).
4 Anne K. Mellor, *Romanticism and Gender* (London: Routledge, 1993), p. 172.
5 The *OED* gives as its second definition of *Cockney* (noun): '"a child that sucketh long" . . . "a mother's darling"; . . . "a child tenderly brought up"; hence a squeamish or effeminate fellow'.
6 Susan Wolfson, 'Feminising Keats', in *Coleridge, Keats, and Shelley*, ed. Peter J. Kitson (Houndmills: Macmillan, 1996), 92–113, at p. 95.
7 'On the Cockney School of Poetry No. IV', *Blackwood's Edinburgh Magazine*, 3 (August 1818), 519–24, at p. 522.
8 Preface to *Blackwood's Edinburgh Magazine*, 19 (January 1826), xvi.
9 *Byron's Letters and Journals*, ed. Leslie A. Marchand, 12 vols (London: Murray, 1973–82), VII (1977), 200; letter dated 12 October 1820.
10 Diane Long Hoeveler, 'Decapitating Romance: Class, Fetish, and Ideology in Keats's *Isabella*', *Nineteenth-Century Literature*, 49 (1994), 321–38, at p. 325.
11 See Jean Hagstrum, *The Romantic Body: Love and Sexuality in Keats, Wordsworth, and Blake* (Knoxville: University of Tennessee Press, 1985), p. 54.
12 So far as I am aware, no source for this story has been identified. Keats may have invented it himself.
13 Ricks, *Keats and Embarrassment*, pp. 120–1.
14 Mellor, *Romanticism and Gender*, p. 176.
15 The image of feet glimpsed beneath water occurs on a number of occasions in Keats, including his earliest surviving poem, *Imitation of Spenser*:

> There saw the swan his neck of arched snow,
> And oar'd himself along with majesty;
> Sparkled his jetty eyes; his feet did show
> Beneath the waves like Afric's ebony,
> And on his back a fay reclined voluptuously.
> (*Imitation of Spenser*, ll. 15–17)

As Miriam Allott notes, Keats found a source for this image in Milton's *Paradise Lost* (VII, 438–40). Keats's interest in the swan's feet is arguably more focused on how these appendages appear beneath the water than Milton's; but even if the imagery in the *Imitation* does not, as the poem's title suggests, stray too far from convention, in later work Keats's fascination with feet in water quickly deconstructs its relationship to 'normal' desire.

16 Sigmund Freud, *On Sexuality: Three Essays on the Theory of Sexuality and Other Works*, trans. James Strachey, ed. Angela Richards, The Pelican Freud Library, 15 vols (Harmondsworth: Penguin, 1953), VII, 352. Further page references to volume VII are given parenthetically in the main body of my discussion.
17 Lewis Dearing, 'A John Keats Letter Rediscovered', *Keats–Shelley Journal*, 47 (1998), 14–16, at p. 16. Further page references are given parenthetically in the main body of text.
18 Roland Barthes, *The Pleasure of the Text*, trans. Richard Miller (Oxford: Blackwell, 1990), p. 58.
19 Motion, *Keats*, p. 89.
20 *Letters*, I, 342.
21 Hoeveler, 'Decapitating Romance', p. 322.
22 Robert Gittings, *John Keats* (Harmondsworth: Penguin, 1968), p. 30.
23 See Motion, *Keats*, p. 21.
24 Wolfson, 'Feminising Keats', p. 106.
25 *Byron's Letters and Journals*, VII, 217; letter dated 4 November 1820.
26 Brown was some eight years older than Keats.

27 Marjorie Levinson, *Keats's Life of Allegory: The Origins of a Style* (Oxford: Blackwell, 1988), p. 120.

2 'Full-grown lambs': immaturity and 'To Autumn'

1. *Byron's Letters and Journals*, VII (1977), 200; letter dated 12 November 1820. 'On the Cockney School of Poetry No. IV', *Blackwood's Edinburgh Magazine*, 3 (1818), 519–24, at p. 522.
2. These comments appeared in reviews of *Lamia . . . and Other Poems* (1820) in the *Guardian*, 6 August 1820, p. 2, and the *London Magazine*, 2 (1820), 315–21, at p. 315.
3. Levinson, *Keats's Life of Allegory*, p. 5. Further page numbers are given parenthetically in the main body of my discussion. The ironic reference to Lockhart and Croker is Charles Cowden Clarke's, Keats's friend; see *An Address to that Quarterly Reviewer who Touched upon Mr. Leigh Hunt's 'Story of Rimini'* (London: Jennings, 1816), p. 18.
4. Helen Vendler, *The Odes of John Keats* (London: Belknap Press, 1983), p. 278.
5. Michael O'Neill, *Romanticism and the Self-Conscious Poem* (Oxford: Clarendon Press, 1997), p. 199.
6. Bate, *John Keats*, p. 584.
7. Motion, *Keats*, p. 462.
8. Vendler, *The Odes of John Keats*, p. 234; Morse Peckham, *The Romantic Virtuoso* (Hannover: University Press of New England, 1995), p. 113.
9. By his own confession in the published Preface to *Endymion*, Keats inhabited an unhealthy and uncertain 'space of life' found between the 'imagination of a boy' and the 'mature imagination of a man'.
10. John Jones, *John Keats's Dream of Truth* (London: Chatto and Windus, 1969), p. 261.
11. Review of *Lamia . . . and Other Poems*, *Monthly Review*, 2nd series, 92 (1820), 305–10, at p. 305.
12. Geoffrey Hartman, *The Fate of Reading and other Essays* (London: University of Chicago Press, 1975), p. 124.
13. 'Puffing' – Keats calling a spade a spade – was one of the strategies through which Leigh Hunt's Cockney community of dilettantes, writers, editors, and painters assisted each other in the London literary and artistic scene; see Jeffrey N. Cox, *Poetry and Politics in the Cockney School: Keats, Shelley, Hunt, and their Circle* (Cambridge: Cambridge University Press, 1998). A portrait of Keats – however small – in a prestigious Royal Academy exhibition would very likely have lent some degree of publicity (or notoriety) to its subject. Its appearance would have represented a major coup for Severn, however. Keats's extreme sensitivity to the charge of boyishness may be gauged from the fact that he could even contemplate obstructing his friend's career by suggesting he withdraw the painting.
14. As Nicholas Roe establishes, reviewers attempted to undermine Keats's cultural, poetical, and political aspirations through repeated allusions to his disqualifying 'childishness'; see *John Keats and the Culture of Dissent* (Oxford: Clarendon Press, 1997), pp. 203–29.
15. Keats read what was long thought to be, but in fact is not, Chaucer's translation of Alain Chartier's 'La Belle Dame sans Mercy' (1424) in Bell's *The Poetical Works of Geoffrey Chaucer* (1782), vol. 10. In the 1782 edition, Chartier's title is spelled 'La bel Dame sans Mercy', exactly incorporating 'beldame'. Possibly the pimping connection between Old Angela and (La) Beldame was strengthened in Keats's mind by the 1782 title.
16. Barbara Johnson, 'Gender Theory and the Yale School', in *Modern Literary Theory: A Reader*, ed. Philip Rice and Patricia Waugh, 3rd edn (London: Arnold, 1996).

17 Arguably, the ambiguity arises due to constraints of ballad metre – four stressed syllables to the line – which Keats places on himself (the poem's subtitle announces his intentions to write a 'genuine' ballad). Keats quite literally runs out of the syllables he needs to clarify the issue of culpability. If he had written: 'She looked at me as if she did love', we would know for certain the Lady was an enchantress, out to deceive the knight from the beginning – but the line would not sound very ballad-like. Johnson does not consider metre as one of the factors affecting the poem's coherency.
18 The Lady thus pimps to herself.
19 Keats felt that because of Brown's flirtation with Fanny Brawne he was being 'done to death by inches'. In so far as Browne was not only older than Keats, but taller, his diagnosis was accurate in more senses than one.
20 Mellor, *Romanticism and Gender*, p. 21.
21 See *Indicator*, 9 August 1820, 345–52, at p. 352; and the *New Monthly Magazine*, 14 (1820), pp. 245, 248.
22 Jack Stillinger, *The Hoodwinking of Madeline and Other Essays on Keats's Poems* (London: University of Illinois Press, 1971), p. 117.
23 Josiah Conder[?], review of *Lamia . . . and Other Poems*, *Eclectic Review*, 2nd series, 14 (1820), 158–71, at p. 159.
24 *Indicator*, 9 August 1820, p. 352.
25 *Eclectic Review*, 2nd series, 14 (1820), p. 169.
26 This loss was to keep him, in legal terms, suspended in status between childhood and adulthood. It also meant that he had to rely on his guardian and older friends for sustenance and rent. 'To Autumn' was composed in the summer of 1820, just as Keats's financial problems were becoming most acute.
27 Compare the account Keats gives almost two years later in a letter to Mary-Ann Jeffrey, dated 9 June 1819, of Brown 'force-feeding' him extracts from his life of David: 'My friend Mr Brown is sitting opposite me . . . He reads me passages as he writes them stuffing my infidel mouth as though I were a young rook' (*Letters*, II, 116). Keats was drawn to images of young birds as a means of alluding to his sense of personal immaturity: to Fanny Brawne on 15 (?) July 1819, he referred to his poetry as the product of a 'half-fledged brain' (*Letters*, II, 130).
28 The *OED* defines 'clammy' as 'soft, moist, and sticky; viscous, tenacious, adhesive'. A 'clammy cell', then, to all extents and purposes, is the same as a 'sticky chamber'.
29 *Byron's Letters and Journals*, VII (1977), 225, 217; letters dated 9 November and 4 November 1820.
30 *Eclectic Review*, 2nd series, 14 (1820), p. 158.
31 George Felton Mathew, *European Magazine*, 71 (1817), 434–7, at p. 435.
32 For the objections of conservative reviewers to Keats's diction, see my '"Handy Squirrels" and Chapman's Homer: Hunt, Keats, and Romantic Philology', *Romanticism*, 4.i (1998), 104–19.
33 Geoffrey Hill, *Collected Poems* (Harmondsworth: Penguin, 1985), p. 19.
34 Possibly, Keats and Fanny Brawne – real-life 'young lovers' – maintain a shadowy presence in lines 16–17. On 1 July 1819, two months or so before 'To Autumn' was composed, Keats, working on the Isle of Wight, entreated Fanny to send him a letter 'immediately': 'make it rich as a draught of poppies to intoxicate me' (*Letters*, II, 123). Keats is clearly thinking of the 'pleasant wonders' of young love here; moreover, he records that he is writing from his 'pleasant Cottage window' that looks out onto a 'beautiful hilly country'; perhaps these hilly bourns contained 'full-grown lambs'.
35 Ricks, *Keats and Embarrassment*, p. 209.
36 Vendler, *The Odes of John Keats*, p. 254.
37 Motion, *Keats*, p. 461.
38 *Eclectic Review*, 2nd series, 14 (1820), p. 169.

138 Notes

39 It is far from certain how Keats would have felt had he known of Woodhouse's (well-meant) remark to Taylor that the poet's strong convictions had made '*half* a Milton of him' (my emphasis): *The Keats Circle: Letters and Papers, 1816–1878*, I, 82.
40 The words in quotation marks are Vendler's description of Keats's style; see *The Odes of John Keats*, p. 294.
41 We could, indeed, point to ways in which new historicist critiques of 'To Autumn' and my reading of the poem to this juncture – which asserts that the ode is childish, but politically so – might be (already) reconciled. At the very least, the two hermeneutics complicate each other in interesting ways. After all, the dilemma contained in 'close bosom-friend' (whether it is to be understood as a 'mature' or 'immature' comment) – always granting that for Keats immaturity could also be a political position – actually makes the phrase *more*, rather than less, 'Keatsian'.
42 The text reprinted here is the version that appeared in Hunt's *Literary Pocket-Book* for 1820 (published at the end of 1819).
43 Leigh Hunt, *Examiner*, 12 (1819), p. 333.
44 I discuss this claim in 'John Keats, Barry Cornwall and Leigh Hunt's *Literary Pocket-Book*', *Romanticism*, 7.ii (2002), 163–76.
45 It had been suspended on 4 March 1817 and was restored on 28 January 1818.
46 I am grateful to Damian Walford Davies for pointing out the relevance of Marvell's poem to my argument.
47 All references to Marvell's poetry are to *Andrew Marvell: The Complete Poems*, ed. Elizabeth Story Donno (Harmondsworth: Penguin, 1972).

3 'Give me that voice again': Keats and puberphonia

1 Marlon B. Ross, *The Contours of Masculine Desire: Romanticism and the Rise of Women's Poetry* (Oxford: Oxford University Press, 1989), p. 157.
2 Interestingly, later portrayals of Apollo (for example, in Book 3 of *Hyperion*) are less concerned with the deity's 'mighty', manly attributes, and emphasize instead his boyish, or even feminine, qualities.
3 Vendler, *Coming of Age as a Poet*, pp. 3, 1. Vendler adds: 'The youthful writer cannot pursue an evolution to adulthood independent of an ongoing evolution of style. To find a personal style *is*, for a writer, to become an adult' (p. 2). This last sentence is resonant in the context of this chapter's argument that Keats 'postponed' finding his poetic voice in an effort to stave off adult responsibilities.
4 Garrett Stewart, 'Keats and Language', in *The Cambridge Companion to Keats*, p. 135.
5 John Barnard, *John Keats* (Cambridge: Cambridge University Press, 1987), p. 1; Motion, *Keats*, p. 112. Gittings sees the poem as a 'summing-up of much that had accumulated in Keats's life and thought all through his apprentice years'; *John Keats*, p. 130. Jerome McGann, by contrast, following Levinson, has drawn attention to an essential naïvety about the poem which he sees as bound up with Keats's 'schoolboy error': Balboa, not Cortez, was the first European to 'discover' the Pacific Ocean. McGann suggests that by including the 'absurd error', Keats 'transports us to the most forbidden world of all – the Rosebud world of adolescence, barred out more securely by the adult consciousness . . . than perhaps any other realm has ever been'; *The Poetics of Sensibility: A Revolution in Literary Style* (Oxford: Clarendon Press, 1996), pp. 122–3. For a cogent argument against reading 'Cortez' as a mistake, see Charles J. Rzepka's essay, '"Cortez – or Balboa, or Somebody Like That": Form, Fact, and Forgetting in Keats's "Chapman's Homer" Sonnet', *Keats–Shelley Journal*, 51 (2002), 35–75. Finding the theme of 'belatedness' central to the sonnet, Rzepka makes the convincing point that

'Cortez, precisely because he represents the poet's mediated relationship to Homer/the Pacific via an original "discoverer", Chapman/Balboa, is the perfect choice for this "second-hand" poet's alienated self-representation' (p. 47).
6 Vendler, *Coming of Age as a Poet*, p. 45.
7 The original reviewers of Keats's *Poems* (1817), where the sonnet made its second appearance, were outraged at the boyish presumption of 'Johnny Keats' for daring to raise his voice in the élite cultural sphere of published poetry.
8 Josiah Conder, *Eclectic Review*, 2nd series, 14 (1820), 158–71, at p. 169. For Conder, Keats's volume was composed, in Roland Barthes' fitting terms, out of 'unweaned', 'milky phonemes'; *The Pleasure of the Text*, p. 5.
9 See McGann's groundbreaking essay, 'Keats and the Historical Method in Literary Criticism', *Modern Language Notes*, 94 (1979), 988–1032, at pp. 1015–17. Also see Nicholas Roe, who argues against McGann's view of *Lamia . . . and Other Poems* (1820) as a volume designed to 'allay conflict'; *Keats and the Culture of Dissent*, pp. 248–9.
10 See Keats's letter to John Hamilton Reynolds, 19 September 1819. The grand, grown-up style, characterized by 'Miltonic intonation', is associated by Keats with 'false beauty proceeding from art', and contrasted with the '*true voice* of feeling' (my emphasis; *Letters*, II, 167).
11 *Twelfth Night*, ed. M. M. Mahood (Harmondsworth: Penguin, 1968), I. v. 150–6.
12 Peter Barry discusses this topic in his recent *English in Practice* (London: Arnold, 2002).
13 *Voice Disorders and their Management*, ed. Margaret Fawcus (London: Croom Helm, 1986), p. 215. Further page references are given in the main body of my discussion.
14 Barnard, *John Keats*, p. 32.
15 Greg Kucich, for example, argues that Calidore's 'allegory of creative development' is associated by Keats with his own 'drama of maturation' and 'poetic growth'; see 'Cockney Chivalry: Hunt, Keats and the Aesthetics of Excess', in *Leigh Hunt: Life, Poetics, Politics*, ed. Nicholas Roe (London: Routledge, 2003), p. 131.
16 Marlon B. Ross sees *Calidore* as a work, like those other fragments the *Hyperion* poems, that is 'concerned with the quest for power'; see 'Beyond the Fragmented World: Keats at the Limits of Patrilinear Language', in *Out of Bounds: Male Writers and Gender(ed) Criticism*, ed. Laura Claridge and Elizabeth Langland (Amherst: University of Massachusetts Press, 1990), p. 114.
17 In his appraisal of *Poems* (1817) for the *Eclectic Review*, the reviewer quipped that *Calidore* was only 'a few good lines which ambitiously aspired to overleap the portfolio' (p. 272). Conder's use of 'overleap' possibly derives from the fact that line 76 – 'Into the court he sprang' – makes Calidore appear to have jumped over the castle walls. But the point to take is that, in Conder's eyes, the poem itself, not just its protagonist, was 'aspiring'.
18 In her essay on Keats, Oliphant declared: 'In poetry his was the woman's part'. See 'John Keats', in Margaret Oliphant, *The Literary History of England in the End of the Eighteenth and Beginning of the Nineteenth Century*, 3 vols (London: Macmillan, 1882), I, 138.
19 The 'portcullis' in *Calidore* seems to have exercised at least one other reader. When Leigh Hunt used Tom Keats's MS to edit *Poems* (1817), he underscored 'portcullis' in the transcript. The cause for Hunt's concern is not clear; at any rate, he let the word stand as Keats wrote it. See *Poems*, p. 549.
20 See Alan Richardson's informative essay, 'Keats and Romantic Science' in *The Cambridge Companion to Keats*.
21 Cooper lectured on, among other things, diseases and injuries of the throat.
22 Motion, *Keats*, pp. 76–7. Also see Roe, *Keats and the Culture of Dissent*, pp. 169–70,

and Donald C. Goellnicht, *The Poet-Physician: Keats and Medical Science* (Pittsburgh: University of Pittsburgh Press, 1984), pp. 23–31.
23 See Hermione de Almeida's excellent opening chapter in *Romantic Medicine and John Keats* (Oxford: Oxford University Press, 1991).
24 See Motion, *Keats*, p. 80.
25 *John Keats's Anatomical and Physiological Note Book*, ed. Maurice Buxton Forman (Oxford: Oxford University Press, 1934). As De Almeida points out, Keats would have required commitment and determination to carry out his daily duties as a surgeon's dresser during his year at Guy's. In a pre-anaesthetic age, even amputations had to be performed with nothing but alcohol to deaden the patient's pain.
26 Cited in Motion, *Keats*, p. 86. In this chapter, I argue that Keats *is* 'articulate' about his anxiety regarding maturing larynxes.
27 For Keats's ownership of this volume see Gittings, *John Keats*, p. 83; also Goellnicht, *The Poet-Physician*, pp. 120–1; and Hillas Smith, *Keats and Medicine* (Newport, Isle of Wight: Cross Publishing, 1995), p. 49. Frederick Tyrrell, Keats's room-mate at Guy's, was later to produce an edition of Cooper's lectures: *The Lectures of Sir Astley Cooper on the Principles and Practice of Surgery*, 3 vols (London: Underwood, 1824–7).
28 *The London Dissector; or, System of Dissection, Practised in the Hospitals and Lecture Rooms of the Metropolis, Explained by the Clearest Rules, for the Use of Students* (Philadelphia, 1818), p. 178. The text of this volume is based on the fifth London edition of 1816.
29 Moyal Andrews and Anne Summers, *Voice Therapy for Adolescents* (Boston, MA: College Hill Press, 1988), p. 2.
30 *London Magazine* (Gold's), 2 (1820), 160–73, at p. 161. Savaging *Endymion*, Croker also associated 'stretching' with Keats. Punning mischievously on the poem's epigraph – 'the stretched metre of an antique song' – he professed to being unable to finish reading *Endymion* despite the 'fullest stretch of our perseverance'; *Quarterly Review*, 19 (1818), 204–8, at p. 204.
31 Jack Stillinger is wrong to call Calidore 'plotless'; *Reading the Eve of St. Agnes: The Multiples of Complex Literary Transaction* (Oxford: Oxford University Press, 1999), p. 104. The scene at the portcullis represents a seminal narrative juncture – not only as far as the plot of Keats's poem is concerned, but also in terms of the maturational trajectory of the would-be knight's (and ultimately Keats's) fictional life.
32 The portcullis could conceivably be construed as 'threat'ning' due to its enormous size; but this characteristic, too, is consonant with the physiology of mutating voices. A medical student, Keats would have been aware that lower phonation during puberty was in part a consequence of the increased proportions of the larynx. (In puberty, the 'larynx descends and the dimensions of the infraglottal sagittal and transverse planes increase. The anterio-posterior dimensions also increase in length, the mucosa becomes stronger, and the epiglottis increases in size'; *Voice Therapy for Adolescents*, pp. 10–11.) In Sir Astley Cooper's day, the larynx was believed to double in size. Since the male voice typically lowers by one octave it was presumed that vocal cords must double in length, which suggested twofold enlargement of the larynx. The actual ratio is considerably less than 1:2.
33 The gatehouse also acts as an echo chamber, a place where voices acquire increased resonance. Compare Andrews and Summers: 'Quality changes in the male voice are related to increased respiratory capacity and enlargement of the resonating cavities above the larynx. The increased resonance capacity is related to adolescent enlargement of the nose, mouth, and maxilla'; *Voice Therapy for Adolescents*, p. 5.
34 While Calidore might be supposed to want to learn from the 'real' knights – which is, in one sense, why he has been called to the castle – it is actually the ladies to

whom he looks at this crucial maturational juncture. As a measure of just how far Keats's childish hero deviates from authorized modes of masculine desire, rather than consume the 'sweet-lipp'd ladies' with a suitably manly gaze, Calidore mimics their traditional feminine qualities: a 'gentle' touch, a soft, whispered voice, 'trembling' lips, and 'glistening' eyes:

> What a kiss,
> What gentle squeeze he gave each lady's hand!
> How tremblingly their delicate ancles spann'd!
> Into how sweet a trance his soul was gone,
> While whisperings of affection
> Made him delay to let their tender feet
> Come to the earth; with an incline so sweet
> From their low palfreys o'er his neck they bent:
> And whether there were tears of languishment,
> Or that the evening due had pearl'd their tresses,
> He feels a moisture on his cheek, and blesses
> With lips that tremble, and with glistening eye,
> All the soft luxury
> That nestled in his arms.
> (*Calidore*, ll. 80–93)

35 Vendler, *Coming of Age as a Poet*, p. 48.
36 Even Chatterton's name might have suggested to Keats an essentially youthful dimension to the poet's discourse: 'Chatter (*v*)': 'To talk rapidly, incessantly, and with more sound than sense. Esp. said of children' (*OED*).
37 Roe, *Keats and the Culture of Dissent*, p. 28.
38 *The Keats Circle: Letter and Papers, 1816–1878*, II, 277.
39 'Her son ... was always guided by the last speaker, by the person who could get hold of and shut him up'; Jane Austen, *Mansfield Park* (Harmondsworth: Penguin, 1994), p. 456.
40 See Greg Kucich, '"The Wit in the Dungeon": Leigh Hunt and the Insolent Politics of Cockney Coteries', *Romanticism on the Net*, 14 (May 1999) at http://users.ox.ac.uk/~scat0385/cockneycoteries.html (accessed 17 January 2003). Hunt had, of course, decorated his cell to resemble a bower.
41 In his review of *Poems* (1817), George Felton Mathew called Keats 'presumptuous'; *European Magazine*, 71 (1817), 434–7.
42 Levinson, *Keats's Life of Allegory*, p. 11.
43 See Barthes, *The Pleasure of the Text*, p. 66. I am suggesting that Keats is frequently a genuinely childish writer, who is often eager to mature, but who deploys childish imagery deliberately for political reasons.
44 As Andrews and Summers point out, in terms of voice 'the adolescent is neither a child nor an adult'; *Voice Therapy for Adolescents*, p. 2.
45 In this respect, the unpublished Preface is closely related to lines 270–300 of *Sleep and Poetry*.
46
> Thy mossy footstool shall the altar be
> 'Fore which I'll bend, bending, dear love, to thee:
> Those lips shall be my Delphos, and shall speak
> Laws to my footsteps, colour to my cheek,
> Trembling or stedfastness to this same voice.
> (*Endymion* IV, 711–15)

47 Z, 'Cockney School of Poetry. No IV.', *Blackwood's Edinburgh Magazine*, 3 (1818), 519–24, at p. 522; Francis Jeffrey, *Edinburgh Review*, 34 (1820), 203–13, at p. 203.

142 Notes

48 *Eclectic Review*, 2nd series, 14 (1820), pp. 170, 169.
49 In reviews of *Poems* (1817) – a collection which Josiah Conder judged to be 'bordering upon childishness' (*Eclectic Review*, 2nd series, 8 (1817), 267–75, at p. 270) – *Endymion*, and the *Lamia* volume (1820), the complaint that Keats spoiled otherwise commendable passages with sudden interludes of childishness emerges as a leitmotiv.
50 *Edinburgh {Scots} Magazine*, 2nd series, 1 (1817), 254–7, at p. 257.
51 'Uncertainty' – as we have seen a key term in the published Preface to *Endymion* – makes a less equivocally political appearance in this arch passage.
52 Reprinted by John Barnard in *John Keats: The Complete Poems*, 2nd edn (Harmondsworth: Penguin, 1977), p. 527; hereafter, *Complete Poems*, page references given parenthetically in the text.
53 In the event, Kean went on tour to America and *Otho the Great* was not staged, causing Keats considerable consternation.
54 *Letters*, II, 188.
55 Motion, *Keats*, p. 437.
56 Also compare Saturn's cavernous voice, which in Book 2 of *Hyperion* 'grew up like organ' (II, 126).
57 In all probability, Keats's own relationship with Fanny Brawne, a woman routinely cited as a primary source for the figure of Lamia, remained unconsummated.
58 Jean Baudrillard, *Seduction*, trans. Brian Singer (1979; New York: St Martin's Press, 1990), p. 53.
59 Girls also undergo a degree of vocal maturation in puberty.
60 Lionel Trilling, *Beyond Culture: Essays on Literature and Learning* (1965; Oxford: Oxford University Press, 1980), p. 57.
61 See *Poems*, p. 465.
62 Far from disrupting sense, the word is meant to bring Lycius *to* his senses.
63 'The same palm which an instant ago was gliding over the material covering the breasts and brushing the pale surfaces of the pronators, now so tense it might burst, sweeps down in several brusque slaps between the legs, onto the vulva'; Jean-François Lyotard, *Libidinal Economy*, trans. Iain Hamilton Grant (Bloomington: Indiana University Press, 1993), p. 74. Lyotard's anatomically precise narrative (pronators, vulva) would have been comprehensible to Keats, who effectively describes the same transition from caress to coercion at *Lamia*, II, 75–7.
64 Lamia finally expires in a fit of *genuine* masculine tyranny, performed by a genuine man, Apollonius.
65 Surprisingly perhaps, Christopher Ricks does not consider Lycius' boyish red face at II, 75–7 in his tour de force critique of blushing in *Keats and Embarrassment*.
66 In Keats's poetry, 'young love' is always the prelude to maturation anxieties.
67 This is not to say that Lamia's transformation into womanhood is without anxiety. In fact, it patently is not.

4 Japing the sublime: naughty boys and immature aesthetics

1 This is Charles Brown's phrase from his own account of the tour, 'Walks in the North' (1840), printed as an addendum to Rollins's edition of Keats's letters.
2 Later, Keats likens his ascent of Ben Nevis to a 'fly crawling up a wainscoat' (*Letters*, I, 352).
3 See *Letters*, I, 312. This chapter departs from Stillinger's edition of Keats to use the version of the walking-tour poems printed by Rollins in *Letters*, retaining Keats's original spelling and punctuation.
4 To illustrate usage contemporary with Keats, the *OED* cites Irving (1809): 'So

insolent . . . a request would have been enough to have raised the gorge of the tranquil Van Twiller himself.'
5 Oliphant, 'John Keats', in *The Literary History of England in the End of the Eighteenth and Beginning of the Nineteenth Century*, I, 138. Further page references are given parenthetically in the main body of text.
6 Motion, *Keats*, p. 265.
7 John Woolford, 'Keats Among the Mountains', *Essays in Criticism*, 49 (1999), p. 28.
8 Strictly speaking, only the letters Keats writes to his brother Tom comprise the 'journal' begun on 25 June 1818. However, since those sent to other correspondents during the walks are similar in tone and purpose, I include them in the journal's narrative.
9 Motion, *Keats*, pp. 296–7.
10 John Glendening, 'John Keats in Scotland: Burns and the Anxieties of Hero Worship', *Keats–Shelley Journal*, 41 (1992), 76–99, at p. 98. Further page references are given parenthetically in the main body of text.
11 Ross, *The Contours of Masculine Desire*, p. 157. Further page references in the main body of text.
12 Gittings, *John Keats*, p. 339.
13 Motion, *Keats*, pp. 281–2.
14 Keats's immaturity during his walking tour is thus a sign precisely of his maturity. I will be explaining the paradox over the course of this chapter.
15 Nicholas Roe and Andrew Motion have shown that Keats's Enfield schooling, conducted under the headmastership of Charles Cowden Clarke's father, was anything but indifferent.
16 See Weiskel's path-clearing discussion in *The Romantic Sublime: Studies in the Structure and Psychology of Transcendence* (Johns Hopkins University Press: Baltimore, 1976).
17 *Coleridge's Miscellaneous Criticism*, ed. T. M. Raysor (London, 1936), p. 12.
18 *The Excursion* (London: Longman, 1814).
19 Not everyone agreed that *The Excursion* was a mature poem. Francis Jeffrey began his infamous review of the poem with the admonition: 'This will never do'; *Edinburgh Review*, 24 (1814), 1–30, at p. 1.
20 *The Thirteen-Book Prelude by William Wordsworth*, ed. Mark L. Reed, 2 vols (London: Cornell University Press, 1991).
21 Peter de Bolla, *The Discourse of the Sublime: Readings in History, Aesthetics and the Subject* (Oxford: Blackwell, 1989), p. 187.
22 Tim Fulford, *Romanticism and Masculinity: Gender, Politics, and Poetics in the Writings of Burke, Coleridge, Cobbett, Wordsworth, De Quincey, and Hazlitt* (Basingstoke: Macmillan, 1999), p. 32.
23 For Ross's discussion of Byron, see *The Contours of Masculine Desire*, pp. 44, 45.
24 Elizabeth Bohls, *Women Travel Writers and the Language of Aesthetics* (Cambridge: Cambridge University Press, 1995), p. 152.
25 Bohls, *Women Travel Writers*, p. 158.
26 Jane Moore, 'Plagiarism with a Difference: Subjectivity in "Kubla Khan" and *Letters Written During a Short Residence in Sweden, Norway and Denmark*', in *Beyond Romanticism: New Approaches to Texts and Contexts 1780–1832*, ed. Stephen Copley and John Whale (London: Routledge, 1992), p. 153.
27 The poem appeared in the second edition of *Lyrical Ballads* (1800).
28 Thomas West, *A Guide to the Lakes in Cumberland, Westmorland, and Lancashire*, 4th edn (London: Robson, 1789), p. 1. Further page references are given parenthetically in the main body of text.
29 Bohls, *Women Travel Writers*, p. 159.
30 William Gilpin, *Observations, Relative Chiefly to Picturesque Beauty, Made in the Year*

1772, On Several Parts of England, Particularly the Mountains and Lakes of Cumberland, and Westmorland, 3rd edn, 2 vols (London: Blamire, 1792), I, xxv.
31 Unsuccessfully, as it turned out.
32 Brougham was unable to save Leigh Hunt from being imprisoned for libelling the Prince Regent.
33 See Charles Brown, 'Walks in the North' (1840), given as a series of lectures (included by Rollins in *Letters*, I, 426ff).
34 Edmund Burke, *A Philosophical Enquiry into the Origin of our Ideas of the Sublime and Beautiful*, 2nd edn (1759; Menston: Scolar Press, 1970), p. 96. Further page references are given parenthetically in the main body of text.
35 For a discussion of 'On First Looking Into Chapman's Homer' and Romantic philology, see this author's *The Politics of Language in Romantic Literature* (London: Palgrave, 2002), pp. 85–7, 89–92. Burke, incidentally, also professed to being stirred more by Pope's Helen than Spenser's 'minute description' of Belphebe (p. 331), another preference that ran directly contrary to Keats's taste.
36 See Charles and Mary Cowden Clarke, *Recollections of Writers* (London: Samson Low, 1878), pp. 129ff.
37 That is, speak out.
38 'Ode to Psyche', l. 43.
39 Gittings, *John Keats*, p. 327.
40 In a letter to Tom Keats written on the same day (2 July), Keats remarked on an 'immense Horse fair at Dumfries', where the 'women [were] nearly all barefoot, with their shoes & clean stockings in hand, ready to put on & look smart in the Towns' (*Letters*, I, 309). We need not dwell overly long on feet here, but Charles Brown's own record of the bare-footed women in 'Walks in the North' is suggestive in the context of my discussion in Chapter 1: 'That neatness of attire, however, in the women made me the more object to their not wearing shoes and stockings. Keats was of an opposite opinion, and expatiated on the beauty of a human foot, that had grown without an unnatural restraint' (*Letters*, I, 439).
41 Barnard, *John Keats: The Complete Poems*, p. 603.
42 Keats writes 'Annan' for 'Arran'.
43 *The Fourteen-Book Prelude by William Wordsworth*, ed. W. J. B. Owen (London: Cornell University Press, 1985).
44 This task was substantially completed by 1839.
45 'Reach' occurs twice within a short space in this letter, once in relation to poetry, as discussed above, and again with reference to reaching Homer (another literary giant) through reading. The latter example indicates the kind of thoughts that were preoccupying Keats at this time.
46 Penelope Hughes-Hallett, *The Immortal Dinner: A Famous Evening of Genius and Laughter in Literary London, 1817* (London: Viking, 2000), p. 75. Wordsworth was also, Hughes-Hallett continues, 'the tallest . . . standing at a precise five foot nine and five-eighths inches . . . and easily the most imposing figure present' (p. 75).
47 Ross, *The Contours of Masculine Desire*, p. 157.
48 See Ayumi Mizukoshi, *Keats, Hunt and the Aesthetics of Pleasure* (London: Palgrave, 2001), p. 41.
49 See *Letters*, I, 334–6.
50 The hero of Scott's *The Antiquary*.
51 Keats had rented rooms at No. 1 Well Walk, Hampstead.
52 See *Letters*, I, 354–7.
53 There is perhaps an ironic echo here of Wordsworth's 'panted up / With eager pace' from the Snowdon section of *The Prelude* (XIII, 31–2). Keats's language also discloses a range of 'boyish' anxieties regarding size, potency, and women (the image of the obese Mrs Cameron 'reeking' up the hill is as enduring as it is revealing of Keats's failure to develop a 'right' feeling towards the opposite sex).

54 'Another domestic of Ben's' (Keats's note).
55 Gittings, *John Keats*, p. 339. Plainly irked at the badness of 'Upon my life, Sir Nevis', Gittings omits Keats's transcription of the poem in the letter as it appears in his edition of the selected letters.
56 Stillinger, *Reading the Eve of St Agnes*, p. 104.
57 If Keats has left London in search of father figures, Wordsworth and Burns, he returns to his adoptive mother, Mrs Wylie.
58 Recorded by Severn in his manuscript, '*My Tedious Life*' (September, 1873), in the Keats Collection, Houghton Library, *54 M-195. See Gittings, *John Keats*, p. 613.

5 'Stifling up the vale': Keats and 'c――ts'

1 See Letters, I, 190 (and note 3). By recording male banter in his correspondence, Keats in turn circulates it further.
2 Jeffrey C. Robinson, for example, detects a tinge of 'homoerotic frisson' in the 'heady, wine-guided' evenings Keats attended. See 'Hunt and the Poetics and Politics of Fancy', in *Leigh Hunt: Life, Poetics, Politics*, ed. Nicholas Roe (London: Routledge, 2003), p. 157.
3 Robert Gittings notes that Keats obtained 'plenty of obstetric experience' at this time. See *John Keats*, p. 83.
4 Hagstrum, *The Romantic Body*, p. 42.
5 John Bayley, *The Uses of Division: Unity and Disharmony in Literature* (London: Chatto and Windus, 1976), p. 132. I do, however, agree with Gerald Enscoe that Keats's concern with the erotic was 'of permanent interest to him'; *Eros and the Romantics: Sexual Love as a Theme in Coleridge, Shelley and Keats* (The Hague: Mouton, 1967), p. 99.
6 As James Barke points out in his introduction to the famous 1965 edition of Robert Burns's bawdy songs, *Merry Muses of Caledonia*, 'this word . . . had an honest use and has an honourable history', *The Merry Muses of Caledonia*, ed. James Barke and Sydney Goodsir Smith (London: Allen, 1965).
7 *Lanfranc's 'Science of Cirurgie'*, edited from the Bodleian Ashmole ms. 1396 and the British Museum Additional ms. 12,056 by Robert v. Fleischhacker (London: Trübner, 1894), p. 172.
8 *The London Dissector; or, System of Dissection, Practised in the Hospitals and Lecture Rooms of the Metropolis, Explained by the Clearest Rules, for the Use of Students*, 4th edn (London: Longman, 1813), p. 63.
9 There are only two known copies of the 1799 first edition in existence.
10 Gittings, *John Keats*, p. 652.
11 A short, four-word phrase from line 9 of the poem was printed by John Hamilton Reynolds in the *Champion* in 1817.
12 For Burns, the female genitalia are a site of liberation; for Keats they are a source of anxiety.
13 Ricks, *Keats and Embarrassment*, p. 36.
14 A similar thing about being 'in a hurry to be gone' could be said of the hero of *The Eve of St Agnes*. Although Porphyro achieves union *with* Madeline (albeit under dubious and psychologically interesting circumstances), immediately afterwards he hurries out of the castle, and out of the text: 'Let us away, my love, with happy speed' (l. 347); 'She hurried at his words' (l. 352). Of course, Porphyro is in a hurry to be gone *with* Madeline, rather than on his own – eagerness to escape is now predicated on the desire to elude the reader's gaze. One might say that Porphyro, in true schoolboy fashion, is reluctant to be seen with his girlfriend. Another way of interpreting events would be to conclude that the scoptophiliac balks at the thought of anyone observing his own voyeurism.
15 The slangy expression 'Stifling up the Vale' – which as far as I have been able to

determine is unique to Keats in this particular combination – actually avoids direct contemplation of (even as it claims to be invoking) the reality of the female genitals in four stages of self-censorship. (1) Keats euphemizes the area of disturbing anatomy as a 'Vale'. (2) The vale has been 'stifled up'. Deployed as a sexual colloquialism, 'stifle' meant 'sexually occupied' – this probably derives from obsolete meanings of 'stifle up': *OED*, 'To choke up, impede the flow of (running water)', 'to choke up (an orifice)'. But it also carried, then as now, the more usual sense of 'suppressed' or 'silenced'. Keats censors himself not only by choosing to represent genital congress euphemistically, but also by choosing this particular euphemism. There is a further meaning of 'stifle up' recorded by the *OED*: 'conceal', 'repress'. We could say that 'Unfelt, unheard, unseen' is as much about concealing the female genitals from view (from the author's as well as the reader's), as it is about *exposing* them, à la Burns. (3) The next stage of suppression is signalled by Keats's decision to expunge the entire line from his second draft and replace it with 'Ah! through their nestling touch'. (4) Keats shrank from publishing the poem – even the toned-down version – during his lifetime, suppressing even the memory of the problematic phrase.

16 The lyric is, or at least asks to be considered as, '*inter*coital' (the term Jean Hagstrum uses to describe the episode where Psyche and Cupid are invoked in *I Stood Tip-toe*, lines 143–6; see *The Romantic Body*, p. 62).
17 Composed 31 January 1818, and not published in Keats's lifetime.
18 See Barnard, *Complete Poems*, p. 590n.
19 Note Keats's (or rather Brown's) use of 'stifle' as a verb denoting sexual intercourse, employed here in a similar sense to its occurrence in 'Unfelt, unheard, unseen'.
20 *Letters*, I, 342.
21 Byron's *Letters and Journals*, VI, 232. Letter dated 25 October 1819.
22 See Gittings, *John Keats*, pp. 650–2.
23 See *Letters*, I, 256, II, 36.
24 Byron's *Letters and Journals*, VII, 217; letter dated 4 November 1820.
25 *European Magazine*, 71 (1817), 434–7, at p. 435. The relentless and strategic construction of Keats as a serial onanist achieved the desired effect, helping to deprive the upstart poet of a polite readership.
26 Ricks, *Keats and Embarrassment*, p. 101.
27 Thomas McFarland, *The Masks of Keats: The Endeavour of a Poet* (Oxford: Oxford University Press, 2000), p. 37.
28 Ibid., p. 36.
29 See Stillinger, *Reading the Eve of St Agnes*, p. 144.
30 Ibid., p. 28.
31 Of course, female readers could just as easily have been titillated by these references, as put off.
32 Barnard, *John Keats*, p. 73.
33 This, even though the fact that they are *acted* acts already distances them from 'bonâ fide' manly behaviour.
34 Cited in Bettina Mathes, 'From Nymph to Nymphomania: "Linear Perspectives" on Female Sexuality', in *The Arts of 17th-Century Science*, ed. Claire Jowitt and Diane Watt (Aldershot: Ashgate, 2002), p. 179.
35 As well as being Keats's anatomy demonstrator at Guy's, Joseph Green (1791–1863) was a friend of Coleridge: it was he who was engaged in conversation with the great man when Keats, walking 'towards highgate' on 11 April 1819, bumped into the pair and joined their company. See *Letters*, II, 88–9.
36 Joseph Henry Green, *The Dissector's Manual* (London: The Author, 1820), p. 185.
37 James Wallace, *Letters on the Study and Practice of Medicine and Surgery, and on Topics Connected with the Medical Profession: Addressed to Students and Young Practitioners of*

Medicine, to Parents and Guardians, and the Public in General (Glasgow: Griffin, 1828), p. 37.
38 This is, we might say, a royal porch to Keats's unconscious fears of female sexuality.
39 Freud, *On Sexuality*, p. 196.
40 Goellnicht, *The Poet-Physician: Keats and Medical Science*, p. 156. Further page references are given parenthetically in the main body of the text.
41 'Vivid', from *vivere*, 'to live', is possibly not the most appropriate word to employ here.
42 Andrew Bennett, *Keats, Narrative and Audience: The Posthumous Life of Writing* (Cambridge: Cambridge University Press, 1994), p. 85.
43 Hoeveler, 'Decapitating Romance', p. 321.
44 I have, of course, tried to do precisely this in my reading of the poem.
45 Hagstrum, *The Romantic Body*, pp. 54, 55.
46 Freud, *On Sexuality*, p. 198.
47 Charles Jeremiah Wells was a school friend of Keats's brother, Tom.
48 John Kingston was the infamous 'comptroller of stamps' who embarrassed Wordsworth at Haydon's immortal dinner.
49 William Haslam nursed Tom Keats in the summer of 1818, earning Keats's lasting gratitude. See Motion, *Keats*, pp. 91–2.

Afterword

1 Bate, *John Keats*, p. 286; Motion, *Keats*, p. 224.
2 'Recommitment' is Motion's word. See *Keats*, p. 225.
3 It may be significant within this context of association that Keats copied the 'Lines on Seeing a Lock of Milton's Hair' into his folio Shakespeare.

Bibliography

Andrews, Moyal and Anne Summers, *Voice Therapy for Adolescents* (Boston, MA: College Hill Press, 1988)
Anon, *The London Dissector; or, System of Dissection, Practised in the Hospitals and Lecture Rooms of the Metropolis, Explained by the Clearest Rules, for the Use of Students*, 4th edn (London: Longman, 1813)
—, *The London Dissector; or, System of Dissection, Practised in the Hospitals and Lecture Rooms of the Metropolis, Explained by the Clearest Rules, for the Use of Students* (Philadelphia, 1818; based on 5th London edn, 1816)
Ashfield, Andrew and Peter de Bolla (eds), *The Sublime: A Reader in British Eighteenth-Century Aesthetic Theory* (Cambridge: Cambridge University Press, 1996)
Barnard, John, *John Keats* (Cambridge: Cambridge University Press, 1987)
Barry, Peter, *English in Practice* (London: Arnold, 2002)
Barthes, Roland, *The Pleasure of the Text*, trans. Richard Miller (Oxford: Blackwell, 1990)
Bate, Walter Jackson, *John Keats* (London: Hogarth, 1992)
Baudrillard, Jean, *Seduction*, trans. Brian Singer (1979; New York: St Martin's Press, 1990)
Bayley, John, 'Keats and Reality', *Proceedings of the British Academy*, 4/8 (1962), 91–125
—, *The Uses of Division: Unity and Disharmony in Literature* (London: Chatto and Windus, 1976)
Bennett, Andrew, *Keats, Narrative and Audience: The Posthumous Life of Writing* (Cambridge: Cambridge University Press, 1994)
Bloom, Harold, *The Anxiety of Influence: A Theory of Poetry*, 2nd edn (1973; Oxford: Oxford University Press, 1997)
Bohls, Elizabeth, *Women Travel Writers and the Language of Aesthetics* (Cambridge: Cambridge University Press, 1995)
Brown, Charles, *Life of John Keats*, ed. D. H. Bodurtha and W. B. Pope (Oxford: Oxford University Press, 1937)
Burke, Edmund, *A Philosophical Enquiry into the Origin of our Ideas of the Sublime and Beautiful*, 2nd edn (1759; Menston: Scolar Press, 1970)
Burns, Robert, *The Merry Muses of Caledonia*, ed. James Barke and Sydney Goodsir Smith (London: Allen, 1965)
Byron, George Gordon, *Byron's Letters and Journals*, ed. Leslie A. Marchand, 12 vols (London: Murray, 1973–82)
Clarke, Charles Cowden, *An Address to that Quarterly Reviewer who Touched upon Mr Leigh Hunt's 'Story of Rimini'* (London: Jennings, 1816)

Clarke, Charles Cowden and Mary Cowden Clarke, *Recollections of Writers* (London: Samson Low, 1878)
Cleland, John, *Fanny Hill: Memoirs of a Woman of Pleasure* (Hollywood, CA: Brandon House, 1963)
Coleridge, Samuel Taylor, *Coleridge's Miscellaneous Criticism*, ed. T. M. Raysor (London: Constable, 1936)
Conder[?], Josiah, Review of *Lamia, Isabella, the Eve of St Agnes, and Other Poems*, *Eclectic Review*, 2nd series, 14 (1820), 158–71
Coote, Stephen, *John Keats: A Life* (London: Hodder and Stoughton, 1995)
Cornwall, Barry [Bryan Waller Procter], *A Sicilian Story, with Diego de Montilla and Other Poems* (London: Ollier, 1820)
—, *Dramatic Scenes and Marcian Colonna* (1819), repr. in *Romantic Context, Poetry, Significant Minor Poetry 1789–1830*, ed. Donald H. Reiman (London: Garland, 1978)
Cox, Jeffrey N., *Poetry and Politics in the Cockney School: Keats, Shelley, Hunt, and their Circle* (Cambridge: Cambridge University Press, 1998)
Cunningham, Valentine, *Reading After Theory* (Oxford: Blackwell, 2002)
de Almeida, Hermione, *Romantic Medicine and John Keats* (Oxford: Oxford University Press, 1991)
de Bolla, Peter, *The Discourse of the Sublime: Readings in History, Aesthetics, and the Subject* (Oxford: Blackwell, 1989)
—, 'The Charm'd Eye', in *Body and Text in the Eighteenth Century*, ed. Veronica Kelly and Dorothea Von Mücke (Stanford, CA: Stanford University Press, 1994)
Dearing, Lewis, 'A John Keats Letter Rediscovered', *Keats–Shelley Journal*, 47 (1998), 14–16
Deleuze, Giles and Félix Guattari, *Anti-Oedipus: Capitalism and Schizophrenia*, Preface by Michel Foucault (1972; London: Athlone Press, 1984)
Enscoe, Gerald, *Eros and the Romantics: Sexual Love as a Theme in Coleridge, Shelley and Keats* (The Hague: Mouton, 1967)
Fairer, David, 'Baby Language and Revolution: The Early Poetry of Charles Lloyd and Charles Lamb', *Charles Lamb Bulletin*, n.s. 74 (1991), 33–51
Foucault, Michel, *The History of Sexuality*, vol. 2: *The Use of Pleasure*, trans. Robert Hurley (Harmondsworth: Penguin, 1992)
Freud, Sigmund, *The Interpretation of Dreams*, trans. James Strachey, ed. Angela Richards, vol. IV in The Pelican Freud Library, 15 vols (Harmondsworth: Penguin, 1976)
—, *On Sexuality: Three Essays on the Theory of Sexuality and Other Works*, trans. James Strachey, ed. Angela Richards, vol. VII in The Pelican Freud Library, 15 vols (Harmondsworth: Penguin, 1977)
Fulford, Tim, *Romanticism and Masculinity: Gender, Politics, and Poetics in the Writings of Burke, Coleridge, Cobbett, Wordsworth, De Quincey, and Hazlitt* (Basingstoke: Macmillan, 1999)
Gallagher, Catherine and Stephen Greenblatt, *Practicing New Historicism* (Chicago: University of Chicago Press, 2000)
Gilpin, William, *Observations, Relative Chiefly to Picturesque Beauty, Made in the Year 1772, On Several Parts of England, Particularly the Mountains and Lakes of Cumberland, and Westmorland*, 3rd edn, 2 vols (London: Blamire, 1792)
Gittings, Robert, *John Keats* (Harmondsworth: Penguin, 1968)
— (ed.), *Letters of John Keats* (Oxford: Oxford University Press, 1970)

Glendening, John, 'John Keats in Scotland: Burns and the Anxieties of Hero Worship', *Keats–Shelley Journal*, 41 (1992), 76–99

Goellnicht, Donald C., *The Poet-Physician: Keats and Medical Science* (Pittsburgh: University of Pittsburgh Press, 1984)

Green, Joseph Henry, *Outlines of a Course of Dissections, for the Use of Students of Anatomy at St Thomas's Hospital* (London: Cox, 1815)

—, *The Dissector's Manual* (London: The Author, 1820)

Hagstrum, Jean, *The Romantic Body: Love and Sexuality in Keats, Wordsworth, and Blake* (Knoxville: The University of Tennessee Press, 1985)

—, *Eros and Vision: The Restoration to Romanticism* (Evanston, IL: Northwestern University Press, 1989)

Hartman, Geoffrey, *The Fate of Reading and other Essays* (London: University of Chicago Press, 1975)

Haydon, Benjamin Robert, *Neglected Genius: The Diaries of Benjamin Robert Haydon, 1808–1846*, ed. John Jolliffe (London: Hutchinson, 1990)

Hitchcock, Tim and Michèle Cohen (eds), *English Masculinities 1660–1800* (London: Longman, 1999)

Hoeveler, Diane Long, 'Decapitating Romance: Class, Fetish, and Ideology in Keats's *Isabella*', *Nineteenth-Century Literature*, 49 (1994), 321–38

Hofkosh, Sonia, *Sexual Politics and the Romantic Author* (Cambridge: Cambridge University Press, 1998)

Hughes-Hallett, Penelope, *The Immortal Dinner: A Famous Evening of Genius and Laughter in Literary London, 1817* (London: Viking, 2000)

Hunt, Leigh, *Foliage; or, Poems Original and Translated* (London: Ollier, 1818)

—, *The Literary Pocket-Book; or, Companion for the Lover of Nature and Art* (London: Ollier, 1819)

Johnson, Barbara, 'Gender Theory and the Yale School', in *Modern Literary Theory: A Reader*, ed. Philip Rice and Patricia Waugh, 3rd edn (London: Arnold, 1996)

Jones, John, *John Keats's Dream of Truth* (London: Chatto and Windus, 1969)

Keats, John, *John Keats's Anatomical and Physiological Note Book*, ed. Maurice Buxton Forman (Oxford: Oxford University Press, 1934)

—, *John Keats: The Complete Poems*, ed. John Barnard, 2nd edn (Harmondsworth: Penguin, 1977)

—, *The Letters of John Keats, 1814–1821*, ed. Hyder Edward Rollins (Cambridge, MA: Harvard University Press, 1958)

—, *The Poems of John Keats*, ed. Miriam Allott (London: Longman, 1970)

—, *The Poems of John Keats*, ed. Jack Stillinger (Cambridge, MA: Belknap Press, 1978)

Kimmel, Douglas C. and Irving B. Weiner, *Adolescence: A Developmental Transition*, 2nd edn (New York: Wiley, 1995)

Kucich, Greg, '"The Wit in the Dungeon": Leigh Hunt and the Insolent Politics of Cockney Coteries', *Romanticism on the Net*, 14 (May 1999) at http://users.ox.ac.uk/~scat0385/cockneycoteries.html (accessed 17 January 2003)

Lacan, Jacques, *Écrits: A Selection* (London: Routledge, 1989)

Lamb, Charles, *The Prose Works of Charles Lamb*, 3 vols (London: Moxon, 1838)

Levinson, Marjorie, *Keats's Life of Allegory: The Origins of a Style* (Oxford: Blackwell, 1988)

Lingis, Alphonso, *Foreign Bodies* (London: Routledge, 1994)

Lockhart, John Gibson, 'On the Cockney School of Poetry No. IV', *Blackwood's Edinburgh Magazine*, 3 (1818), 519–24

Lyotard, Jean-François, *Libidinal Economy*, trans. Iain Hamilton Grant (Bloomington: Indiana University Press, 1993)
McFarland, Thomas, *The Masks of Keats: The Endeavour of a Poet* (Oxford: Oxford University Press, 2000)
McGann, Jerome, 'Keats and the Historical Method in Literary Criticism', *Modern Language Notes*, 94 (1979), 988–1032
—, *The Poetics of Sensibility: A Revolution in Literary Style* (Oxford: Clarendon Press, 1996)
Marggraf Turley, Richard, *The Politics of Language in Romantic Literature* (London: Palgrave, 2002)
—, 'John Keats, Barry Cornwall and Leigh Hunt's *Literary Pocket-Book*', *Romanticism*, 7.ii (2002), 163–76
Marvell, Andrew, *Andrew Marvell: The Complete Poems*, ed. Elizabeth Story Donno (Harmondsworth: Penguin, 1972)
Mathes, Bettina, 'From Nymph to Nymphomania: "Linear Perspectives" on Female Sexuality', in *The Arts of 17th-Century Science*, ed. Claire Jowitt and Diane Watt (Aldershot: Ashgate, 2002)
Mathew, George Felton, *European Magazine*, 71 (1817), 434–7
Mellor, Anne K., *Romanticism and Gender* (London: Routledge, 1993)
Mizukoshi, Ayumi, 'The Cockney Politics of Gender: The Cases of Hunt and Keats', *Romanticism on the Net*, 14 (May 1999) at http://users.ox.ac.uk/~scat0385/cockneygender.html (accessed 5 February 2003)
—, *Keats, Hunt and the Aesthetics of Pleasure* (London: Palgrave, 2001)
Monckton Milnes, Richard (ed.), *Life, Letters, and Literary Remains of John Keats*, 2 vols (London: Moxon, 1848)
Moore, Jane, 'Plagiarism with a Difference: Subjectivity in "Kubla Khan" and *Letters Written During a Short Residence in Sweden, Norway and Denmark*', in *Beyond Romanticism: New Approaches to Texts and Contexts 1780–1832*, ed. Stephen Copley and John Whale (London: Routledge, 1992)
Moore, Keith L., *Clinically Oriented Anatomy*, 3rd edn (London: Williams and Wilkins, 1992)
Motion, Andrew, *Keats* (London: Faber and Faber, 1997)
Mudge, Bradford K., 'Romanticism, Materialism, and the Origins of Modern Pornography', *Romanticism on the Net*, 23 (August 2001) at http://users.ox.ac.uk/~scat0385/23mudge.html (accessed 27 February 2003)
Najarian, James, *Victorian Keats: Manliness, Sexuality, and Desire* (London: Palgrave, 2002)
Oliphant, Margaret, *The Literary History of England in the End of the Eighteenth and Beginning of the Nineteenth Century*, 3 vols (London: Macmillan, 1882)
O'Neill, Michael, *Romanticism and the Self-Conscious Poem* (Oxford: Clarendon Press, 1997)
Peckham, Morse, *The Romantic Virtuoso* (Hannover: University Press of New England, 1995)
Phillips, Kim M. and Barry Reay (eds), *Sexualities in History: A Reader* (London: Routledge, 2002)
Quennell, Peter (ed.), *Byron: A Self-Portrait: Letter and Diaries, 1798–1824*, 2 vols (London: J. Murray, 1950)
Reiman, Donald H. (ed.), *The Romantics Reviewed: Contemporary Reviews of British Romantic Writers*, 9 vols (New York: Garland, 1972)

Reynolds, Nicole, '"And seal the hushed casket of my soul": The Enchantment of the Tomb in John Keats's "Eve of St. Agnes"', *Prometheus Unplugged* at http://prometheus.cc.emory.edu/panels/2A/N.Reynolds.html (accessed 27 February 2003)

Richardson, Alan, 'Keats and Romantic Science', in *The Cambridge Companion to Keats*, ed. Susan Wolfson (Cambridge: Cambridge University Press, 2001)

Richardson, Joanna, *The Everlasting Spell: A Study of Keats and his Friends* (London: Jonathan Cape, 1963)

Ricks, Christopher, *Keats and Embarrassment* (Oxford: Clarendon Press, 1974)

———, *Allusion to the Poets* (Oxford: Oxford University Press, 2002)

Ridley, M. R., *Keats's Craftsmanship* (Oxford: Clarendon Press, 1933)

Robinson, Jeffrey C., *Reception and Poetics in Keats: 'My Ended Poet'* (London: Macmillan, 1998)

—, 'Leigh Hunt and the Poetics and Politics of the Fancy', in *Leigh Hunt: Life, Poetics, Politics* (London: Routledge, 2003)

Roe, Nicholas (ed.), *Keats and History* (Cambridge: Cambridge University Press, 1995)

—, 'A Cockney Schoolroom: John Keats at Enfield', in *Keats: Bicentenary Readings*, ed. Michael O'Neill (Edinburgh: Edinburgh University Press, 1997)

—, *John Keats and the Culture of Dissent* (Oxford: Clarendon Press, 1997)

— (ed.), *Leigh Hunt: Life, Poetics, Politics* (London: Routledge, 2003)

Rollins, Hyder Edward (ed.), *The Keats Circle: Letters and Papers, 1816–1878*, 2 vols (Cambridge, MA: Harvard University Press, 1948)

—, *The Letters of John Keats, 1814–1821*, 2 vols (Cambridge, MA: Harvard University Press, 1958)

Ross, Marlon B., *The Contours of Masculine Desire: Romanticism and the Rise of Women's Poetry* (Oxford: Oxford University Press, 1989)

—, 'Beyond the Fragmented World: Keats at the Limits of Patrilinear Language', in *Out of Bounds: Male Writers and Gender(ed) Criticism*, ed. Laura Claridge and Elizabeth Langland (Amherst: University of Massachusetts Press, 1990)

Rossetti, William Michael, *Life of John Keats* (London: Walter Scott, 1887)

Rzepka, Charles J., '"Cortez – or Balboa, or Somebody Like That": Form, Fact, and Forgetting in Keats's "Chapman's Homer" Sonnet', *Keats–Shelley Journal*, 51 (2002), 35–75

Sedgwick, Eve Kosofsky, *Between Men: English Literature and Male Homosocial Desire* (New York: Columbia University Press, 1985)

Sha, Richard C., 'Scientific Forms of Sexual Knowledge in Romanticism', *Romanticism On the Net*, 23 (August 2001) at http://users.ox.ac.uk/~scat0385/23sha.html (accessed 20 February 2003)

Shakespeare, William, *Twelfth Night*, ed. M. M. Mahood (Harmondsworth: Penguin, 1968)

Sharrock, Roger, 'Keats and the Young Lovers', *A Review of English Literature*, 2 (1961), 76–86

Smith, Hillas, *Keats and Medicine* (Newport, Isle of Wight: Cross Publishing, 1995)

Sperry, Stuart M., *Keats the Poet* (Princeton, NJ: Princeton University Press, 1973)

Stewart, Garrett, 'Keats and Language', in *The Cambridge Companion to Keats*, ed. Susan Wolfson (Cambridge: Cambridge University Press, 2001)

Stillinger, Jack, *The Hoodwinking of Madeline and Other Essays on Keats's Poems* (London: University of Illinois Press, 1971)

—, *Reading the Eve of St Agnes: The Multiples of Complex Literary Transaction* (Oxford: Oxford University Press, 1999)
—, 'The "Story" of Keats', in *The Cambridge Companion to Keats*, ed. Susan Wolfson (Cambridge: Cambridge University Press, 2001)
Trilling, Lionel, 'The Fate of Pleasure: Wordsworth to Dostoevsky', *The Partisan Review* (1963), 167–91
—, *Beyond Culture: Essays on Literature and Learning* (1965; Oxford: Oxford University Press, 1980)
Veeser, H. Aram, *The New Historicism* (London: Routledge, 1989)
Vendler, Helen, *The Odes of John Keats* (London: Belknap Press, 1983)
—, *Coming of Age as a Poet: Milton, Keats, Eliot, Plath* (Cambridge, MA: Harvard University Press, 2003)
Voller, Jack G., *The Supernatural Sublime: The Metaphysics of Terror in Anglo-American Romanticism* (DeKalb: Illinois University Press, 1994)
Wallace, James, *Letters on the Study and Practice of Medicine and Surgery, and on Topics Connected with the Medical Profession: Addressed to Students and Young Practitioners of Medicine, to Parents and Guardians, and the Public in General* (Glasgow: Griffin, 1828)
Watt, Diane, 'Oedipus, Apollonius, and Richard II: Sex and Politics in Book 8 of John Gower's *Confession Amantis*', *Studies in the Age of Chaucer*, 24 (2002), 181–208
West, Thomas, *A Guide to the Lakes in Cumberland, Westmorland, and Lancashire*, 4th edn (London: Robson, 1789)
Wolfson, Susan, 'Feminising Keats', in *Coleridge, Keats, and Shelley*, ed. Peter J. Kitson (Houndmills: Macmillan, 1996)
— (ed.), *The Cambridge Companion to Keats* (Cambridge: Cambridge University Press, 2001)
Wollstonecraft, Mary, *Letters Written during a Short Residence in Sweden, Norway and Denmark* (1796; Harmondsworth: Penguin, 1987)
Woolford, John, 'Keats Among the Mountains', *Essays in Criticism*, 49 (1999), 22–43
Wordsworth, William, *The Excursion* (London: Longman, 1814)
—, *The Fourteen-Book Prelude by William Wordsworth*, ed. W. J. B. Owen (London: Cornell University Press, 1985)
—, *The Thirteen-Book Prelude by William Wordsworth*, ed. Mark L. Reed, 2 vols (London: Cornell University Press, 1991)
Wordsworth, William and Samuel Taylor Coleridge, *Lyrical Ballads*, ed. R. L. Brett and A. R. Jones (London: Methuen, 1965)
Zylinska, Joanna, *On Spiders, Cyborgs and Being Scared: The Feminine and the Sublime* (Manchester: Manchester University Press, 2001)

Index

Abbey, Richard 32
Allott, Miriam 20, 135n.15
Austen, Jane: *Mansfield Park* 57

Bailey, Benjamin 57, 124
Barnard, John 47, 49, 93, 109, 114
Barthes, Roland 17, 60, 139n.8
Bate, Walter Jackson 6, 7, 27–8, 126, 127
Baudrillard, Jean 67
bawdy 117; *see also under* Keats, John
Bayley, John 3, 60, 105
Bennett, Andrew 121
Black Dwarf 43
Blackwood's Edinburgh Magazine 7, 11, 33
Blancaert's *Reformirte Anatomie* 115
Bloom, Harold 60
Bohls, Elizabeth 81–2, 84
Brawne, Fanny 25
Brougham, Henry 85
Brown, Charles 25, 32, 73, 99, 109–10; 'Life of John Keats' 134n.15
Burke, Edmund 73, 74, 80, 101; *A Philosophical Enquiry* 82, 86, 87–9
Burns, Robert 114; his cottage 94, 96, 110–11; 'Cumnock Psalms' 106–9; 'Dainty Davie' 108–9; *The Merry Muses of Caledonia* 10, 106, 108; 'Nine Inch Will Please a Lady' 108; 'Put Butter in my Donald's Brose' 108
Burton, Robert: *Anatomy of Melancholy* 108
Byron, Lord 58; *Childe Harold's Pilgrimage* 80; *Don Juan* 111–12; and Keats 25, 27, 36, 53, 114

Cap of Liberty 43
Carlile, R. 43
Cato Street Conspiracy 61
Chapman, George 88; *see also* Keats's poetry: 'On First Looking into Chapman's Homer'
Chartier, Alain 136n.15
Chatterton, Thomas 25, 38, 55–7, 62; and chattering 141n.36
Cinderella 15, 72
Clarke, Charles Cowden 88, 107, 136n.3; *see also* Keats's poetry: 'To Charles Cowden Clarke'
Coleridge, Samuel Taylor 78
Conder, Josiah 33, 36, 38, 48, 62
Condillac, Etienne Bonnot de ix, 7
Cooper, Astley 10, 52
Coote, Stephen 2
Cornwall, Barry [Bryan Waller Procter]: *A Sicilian Story; with Diego Montilla, and Other Poems* 41, 42; 'Spring' 41–5
Croker, John Wilson 7, 27, 29, 36, 140n.30

de Almeida, Hermione 118
de Bolla, Peter 79
Dearing, Lewis 15–16
Dilke, Charles 66
Dylan, Bob 39

Eclectic Review see Conder, Josiah
Edinburgh (Scots) Magazine 62
European Magazine 36, 112

Fawcus, Margaret 49
Freud, Sigmund 119, 123; 'On Fetishism' 8, 11, 14, 16–17, 21–3

Index   155

Frogley, Mary 19–20
Fulford, Tim 80

George III, 126
Gilpin, William 74; *Observations, Relative Chiefly to Picturesque Beauty* 85
Gittings, Robert 6, 22, 77, 90, 100, 101, 107, 112
Glendening, John 76
Goellnicht, Donald 118, 120–1
Grand Tour 74–5
Green, Joseph Henry 52; *Dissector's Manual* 115, 121; *Outlines of a Course of Dissections* 115, 121
Guardian 27
Guy's Hospital, 10, 52, 104, 116, 122

habeas corpus 43, 63
Hagstrum, Jean 12, 25, 104, 122, 123
Hammond, Thomas 9, 52, 104, 116, 119
Hartman, Geoffrey 28
Haslam, William 124
Haydon, Benjamin Robert 22, 95
Heisenberg, Werner: uncertainty principle 48
Hill, Geoffrey 36
Hoeveler, Diane Long 12, 22, 121
Hone, William 43
Hughes-Hallett, Penelope 95
Hunt, Henry 43
Hunt, Leigh 61, 78; *Examiner* 58; *Foliage* 1; imprisoned for libel 6, 36, 57–8; *Indicator* 33; *Literary Pocket-Book* 41; and Milton's hair 127; 'To William Hazlitt' 1, 7; *see also under* Keats, John

'immortal dinner' 95, 124

Jeffrey sisters, Marian and Sarah 24
Johnson, Barbara 31
Jones, John 28

Kean, Edmund 63–4
Keats, Fanny 34–5
Keats, Frances 22
Keats, George 19–20, 64–8
Keats, Georgiana 64, 66

Keats, John: and aesthetics 7, 9, 74–5, 81, 85–6, 89, 92, 95, 96, 98, 128; and ambiguity 28, 31, 33, 38, 41, 42, 45; and anatomy 9, 23, 52, 104, 115–16, 119, 120, 124; *see also Dissector's Manual*; *London Dissector*; and aspiration 50, 53, 60, 139n.17; and ballad metre 137n.17; and bawdy 97, 104, 107–8, 109–10, 113; and beldames 32; and blushing 37; and boyishness, 'genuine' 2, 8, 10, 16, 29, 40–1, 59, 128; and boyishness, strategic 1, 2, 3, 6–7, 8, 9, 10, 27, 33, 40, 55, 59–60, 61–2, 75, 78, 100, 103, 128; and breasts 20, 34, 44; and Byron, Lord 111–12; and canonicity 27–8, 33, 38, 39–40; and 'cant' 111–12, 124–5; and castration 13–14, 15–16, 22, 114; and censorship 106–7, 110–11, 113–14, 122–4, 145–6n.15; and 'Chamber of Maiden-Thought' 4, 30–1, 34, 35, 36, 49–50, 62; and 'Cockney' jargon 36, 63; and 'C——t' 106, 111–12, 124; and 'Duchess of Dunghill' 86–7, 88–9; and effeminacy 11, 24, 25, 27; and English language 38–9, 88; and feet 8, 11–26, 144n.40 (male feet 25); and female sexuality 8, 11, 12, 13; and fetishism 12, 13, 15–16, 18, 19–20, 21, 22, 24; *see also under* Freud, Sigmund; and finding his voice 5, 46–7, 53; and food 26; *see also* Keats, John: overfeeding; and giving birth *see* Keats, John: pregnancy; and homosociality 104, 114, 124; and humour 24, 101–2, 110–11, 113, 122; and Hunt, Leigh 1, 7, 29, 56–7, 78, 139n.19; and immaturity 2, 4, 7, 11–12, 26, 27, 29–30, 33, 40, 45, 61–2, 74, 103, 106, 127, 138n.41, 143n.14; and manliness 8–9, 11, 16–17, 24–6, 54, 60, 65, 70–1, 75, 77, 80, 108, 128, 146n.33; and maturation, 4, 7, 9, 28, 34, 49, 53, 65–8, 77, 79, 119, 125; and maturity 2–4, 6–7, 8, 27–40, 47, 64, 73, 75–8, 95–6, 103, 126–7; medical books 52, 116, 118; and medical

studies 9–10, 52; and Milton, John 29, 39, 48, 126–8, 135n.15; and mothers 14, 20–4, 34, 41–2, 44, 145n.57; and 'namby-pamby' phrases 2, 63, 128; and narratives of personal/poetic evolution 2–5, 6–7, 9, 11, 14–15, 28, 29, 30, 32, 46, 71, 76; *see also* Keats's poetry: *Calidore*; Keats, John: 'Chamber of Maiden-Thought'; and naughtiness 74–5; and 'Negative Capability' 48; and obstetrics 9, 13, 104, 110, 119; and Oedipal triangulation 21; and overfeeding 73, 102; and parapraxis 16, 42, 69–70; and parenthood 66–7, 72, 119; and phallic anxiety 20–1, 23, 25, 49; and pitch 65–6; and plot(ting) 61, 140n.31; and poetic afterlife 24, 38, 39; and political consciousness 4; and poverty 74, 75, 87, 89, 92; and pregnancy 13, 35, 111, 119, 124, 127; and Procter, Bryan Waller *see* Cornwall, Barry; and puberphonia 8, 49, 55, 71; and 'reach' in poetry 95, 144n.45; and review of *Richard III* 63; *see also* Kean, Edmund; and Reynolds *see* Reynolds, John Hamilton; and 'right feeling' towards women 2, 8, 10, 12, 14, 21, 23, 25, 26, 66, 114, 124, 144n.53; and 'Saturday club', 9, 124; and 'school boy' taste 33, 62; and Severn *see* Severn, Joseph; and social/medical knowledge of women 104–5, 110, 118, 122–3, 124; and speaking out 46–7, 58–9, 61–2; and stature 24–6, 58, 137n.19; and steadiness 34; and sublime rhetoric 9, 73–4, 77–8, 81–3, 87, 89–90, 92, 95, 96, 97, 99, 101; and throats 38, 52, 69, 73; and 'T wang-dillo-dee' 5–6, 7; and voice break 46–7, 49, 51–5, 56, 60, 62–3, 68, 70; and vowels 57; and voyeurism 13, 19, 25–6, 109, 145n.14; and walking tour 9, 73–103; and Wollstonecraft, Mary 84, 90–1; and Wordsworth, William 30, 79, 81, 86, 95–6
Keats, Tom 109–10

Keats's poetry: 'Addressed to Haydon' 62; 'Ah! ken ye what I met the day' 77; 'All gentle folks who owe a grudge' 98; *Calidore: A Fragment* 6, 49–54, 66, 68–9, 72, 140–1n.34; *The Cap and Bells; or, The Jealousies* 7, 8, 21–2, 29, 42; *Endymion* (and Prefaces) 8, 11, 15–19, 21–2, 25, 40, 48, 60–1, 67–8, 73, 115, 122, 126; *The Eve of St Agnes* 8, 25–6, 30–2, 33, 50, 54, 111, 113–14, 122; *The Fall of Hyperion* 6, 8, 14, 20–4, 25, 48, 120; *Hyperion* 6, 20, 46, 71, 75; *Imitation of Spenser* 135n.15; *I Stood Tip-toe* 8, 46, 58–60; *Isabella; or, The Pot of Basil* 112–13, 120–2; 'La Belle Dame sans Merci' 11, 31–2; *Lamia* 11, 12, 31, 62, 65, 67–72, 118–19; *Lamia . . . and Other Poems* 2, 28, 33, 38, 48; 'Lines on Seeing a Lock of Milton's Hair' 126–8; 'O blush not so!' 105; 'Ode on a Grecian Urn' 40; 'Ode on Indolence' 38; 'Ode to a Nightingale' 34, 44; 'Oh Chatterton! how very sad thy fate!' 55–7; 'On First Looking into Chapman's Homer' 46–7; 'On Sitting Down to Read *King Lear* Once Again' 126–7; *Otho the Great* 63, 64; 'Pensive they sit, and roll their languid eyes' 64; *Sleep and Poetry* 6, 8, 46, 58–9, 61; 'A Song about Myself' 74, 77, 92–3; 'Specimen of an Induction to a Poem' 11, 54; 'This mortal body of a thousand days' 96; 'To Autumn' 2, 4, 8, 27–45, 75, 137n.34; 'To Charles Cowden Clarke' 5; 'To George Felton Mathew' 4–5; 'To [Had I a man's fair form]' 24; 'To [Mary Frogley]' 19–20; 'Unfelt, unheard, unseen' 107–9, 145–6n.15; 'Upon my life, Sir Nevis, I am piqued' 77, 99–101; 'Written on the Day That Mr Leigh Hunt Left Prison' 56–7
Kingston, John 124
Kucich, Greg 139n.15

Lafranc's *Cirurgia* 106
Lake District, 83, 84, 86, 95; *see also* Keats, John: walking tour

landscape, politics of 74; *see also* sublime
Leavis, F. R. 48
Levinson, Marjorie 4, 26, 27, 36, 58, 60
Liverpool, Lord 43
Locke, John 7
Lockhart, John Gibson ('Z') 7, 11, 27, 29, 36
London Dissector 52, 106, 115–19
London Magazine 27, 53
Lowther, Lord 85–6, 98, 103
Lyotard, Jean-François 70–1, 142n.63

McFarland, Thomas 113
McGann, Jerome 42, 48, 138n.5
Marvell, Andrew 44–5
Mathes, Bettina 115
Mathew, George Felton 5, 36, 112
medical vocabulary 115–18
Mellor, Anne 11, 32
Milnes, Richard Monckton 5, 57; *Life, Letters, and Literary Remains of John Keats* 2, 107
Milton, John 44; *see also under* Keats, John
Mizukoshi, Ayumi 97
Monthly Review 28, 33, 40
Moore, Jane 83
Motion, Andrew 3, 6, 7, 19, 28, 37, 65, 75, 76–8, 93, 103, 126
Mr Kipling cakes 39
Murray, John 25, 36

new historicism 4, 28, 41, 76, 138n.41
nymphs 115

Oliphant, Margaret 75, 77
O'Neill 27

Peckham, Morse 28
Peterloo 4, 42–3, 61
Political Register 43
Pope, Alexander 88
Prince Regent 57
Procter, Bryan Waller *see* Cornwall, Barry

Quarterly Review 7, 33

Redhall, Mr 106, 108, 110, 124
Reynolds, John Hamilton 105
Rice, James 124
Richardson, Joanna 8
Ricks, Christopher 3, 13, 37, 108, 113
Ridley, M. R. 2
Robinson, Jeffrey C. 1, 6, 145n.2
Roe, Nicholas 4, 28, 32, 34, 42, 56, 136n.14
Rollins, Hyder Edward 106
Ross, Marlon B. 46, 76, 80, 95–6
Rzepka, Charles J. 138–9n.5

Sedgwick, Eve Kosofsky 104
Seditious Meetings Act 43
Severn, Joseph 103; portrait of Keats 29, 136n.13
Shakespeare, William 48, 126–7
Sharrock, Roger 3
Shelley, Percy Bysshe 75
Smith, Adam: 'The Origin of Language' 39
Smith, Hillas 120
Spenser, Edmund 7, 20, 52
Stewart, Garrett 46
Stillinger, Jack 2, 32, 101, 107, 114, 123
sublime, 78–9, 82–3; *see also* Burke, Edmund; Keats, John; Wollstonecraft, Mary; Wordsworth, William

Taylor, John 113–15
Tennyson, Alfred 37, 40; *Maud* 122–3
Thomas, Dylan 37
travel narratives 74
Trilling, Lionel 3, 69

Vendler, Helen 4, 27, 28, 37, 40, 46, 56, 134n.10, 138n.3

Wallace, James 116
Ward, Aileen 6
Weiskel, Thomas 78
Wells, Charles, 124
West, Thomas 74; *Guide to the Lakes* 84
White, Kirke 55
Wolfson, Susan 11, 24
Wollstonecraft, Mary: *Letters Written During a Short Residence* 81–5, 90–1

Woodhouse, Richard 113–14
Wooler, T. J. 43
Woolford, John 75, 77–8, 103
Wordsworth, William 55; *The Excursion* 78–9; and Lowther, support of 86; *Poems on the Naming of Places* 83–4; 'Preface' to *Lyrical Ballads* 39; *The Prelude* 79, 94–5; and sublime style 77–80; and walking 95; *see also under* Keats, John
Wylie, Mrs 101

eBooks – at www.eBookstore.tandf.co.uk

A library at your fingertips!

eBooks are electronic versions of printed books. You can store them on your PC/laptop or browse them online.

They have advantages for anyone needing rapid access to a wide variety of published, copyright information.

eBooks can help your research by enabling you to bookmark chapters, annotate text and use instant searches to find specific words or phrases. Several eBook files would fit on even a small laptop or PDA.

NEW: Save money by eSubscribing: cheap, online access to any eBook for as long as you need it.

Annual subscription packages

We now offer special low-cost bulk subscriptions to packages of eBooks in certain subject areas. These are available to libraries or to individuals.

For more information please contact webmaster.ebooks@tandf.co.uk

We're continually developing the eBook concept, so keep up to date by visiting the website.

www.eBookstore.tandf.co.uk